# AQA History

## AS
Unit 1

# USA, 1890–1945

**Exclusively endorsed by AQA**

Chris Rowe

Series editor
Sally Waller

Nelson Tho

Published in 2008 by:
Nelson Thornes Ltd
Delta Place
27 Bath Road
CHELTENHAM
GL53 7TH
United Kingdom

08 09 10 11 12 / 10 9 8 7 6 5 4 3 2

A catalogue record for this book is available from the British Library

978-0-7487-8272-7

Illustrations by Bob Moulder (c/o Graham-Cameron Illustration) Gary Rees (c/o
Linda Rogers Associates) and David Russell Illustration

Page make-up by Thomson Digital

Printed in Croatia by Zrinski

# Contents

# AQA introduction

## Nelson Thornes and AQA

Nelson Thornes has worked in collaboration with AQA to ensure that this book offers you the best support for your AS or A level course and helps you to prepare for your exams. The partnership means that you can be confident that the range of learning, teaching and assessment practice materials has been checked by the senior examining team at AQA before formal approval, and is closely matched to the requirements of your specification.

## How to use this book

This book covers the specification for your course and is arranged in a sequence approved by AQA.

The features in this book include:

## Timeline

Key events are outlined at the beginning of the book. The events are colour-coded so you can clearly see the categories of change.

### Learning objectives

At the beginning of each section you will find a list of learning objectives that contain targets linked to the requirements of the specification.

## Key chronology

A short list of dates usually with a focus on a specific event or legislation.

## Key profile

The profile of a key person you should be aware of to fully understand the period in question.

## Key term

A term that you will need to be able to define and understand.

## Did you know?

Interesting information to bring the subject under discussion to life.

## Exploring the detail

Information to put further context around the subject under discussion.

## A closer look

An in-depth look at a theme, person or event to deepen your understanding. Activities around the extra information may be included.

## Sources

Sources to reinforce topics or themes and may provide fact or opinion. They may be quotations from historical works, contemporaries of the period or photographs.

## Cross-reference

Links to related content within the book which may offer more detail on the subject in question.

## Activity

Various activity types to provide you with different challenges and opportunities to demonstrate both the content and skills you are learning. Some can be worked on individually, some as part of group work and some are designed to specifically "stretch and challenge".

## Question

Questions to prompt further discussion on the topic under consideration and are an aid to revision.

## Summary questions

Summary questions at the end of each chapter to test your knowledge and allow you to demonstrate your understanding.

## AQA Examiner's tip

Hints from AQA examiners to help you with your study and to prepare for your exam.

## AQA Examination-style questions

Questions at the end of each section in the style that you can expect in your exam.

*Learning outcomes*

Learning outcomes at the end of each section remind you what you should know having completed the chapters in that section.

## Web links in the book

Because Nelson Thornes is not responsible for third party content online, there may be some changes to this material that are beyond our control. In order for us to ensure that the links referred to in the book are as up-to-date and stable as possible, the web sites provided are usually homepages with supporting instructions on how to reach the relevant pages if necessary.

Please let us know at **webadmin@nelsonthornes. com** if you find a link that doesn't work and we will do our best to correct this at reprint, or to list an alternative site.

# Introduction to the History series

When Bruce Bogtrotter in Roald Dahl's *Matilda* was challenged to eat a huge chocolate cake, he just opened his mouth and ploughed in, taking bite after bite and lump after lump until the cake was gone and he was feeling decidedly sick. The picture is not dissimilar to that of some A level history students. They are attracted to history because of its inherent appeal but, when faced with a bulging file and a forthcoming examination, their enjoyment evaporates. They try desperately to cram their brains with an assortment of random facts and subsequently prove unable to control the outpouring of their ill-digested material in the examination.

The books in this series are designed to help students and teachers avoid this feeling of overload and examination panic by breaking down the AQA history specification in such a way that it is easily absorbed. Above all, they are designed to retain and promote students' enthusiasm for history by avoiding a dreary rehash of dates and events. Each book is divided into sections, closely matched to those given in the specification, and the content is further broken down into chapters that present the historical material in a lively and attractive form, offering guidance on the key terms, events and issues, and blending thought-provoking activities and questions in a way designed to advance students' understanding. By encouraging students to think for themselves and to share their ideas with others, as well as helping them to develop the knowledge and skills they will need to pass their examination, this book should ensure that students' learning remains a pleasure rather than an endurance test.

To make the most of what this book provides, students will need to develop efficient study skills from the start and it is worth spending some time considering what these involve:

- Good organisation of material in a subject-specific file. Organised notes help develop an organised brain and sensible filing ensures time is not wasted hunting for misplaced material. This book uses cross-references to indicate where material in one chapter has relevance to material in another. Students are advised to adopt the same technique.

- A sensible approach to note-making. Students are often too ready to copy large chunks of material from printed books or to download sheaves of printouts from the internet. This series is designed to encourage students to think about

the notes they collect and to undertake research with a particular purpose in mind. The activities encourage students to pick out information that is relevant to the issue being addressed and to avoid making notes on material that is not properly understood.

- Taking time to think, which is by far the most important component of study. By encouraging students to think before they write or speak, be it for a written answer, presentation or class debate, students should learn to form opinions and make judgements based on the accumulation of evidence. These are the skills that the examiner will be looking for in the final examination. The beauty of history is that there is rarely a right or wrong answer so, with sufficient evidence, one student's view will count for as much as the next.

## Unit 1

The topics offered for study in Unit 1 are all based on 'change and consolidation'. They invite consideration of what changed and why, as well as posing the question of what remained the same. Through a study of a period of about 50 to 60 years, students are encouraged to analyse the interplay of long-term and short-term reasons for change and to consider not only how governments have responded to the need for change but also to evaluate the ensuing consequences. Such historical analyses are, of course, relevant to an understanding of the present and, through such historical study, students will be guided towards a greater appreciation of the world around them today, as well as developing their understanding of the past.

Unit 1 is tested by a 1 hour 15 minute paper containing three questions, from which students need to select two. Details relating to the style of questions, with additional hints, are given in Table 1 and links to the examination requirements are provided throughout this book. Students should familiarise themselves with these and the marking criteria given below before attempting any of the practice examination questions at the end of each section.

Answers will be marked according to a scheme based on 'levels of response'. This means that the answer will be assessed according to which level best matches the historical skills displayed, taking both knowledge and understanding into account. All students should have a copy of these criteria and need to use them wisely.

**Table 1** *Unit 1: style of questions and marks available*

| Unit 1 | Question | Marks | Question type | Question stem | Hints for students |
|---|---|---|---|---|---|
| Question 1, 2 and 3 | (a) | 12 | This question is focused on a narrow issue within the period studied and requires an explanation | Why did… Explain why… In what ways… (was X important) | Make sure you explain 'why', not 'how', and try to order your answer in a way that shows you understand the inter-linkage of factors and which were the more important. You should try to reach an overall judgement/conclusion |
| Question 1, 2 and 3 | (b) | 24 | This question links the narrow issue to a wider context and requires an awareness that issues and events can have different interpretations | How far… How important was… How successful… | This answer needs to be planned as you will need to develop an argument in your answer and show balanced judgement. Try to set out your argument in the introduction and, as you develop your ideas through your paragraphs, support your opinions with detailed evidence. Your conclusion should flow naturally and provide supported judgement |

## Marking criteria

### Question 1(a), 2(a) and 3(a)

**Level 1** Answers will contain either some descriptive material that is only loosely linked to the focus of the question or some explicit comment with little, if any, appropriate support. Answers are likely to be generalised and assertive. The response will be limited in development and skills of written communication will be weak. *(0–2 marks)*

**Level 2** Answers will demonstrate some knowledge and understanding of the demands of the question. They will **either** be almost entirely descriptive with few explicit links to the question **or** they will provide some explanations backed by evidence that is limited in range and/or depth. Answers will be coherent but weakly expressed and/or poorly structured *(3–6 marks)*

**Level 3** Answers will demonstrate good understanding of the demands of the question providing relevant explanations backed by appropriately selected information, although this may not be full or comprehensive. Answers will, for the most part, be clearly expressed and show some organisation in the presentation of material. *(7–9 marks)*

**Level 4** Answers will be well focused, identifying a range of specific explanations backed by precise evidence and demonstrating good understanding of the connections and links between events/issues. Answers will, for the most part, be well written and organised. *(10–12 marks)*

### Question 1(b), 2(b) and 3(b)

**Level 1** Answers may **either** contain some descriptive material which is only loosely linked to the focus of the question **or** they may address only a part of the question. Alternatively, there may be some explicit comment with little, if any, appropriate support. Answers are likely to be generalised and assertive. There will be little, if any, awareness of differing historical interpretations. The response will be limited in development and skills of written communication will be weak. *(0–6 marks)*

**Level 2** Answers will show some understanding of the focus of the question. They will **either** be almost entirely descriptive with few explicit links to the question **or** they may contain some explicit comment with relevant but limited support. They will display limited understanding of differing historical interpretations. Answers will be coherent but weakly expressed and/or poorly structured. *(7–11 marks)*

**Level 3** Answers will show a developed understanding of the demands of the question. They will provide some assessment, backed by relevant and appropriately selected evidence, but they will lack depth and/or balance. There will be some understanding of varying historical interpretations. Answers will, for the most part, be clearly expressed and show some organisation in the presentation of material. *(12–16 marks)*

**Level 4** Answers will show explicit understanding of the demands of the question. They will develop a balanced argument backed by a good range of appropriately selected evidence and a good understanding of historical interpretations. Answers will, for the most part, show organisation and good skills of written communication. *(17–21 marks)*

**Level 5** Answers will be well focused and closely argued. The arguments will be supported by precisely selected evidence leading to a relevant conclusion/judgement, incorporating well-developed understanding of historical interpretations and debate. Answers will, for the most part, be carefully organised and fluently written, using appropriate vocabulary. *(22–24 marks)*

# Introduction to this book

## The USA in 1890

### The land of the free

The history of the USA is a story of apparently limitless growth and never-ending change. The new nation that was born out of the American Revolution was an 18th century society based on the Thirteen Colonies. By 1890, this society had been transformed out of all recognition by territorial expansion, population growth and the impact of industrialisation and modernity – and the rate of change was set to accelerate even faster after 1890. However, there was continuity as well as change. The principles set out by the Founding Fathers remained influential for more than two centuries afterwards.

One example of this was the way Americans saw their relationships with the wider world. Despite its growth and potential, the USA was not a Great Power in 1890 and it did not wish to be. The American Revolution was based on a revolt against the British Empire, against monarchy and colonialism. The new nation was based on the ideals of the Brotherhood of Man; it rejected war, alliances and standing armies. The ideas of independence and neutrality were deeply rooted. In 1796 the first American president, George Washington, warned against the dangers of entanglement in treaties with foreign powers.

> The great rule for our United States in regard to foreign nations is to extend our commerce with them but to have as little political connection as possible. Our detached and distant situation enables us to have our neutrality respected. Why should we give away the advantages of such a unique situation? Why should we entangle our peace and prosperity in European ambitions and rivalries? It is our true policy to steer clear of permanent alliances with any portion of the foreign world.

**1**

*George Washington, **Farewell Address to the American People**, 1796*

These ideas of neutrality and anti-colonialism, of protecting the Americas against outside interference, provided the basis of the Monroe Doctrine set out by President James Monroe in 1823, at a time when the USA was nervous about European interference in the newly independent states of Latin America. The Monroe Doctrine warned the European powers that any military interventions in Latin America would be seen as hostile action against the USA. It became a foundation stone of American foreign policy all the way to 1890 and beyond.

The USA was founded on a strong sense of history and national identity. The keystone of this, of course, was the American Revolution and the War of Independence. The ideals of 'Jeffersonian democracy' were set out in the Declaration of Independence of 1776 and the American Constitution of 1787. Ever since, almost all Americans have believed that their form of republican democracy represents something newer and better than the political models of 'Old Europe'.

There were also other influences from further in the past. The first settlements of British colonies had been established in Virginia in 1607. Most Americans, however, preferred to look back to Pilgrim Fathers, who had landed in Massachusetts in the 1620s and 1630s, as religious idealists setting up a 'city on a hill' as a pure society and an example to the world. The colonial period in American history was seen as a formative experience, carving out a new society from the wilderness and moulding the individualism and self-reliance that was needed for life on the frontier.

The colonial frontier experience also shaped attitudes towards Native Americans, who were generally regarded as backward peoples standing in the way of 'civilisation' and progress. One of the driving forces behind the American Revolution was the urge to open up the West for expansion and settlement.

Another significant influence from the colonial past was slavery and the plantation society of the southern colonies. Before the American Revolution, wide social and economic differences had already existed between North and South. As the new nation expanded after independence, these differences became much more troublesome.

The American Civil War of 1861–5 was the defining experience of the USA in the 19th century. It would be impossible to understand the situation of the USA in 1890 without recognising the significance of the causes and consequences of the Civil War. The causes of the war lay mostly in the rapid economic and industrial development of the North while the traditional society of the South continued to hold on to its old ways. The question of slavery or its abolition was not only a moral issue, it was a clash of cultures. The conflict between North and South was also intensified by westward expansion because the emergence of new western states destabilised the fragile political balance between North and South.

The consequences of the Civil War widened the divide between North and South. In the years before 1890, the North East was transformed by industrialisation and urbanisation. The West and the Middle West were transformed by intensive settlement and the end of the frontier life. However, these deep and rapid changes had little impact on the South. Few immigrants went to the South. Industrialisation and the growth of big business were limited. The South remained isolated and alienated.

Many southerners were embittered, clinging to their memories of a lost way of life and nursing their grievances against the consequences of defeat and the northern **carpet-baggers** who were perceived to have looted the wealth of the South in the aftermath of the Civil War. Although the years between 1865 and 1877 were known proudly in the North as the Age of Reconstruction, they were seen in the South as years of suffering and broken promises.

The South remained a world apart. Despite the abolition of slavery, racial segregation was still entrenched. White dominance excluded African-Americans from the political process and took away their voting rights. **Disenfranchisement** reached a peak in the 1880s. The political life of the South was firmly in the hands of white **segregationists**. The rest of the country took little interest and the main political parties accepted the status quo.

One important consequence of the Civil War was political. Abraham Lincoln and the Republican Party had led the North to victory by 1865, and the Republican Party held power through the years of Reconstruction.

## Key terms

**Carpet-baggers:** a derogatory term for northerners who moved to the South after the Civil War to make a profit from Reconstruction.

**Disenfranchisement:** preventing people from registering to vote.

**Segregationists:** people who believe that different human races should be kept separate. In the US context at the end of the 19th century, this meant whites keeping African-Americans in inferior social, political and economic conditions.

The result was the white South voted overwhelmingly for the Democratic Party. The 'Solid South' became a major part of the electoral base of the Democrats and this voting pattern continued until the 1960s. This meant that little pressure was put on southern politicians to change their ways. The South's isolation would not be overcome until generations later, with the migration of African-Americans from the rural South to the cities of the North in the 1950s and the rise of the civil rights movement.

Between 1865 and 1890, the rest of the country experienced massive change – through industrial growth, the completion of the settlement of the West and the impact of mass immigration.

The USA was already a booming economic power by 1890. At about this time, Germany was becoming Europe's 'superpower', overtaking Britain as the top producer of steel and leading the way in key new industries such as electrical engineering, chemicals and armaments. Yet America's productive capacity was already far greater than Germany's and the USA possessed almost unlimited natural resources in both the energy and raw materials for industry and in the capacity for agricultural development.

In 1890 and for generations afterwards, Europeans were fascinated by the images and myths of the American West. Buffalo Bill's Wild West Show was already a popular touring attraction; soon after 1890 'Westerns' would become the staple diet of feature films in the cinema. However, by 1890 the days of the Old West (which had only begun in the 1840s) were already nearly over.

The continuous expansion of the railways meant that wagon trains and long-distance cattle drives were things of the past. Lawless frontier towns were becoming modernised. The great age of buffalo hunting was over because the vast herds of buffalo, estimated to have numbered 60 million, had been hunted to the edge of extinction. Settler society was filling the empty spaces of the Great Plains. A rush of western states achieved statehood. Native Americans, who had once roamed free over the Great Plains, were confined to shrinking reservations.

In 1890, at the Battle of Wounded Knee Creek, the last rebellion by the independent Sioux nation was crushed and about 200 Sioux warriors were killed. It was a symbolic end to the old American frontier. The 1890 US census announced that 'Up to and including 1880, the country had a frontier of settlement but at present the unsettled area has been so broken into isolated bodies of settlement that there can hardly be said to be a frontier line.'

## Key chronology

**Landmarks in the development of the USA**

**1607** First permanent English colonial settlement is established at Jamestown, Virginia.

**1620** Arrival of the Pilgrim Fathers in New England.

**1664** Capture of New York from the Dutch.

**1763** French defeated in the Seven Years War.

**1775** Outbreak of the American War of Independence.

**1787** Founding of the US Constitution.

**1825** Erie Canal built.

**1846** Beginning of the Oregon Trail.

**1849** California Gold Rush and the acceleration of opening of the West.

**1865** Victory of the North over the South in the American Civil War.

**1869** Completion of the first transcontinental railroad, the Union Pacific.

**1877** End of the era of Reconstruction.

**1890** Battle of Wounded Knee Creek and the end of the Indian wars.

---

Up to our own day, the American history has been in large degree the history of the colonisation of the Great West. The frontier produced men of a practical turn of mind, full of restless energy and the exuberance that comes with freedom. Now, the paths of the pioneers have widened into broad highways. The forest clearing has been expanded into affluent towns. The ideals of the pioneer in his log cabin will now enlarge into civic life for the common good.

**2**
*Frederick Jackson Turner addressing the American Historical Association in 1893*

---

Mass immigration had not yet reached its peak in 1890. In the years to 1914, a flood of immigrants would arrive: Jews from the Russian Empire; peasants from southern Italy, Spain, Portugal and south-east

Europe. The influx of these people would accelerate the growth and modernisation of the USA at terrifying speed. However, by 1890 American society had already been transformed by the earlier generations of immigrants: Irish in Boston, Scandinavians in the Great Lakes region, Chinese labourers brought in to help build the transcontinental railways. People from just about everywhere settled in the great metropolises of Chicago and New York.

The fact that the USA was already a 'melting pot' of many different nationalities meant that it was important to prevent European loyalties from creating divisions in American society. By 1890, millions of new American citizens had come from backgrounds in the empires of Germany, Russia or Austria-Hungary. Great numbers of Irish immigrants had strong anti-British feelings. The USA had little interest or influence in foreign affairs.

On the other hand, the USA already had the potential to become a great power by 1890 and several factors were pushing towards this. Above all, the vast economic growth of the USA during the 19th century resulted in a massive increase in overseas trade. The expansion of the American economy led to the demand for markets abroad and to the idea that the USA must establish a powerful navy to protect and expand American trade. By 1898, when the Spanish–American War began, these ideas would involve the USA more deeply in international affairs.

## Timeline

The colours represent events relating to the USA during the period: Red: Political, Green: Economic, Blue: Social, Black: International/the USA's place in the world

| 1890 | 1896 | 1898 | 1901 | 1904 | 1905 |
|---|---|---|---|---|---|
| The accession of Idaho and Wyoming brings the number of states in the Union to 44 <br><br> The US census notes that there is no longer a moving frontier in the American West <br><br> The Sherman Antitrust Act is passed by Congress | William McKinley's election victory marks the beginning of a lengthy period of Republican political dominance | Victory in the Spanish–American War marks the rise of 'American imperialism' and establishes control over Cuba and the Philippines | Theodore Roosevelt becomes president after the assassination of McKinley <br><br> The Platt Amendment is passed by Congress | Theodore Roosevelt proclaims the Roosevelt Corollary to the Monroe Doctrine after establishing US influence over Panama | President Roosevelt acts as mediator in the Treaty of New Hampshire, ending the Russian–Japanese War |

| 1919 | 1920 | 1922 | 1923 | 1924 |
|---|---|---|---|---|
| Woodrow Wilson is received in Europe as a conquering hero at the start of the Paris Peace Conference <br><br> The Volstead Act brings in the era of Prohibition <br><br> The Attorney General, A. Mitchell Palmer, makes thousands of arrests of suspected radicals in the 'Red Scare' | Two radicals, Sacco and Vanzetti, are sentenced to death for murder. Their case causes controversy and becomes a national sensation <br><br> Woodrow Wilson's attempts to persuade Congress to ratify the Treaty of Versailles and to approve American membership of the League of Nations ends in failure <br><br> The Republican Warren G. Harding wins the presidential election, promising that he would return the USA to 'normalcy' | The Washington Naval Conference establishes agreed international restrictions on building battleships | Warren G. Harding dies in office. Calvin Coolidge becomes president | The election victory of Calvin Coolidge continues the period of Republican political dominance <br><br> The Dawes Plan, backed mostly by American loans, restructures Germany's reparations payments <br><br> Quotas for immigration into the USA are tightened up by the National Origins (Quota) Act |

| 1931 | 1932 | 1933 | 1935 | 1936 |
|---|---|---|---|---|
| The Great Depression begins, many banks fail, unemployment rises sharply and wheat prices drop even further <br><br> Al Capone's career in crime ends when he is imprisoned on charges of tax evasion | The depression intensifies. Unemployment reaches nearly 25 per cent <br><br> Herbert Hoover loses the presidential election to Franklin D. Roosevelt. The Democrats win control of both the House and the Senate | Hitler comes to power in Germany <br><br> Congress repeals the Volstead Act, ending Prohibition <br><br> Franklin D. Roosevelt launches the New Deal in the Hundred Days after his inauguration | President Roosevelt launches the Second New Deal <br><br> Huey Long, Governor of Louisiana and a strong opponent of Roosevelt's policies, is assassinated in Baton Rouge <br><br> The drought conditions of the dust bowl reach the worst levels yet | Franklin D. Roosevelt wins re-election |

## 1912

New Mexico and Arizona achieve statehood, bringing the number of states in the Union to 48

The Republican Party splits. Theodore Roosevelt runs for president on behalf of the 'Bull Moose' Progressive Party, ensuring the defeat of President Taft

Woodrow Wilson wins the presidency for the Democrats

## 1914

War begins in Europe. The USA proclaims neutrality

President Wilson sends US forces to occupy the port of Vera Cruz in Mexico

## 1915

The sinking of the *Lusitania* worsens US relations with Germany

The epic silent film *Birth of a Nation*, directed by D. W. Griffith, gains a national audience and gives a favourable impression of the Ku Klux Klan

## 1917

Germany resumes unrestricted submarine warfare. Together with discovery of the Zimmermann Telegram, this pushes the USA into entering the First World War on the side of the Allies

Congress passes the Espionage Act

## 1918

The First World War ends

The Spanish Flu pandemic begins, leading to millions of civilian deaths

## 1925

Support for the Ku Klux Klan dips sharply after a series of scandals involving Klan leaders

The 'Monkey Trial' in Dayton, Tennessee dramatises the conflicts over the teaching of Darwin's theory of evolution in schools

## 1927

Sacco and Vanzetti are finally executed after long years of judicial appeals

The aviator Charles Lindbergh becomes a national hero after his solo flight across the Atlantic

The era of talking pictures begins with *The Jazz Singer*

## 1928

The US stock market reaches record heights

The Kellogg-Briand Pact, sponsored by foreign ministers of the USA and France, attempts to secure international agreement to renounce war

Herbert Hoover becomes president after defeating Democratic candidate Al Smith

## 1929

The stock market boom continues until the autumn. In October, the Wall Street Crash causes massive losses for speculators

## 1930

Dust storms affect Arkansas at the start of years of drought in the South and West

## 1937

After years of cautious economic recovery, there is a slowdown. The Roosevelt Recession begins

The Ludlow Amendment shows the strength of isolationism in Congress

The Japanese invasion of China causes alarm to US policymakers

## 1940

The war in Europe affects politics in the USA and brings pressure on President Roosevelt from isolationists like Charles Lindbergh

Roosevelt controversially runs for a third term as president and wins re-election

## 1941

After considerable controversy, the Lend-Lease agreement is concluded with Britain

Relations between the USA and Japan deteriorate

After the surprise Japanese attack on Pearl Harbor, the USA declares war on Japan

## 1944

American war production reaches maximum output

Landings by Allied forces in Normandy begin the liberation of Occupied Europe

Franklin D. Roosevelt is elected for a fourth term

## 1945

At the Yalta Conference, Roosevelt, Churchill and Stalin make agreements about the post-war world. Roosevelt dies shortly afterwards and is succeeded by Harry Truman

After Germany's surrender, the war with Japan continues until August, when two atomic bombs are dropped on Hiroshima and Nagasaki. The war ends

# 1 Politics, economy and society

*In this chapter you will learn about:*

- the American political system – how power was shared between the federal government and the states, the nature of the main political parties and the role of the presidents – and how that system developed in the years that followed

- how society was changed by the impact of mass immigration

- the rise of big business and its impact on the economy and politics.

Look at the United States today. We have made mistakes. We shall make mistakes in the future and fall short of our own best hopes. But none the less, is there any nation on the face of the earth which can compare with us in ordered liberty, in peace and in the largest freedom? Contrast the United States with any country in the world today and ask yourself whether the situation of the United States is not the best to be found. The United States is the world's best hope. Strong, generous and confident, we have nobly served mankind. Beware how you trifle with this marvellous inheritance, this great land of ordered liberty, for if we stumble and fall, then freedom and liberty everywhere will go down in ruins.

**1**     *Henry Cabot Lodge, August 1919*

**Fig. 1** *A French postcard of New York harbour*

### Key profile

#### Henry Cabot Lodge

Henry Cabot Lodge (1860–1924) was senator for Massachusetts from 1893. He was a strong believer in an expansionist foreign policy for the USA and was influential in leading American political opinion in foreign affairs. At the end of the First World War he came into bitter conflict with Woodrow Wilson over American commitment to the League of Nations.

Henry Cabot Lodge was the long-serving senator for Massachusetts. He made the speech in Source 1 in Washington, DC in August 1919 as part of his campaign against President Woodrow Wilson and the idea of a League of Nations.

By 1919, after victory in the First World War, the USA was vastly more powerful than it had been in 1890. Its economy was more developed, its population had almost doubled and its importance in world affairs was much greater. However, the key theme of Lodge's speech is the thread of idealism and moral certainty running through it. From the founding of the American Republic after the War of Independence onwards, Americans believed that their country and its political system stood for something special, different from and better than the Old World.

In 1890, the USA was only beginning its rise towards world power but was already convinced of its superiority over other ways of life and political systems. Other people were convinced, too. Millions of immigrants had streamed across the ocean hoping for a better life as American citizens. Between 1890 and the 1920s, even more millions would follow, most of them sailing past the Statue of Liberty as they came into New York harbour.

> Not like the brazen giant of Greek fame,
> With conquering limbs astride from land to land;
> Here at our sea-washed, sunset gates shall stand
> A mighty woman with a torch, whose flame
> Is the imprisoned lightning, and her name
> Mother of Exiles. From her beacon-hand
> Glows world-wide welcome; her mild eyes command
> The air-bridged harbor that twin cities frame.
> 'Keep, ancient lands, your storied pomp!' cries she
> With silent lips. 'Give me your tired, your poor,
> Your huddled masses yearning to breathe free,
> The wretched refuse of your teeming shore.
> Send these, the homeless, tempest-tost to me,
> I lift my lamp beside the golden door!'

**2** *Poem by Emma Lazarus and inscribed on the plinth of the Statue of Liberty*

## The political system and the role of the president

The workings of the US political system have influenced some of the key moments in American history – from the Civil War to **Prohibition**; from Woodrow Wilson's fight for the League of Nations to Franklin D. Roosevelt's fight for the New Deal.

### Historical context

The political system of the USA was already more than 100 years old by 1890. The written Constitution established at Philadelphia in 1787 provided the original model for modern **republican democracy**. However, it should be remembered that this system was designed to fit the conditions of the late 18th century, when the Thirteen Colonies broke away from British colonial rule. The Constitution of 1787 proved to be both durable and flexible in adapting to change but Thomas Jefferson and the Founding Fathers were not only motivated by the spirit of the American Revolution. They were also influenced by the specific conditions of their time.

The right to bear arms, for example, is regarded by many present-day commentators as out of date and dangerous in a modern urban society, but it made perfect sense in the individualistic frontier society of the 1780s. The fact that there is such a long interval between the election in November and the inauguration of the president in the following year

**Key terms**

**Prohibition:** a legal ban on making, selling or transporting alcoholic drinks.

**Republican democracy:** this political system is based on the rejection of monarchy and the idea of government by equal citizens, elected by the people.

**Fig. 2** *The USA*

may seem pointless now but was absolutely necessary then, as it allowed time for delegates to the Electoral College to make what might be a long and difficult journey to their state capital. There were times, such as during the transition from Herbert Hoover to Franklin D. Roosevelt in 1933, when this time delay had important political consequences.

Between 1787 and 1890, there were several amendments to the American Constitution and the political system had to be adapted to reflect changing circumstances. In the early years after independence, for example, the 'federalists', led by Alexander Hamilton, attempted to extend the powers of the president and the **federal government** at the expense of state's rights. In the event, the federalists did not achieve their aims and the ideas of the 'Jeffersonians' – those in favour of limited powers for the federal government – were followed.

In the 1860s, the balance shifted. The victory of the North in the American Civil War prevented the southern states from **seceding from the Union**. As a result, the powers of the presidency and the Supreme Court were increased. The Civil War had a huge impact on the political system in other ways. It led to the abolition of slavery. As Abraham Lincoln was a Republican, his party was seen in the defeated South as an enemy. It was after the Civil War that the present two-party system, Democrats against Republicans, began to take shape.

## Key terms

**Federal government:** the central government in Washington, DC, which deals with national issues such as war and foreign affairs. 'Federalists' wanted the powers of central government to be stronger; 'Jeffersonians' wanted central government to interfere with people's lives as little as possible.

**Seceding from the Union:** breaking away completely – to declare independence from the USA. Whether states had the right to do this, or whether the other states had the right to prevent it, was a complex constitutional question.

## Key profile

### Abraham Lincoln

Abraham Lincoln (1809–1865) was a little-known Republican lawyer from the mid-West. He was elected as president in 1860 and led the North to victory in the American Civil War of 1861–5. In 1863, his speech at Gettysburg committed the USA to the abolition of slavery. Lincoln was assassinated in 1865, shortly after the end of the war. Since then, he has always been regarded as one of the greatest American presidents – although not in the defeated South.

The Civil War opened the way for the westward expansion of the USA. Transcontinental railroads were completed. The Great Plains were brought under cultivation. The frontier moved ever further west until 1890, the year that it was officially declared that there was no longer a moving frontier. The settlement of the West greatly enlarged the number of states in the Union. In 1787 there had been only 13 states; by 1861 there were 34. Between 1863 and 1890, 10 new states joined, 6 of them in 1889 and 1890.

These western states (Nevada, Colorado, North and South Dakota, Montana, Washington state, Idaho and Wyoming) sent to Congress politicians who represented individualist, local concerns. Between 1896 and 1912, four more territories achieved statehood: Utah, Oklahoma, New Mexico and Arizona. The political balance of the USA had changed.

## The political system

The USA was a federal republic, sharing power between central government and the states – the 13 former colonies of 1787. The desire to get away from the arbitrary monarchical rule of George III meant that strict limits were placed on the powers of the federal government and the president. The federal government could not interfere in most issues affecting people's daily lives such as education, roads and policing. The powers of the legislatures and governors in the individual states were extensive. There was also a strong tradition of local democracy. City mayors and other public officials like sheriffs and fire chiefs got their jobs through direct elections and were accountable to the people who voted for them.

The powers of the federal government were limited to things like war, foreign policy and interstate commerce. It is important to keep in mind the lasting effects of these limits on the power and reach of the federal government. It helps to explain why Al Capone was not imprisoned in 1931 for the numerous murders he had committed: murder was a state crime and Capone knew that the corrupt state authorities would never come after him. He was charged instead with tax evasion which could be prosecuted by federal agencies. Similarly, when natural disasters occur, state governors are often anxious for the president to declare a state of emergency because this enables the federal government to provide money to help with what would otherwise be a state problem.

The balance of power between the states and the federal government was a key aspect of the American Civil War. The main constitutional issue in 1861 was whether the southern states of the Confederacy had the right to secede – to break away from the USA altogether. The outcome of the Civil War decided the issue against the states and by 1890 the powers of the federal government were stronger than they had been in 1787. However, the rights of the states remained strong. In 1936 and 1937, Franklin D. Roosevelt found himself in constitutional trouble when parts of his New Deal legislation were ruled illegal because they infringed state rights.

The Constitution was guided by two great principles: the separation of powers and the system of 'checks and balances'. The separation of powers set out clear boundaries between the executive (the presidency), the legislature (Congress) and the judiciary (the Supreme Court). The checks and balances were designed to prevent any one arm of government from becoming too powerful and acting in an authoritarian way. The president could pass legislation and carry on the government only with the approval of Congress, but the president had the power to use his presidential veto to block acts of Congress if he deemed them unacceptable. Congress was given sufficient powers to balance, but not overrule, presidential authority. The role of the Supreme Court was

### Key chronology

**The western states by date of statehood**

| | |
|---|---|
| **1859** | Oregon |
| **1861** | Kansas |
| **1864** | Nevada |
| **1867** | Nebraska |
| **1876** | Colorado |
| **1889** | North and South Dakota, Montana |
| **1890** | Idaho and Wyoming |

### Cross-reference

For more on the **New Deal**, see pages 107–10.

to uphold the Constitution and to protect the rights of the individual against unconstitutional action by government.

### The presidency

The president was head of state, to serve a term of four years. The vice-president had little direct power; his role was to provide an approved replacement if the president should be removed by death or incapacity. The president nominated key appointments – Supreme Court justices and high government posts such as the secretary of state and the secretary of the treasury – but the system of checks and balances ensured that these appointments had to be ratified (that is, approved by majority voting) by Congress.

The president could rely on his 'inner circle' of advisers but this was on a small scale. The idea of the 'administration' – the massive White House political machine popularised by *The West Wing* – did not exist until much later. In the 1790s, any communications between the different regions were limited and slow; the concept of 'public opinion' did not yet have much significance. By 1890, the situation was beginning to change, with railways, telegraph services and major regional newspapers. However, the system of daily 'news management' was still in its infancy.

### Congress

Congress was what constitutional experts call a bicameral legislature, with two separate bodies: the House of Representatives and the Senate. Congressmen were elected to the House of Representatives and had to face election every two years. The number of congressmen from any state varied according to the size and population of the state. Congressional committees met to monitor specific areas of government.

Balancing the power of the House of Representatives was the Upper House, or Senate. Two senators represented each state, large or small, and served for a term of six years. In 1890, there was not yet a system of direct elections to the Senate; until 1913 they were selected by each state.

There was a careful balance between the presidency and Congress. Congress could block laws proposed by the White House if a majority voted against; equally, the president could use his veto to block measures initiated by Congress. At times, as with the Republicans in 1896 and Franklin D. Roosevelt in 1932, a president might be in a strong position because his party had a strong majority in both houses of Congress, but this situation did not always apply. In any case, the main political parties were rarely united or obedient. Managing Congress required political skill and compromises.

### The Supreme Court

Above the political battlefield was the Supreme Court – the defender of the Constitution, which had the last word on whether or not the actions of politicians were lawful. For example, Congress had the power to pass legislation – but legislation might be overturned if the Supreme Court deemed it unconstitutional.

The political balance in the Supreme Court was important. In theory, the court was impartial but, at different times, a majority of the nine justices might be more liberal or more conservative. In the 1930s, for example, the Supreme Court reflected the fact that most of the justices had been appointed during the long period of Republican dominance up to 1933. This created difficulties for President Franklin D. Roosevelt in pushing through the more radical measures in his Second New Deal. Presidents could influence the make-up of the Supreme Court if vacancies happened to occur during their presidency but were usually careful to avoid open confrontations.

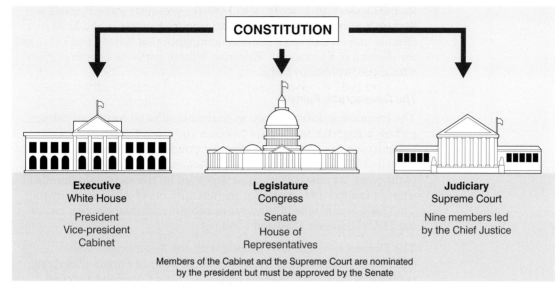

**Fig. 3** *The American political system*

## The political parties

The USA had a clearly defined two-party system by 1890. Both major parties were strongly influenced by the American Civil War. The Republicans were originally formed as an anti-slavery movement in 1854 and were led to victory in the Civil War by Abraham Lincoln. After 1865, the Republicans gradually moved away from their liberal traditions and increasingly came to represent the conservative elements of American politics, often closely linked to big business. The Democrats came to be associated with more reformist elements, supported by sectional interests such as small farmers, in the southern and western states – and, later, with links to trades unions.

Neither the Republicans nor the Democrats were united parties. Both were loose coalitions linking together quite varied interest groups. Local issues were extremely important. Any politician at national level had to have a strong local power base and was always concerned to represent local interests. This did not only apply to individuals. Many issues that became important in national politics had their roots in local campaigns, such as the campaign for Prohibition and the origins of progressivism.

Partly because of these strong local influences, there was no clear-cut divide between right and left. Both parties contained conservative elements as well as reformers. One peculiarity of Democrat voting strength, for example, was solid support from white segregationists in the South. This reflected southern resentment of Republicans carried over from the American Civil War. After 1865, where African-Americans had the vote they were likely to vote Republican, although neither party did much to support their cause. Both major parties appealed almost exclusively to white voters.

In 1890, the two parties were still in the process of change and development, subject to volatile political swings reflecting the rapid changes in American society, especially mass immigration. In the following decades, several political movements – socialism, populism and progressivism – seemed likely to gain mass support, but in the event the dominance of the Republican–Democrat two-party system was never broken.

In 1890, the parties were evenly matched. From 1885 to 1889 and again from 1893 to 1897, President Grover Cleveland held the White House

### Cross-reference

For more on **progressivism**, see pages 17–8.

**Populism** is covered in more detail on page 17.

**Grover Cleveland** is looked at in more detail on pages 19–20.

### Activity

**Group activity**

Working in two groups, make a list of the main ideas and principles promoted by the Republican and Democratic parties. Choose the key differences between the two parties.

for the Democrats; from 1889 to 1893 the president was a Republican, Benjamin Harrison. The Republicans won back power in the 1896 election and established a political dominance that lasted until 1912, and the election of a Democrat, Woodrow Wilson, partly as a result of splits within the Republican Party.

### The Democratic Party

The Democratic Party claimed to be the oldest of all American political parties, going back to Thomas Jefferson and the 1796 election when the Jeffersonians opposed the federalist policies of Alexander Hamilton. The Civil War caused deep political divisions and led to a re-alignment of the party. Its new political base depended on the sectional interests of western farmers and, especially, the resentments of white southerners. The 'Solid South' voted Democrat in every presidential election except one (1928) between 1880 and 1960.

The Democrats could not compete with the Republicans, who controlled the presidency from 1860 to 1884 until Grover Cleveland, governor of New York, became president. After Cleveland's second defeat in 1896, the Democrats endured more long years in opposition, as a party of protest.

■ **Exploring the detail**

**The role of secretary of state**

The position of secretary of state, which in other countries might be called foreign secretary, was one of the most important posts in government, usually held by either a close ally of the president or a rival whose strong party support meant he had to be rewarded with a plum job.

■ **Cross-reference**

See page 69 for more details on the 'Monkey Trial'.

■ A closer look

### William Jennings Bryan

The dominant political personality in the Democratic Party in their years of opposition was William Jennings Bryan (1860–1925). A westerner from Nebraska (with strong support in the South) and legendary public speaker, Bryan's nickname, 'the Great Commoner', reflected his image as a Populist and a moralist – as the champion of the people against big business and big government. Bryan ran for president in 1896, 1900 and 1908 and was briefly secretary of state under Woodrow Wilson. Right at the end of his life, he came to prominence again as the legal champion of the anti-Darwinists in the 'Monkey Trial' of 1925.

Bryan's moral crusades included the campaign to introduce Prohibition; support for the anti-Darwinists who opposed the teaching of evolution in schools; anti-imperialism; and support for 'Silverites' – those who believed, especially in the 1890s, that the mass circulation of silver coins would end the 'shortage of money' and drag America out of recession. He had strong support in the South and the Plains states but always faced hostility from business and big-city voters. Bryan was unlucky in that his rise coincided with a swing to the Republicans, who won four consecutive victories in presidential elections from 1896. There were also internal party divisions, partly caused by attitudes to Bryan himself. His strong support for populism alienated many traditional Democrat politicians.

As industrialisation went further and faster, the Democratic Party became more and more associated with the opponents of big business, especially the emerging labour unions. However, most of the Democratic Party's leaders held conservative social views and reliance on the 'Solid South' meant that there was no support for the advancement of African-Americans. In the end, Bryan's career was one of opposition rather than of power.

Divisions within the Democratic Party widened after 1900 because of the long run of electoral defeats and the rising influence of progressivism. In 1912, Woodrow Wilson, a southerner and a Progressive, won the three-sided race against William Howard Taft and Theodore Roosevelt, and so became only the second Democratic president since the Civil War.

### The Republican Party

The Republican Party was moulded by the Civil War. The party was formed in 1854 as part of the anti-slavery movement. Abraham Lincoln, elected in 1860, led the North to victory during the Civil War and laid the foundations of Republican political dominance in the years that followed. At that time, the Republicans were not especially conservative or pro-business. This changed in the 1880s and 1890s. The 1896 presidential election brought about a political revolution and handed power to the Republicans for a generation. The Democrats did not win back the White House until 1912.

### A closer look

#### Mark Hanna, big business and the 1896 election

Mark Hanna's reputation as a brilliant and inventive political analyst has lasted more than a century. He was the political hero and role model for Karl Rove, the man behind the targeted campaigning that produced victories for George W. Bush in 2000 and 2004, and often referred to as 'Bush's Brain'. Mark Hanna symbolised the growing influence of big business in American politics and laid the foundations for the political dominance of the Republicans between 1896 and 1912. This dominance was partly due to the splits within the Democrats but was also masterminded by Mark Hanna, the man credited with devising the tactics that built a winning platform for Republican success.

Hanna himself built a huge business empire in coal, iron, shipping and banking. He was a brilliant fundraiser and used his influence to build the career of William McKinley, first as the governor of Ohio in 1892 and then as a presidential candidate. In 1896, he spent more than $100,000 of his own money in promoting McKinley: the outcome of the Republican Convention in St Louis was decided before it began.

Hanna then raised vast sums of money from big business, estimated as high as $16 million, to help ensure McKinley defeated Williams Jennings Bryan, often using negative tactics and employing 1,400 Republican campaign workers to send letters to voters. Victory in 1896 was consolidated by another decisive win in 1900. Figure 4 reveals the geographical extent of Republican success. Mark Hanna had political ambitions of his own and may well have been the Republican presidential candidate in 1904 but for his sudden and unexpected death.

Conservative, pro-business Republicans were powerful within the party from the 1890s but the Republican Party also had a reformist wing that was influenced by the ideas of progressivism. This wing promoted ideas such as **anti-trust laws**, social justice and conservation. The leading figure was Theodore Roosevelt, vice-president from 1901 and president in his own right from 1901 to 1909.

Conservative Republicans like Mark Hanna were not at all enthusiastic about Theodore Roosevelt. They saw Roosevelt as politically unreliable.

### Key term

**Anti-trust laws:** legislation to prevent big business from fixing prices.

### Activity

#### Source analysis

Study Figure 4. Why do you think the Republicans did well in some geographical regions but not in others?

### Cross-reference

For more information about **Theodore Roosevelt**, see pages 34–41.

However, party divisions did not come out in the open because Roosevelt was so successful and popular among the electorate. The Republicans maintained their political dominance until 1912 but, even then, the reason why they lost the presidency to Woodrow Wilson was not a massive switch in voting strength. It was caused mostly by internal party divisions and the decision of the former president, Theodore Roosevelt, to run as a progressive candidate against the incumbent, President William Howard Taft. After two terms of Woodrow Wilson, the Republicans began another period of political dominance from 1920.

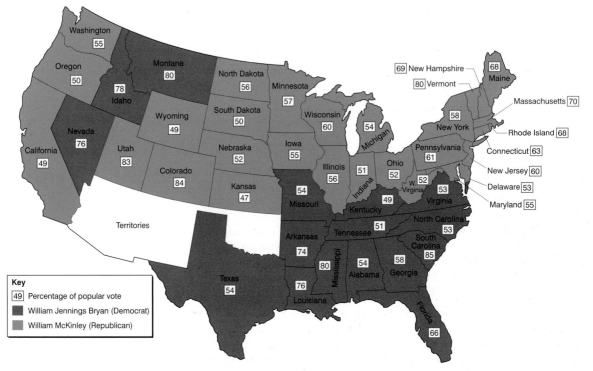

**Fig. 4** *The 1896 presidential election*

## Activity

### Group activity

Working in two groups, make two lists: one giving the reasons why the Republicans were so dominant between 1896 and 1912, and one giving the reasons why the Democrats were unsuccessful. Arrange the top three factors in each list in order of importance.

## Cross-reference

The **rise of socialism** is covered in more detail on pages 30–33.

### Other political movements

The stranglehold of the two main parties was maintained throughout the period from 1890 to 1920 but there were strong challenges from rival political movements. At different times, it seemed possible that any or all of socialism, populism or progressivism would make a breakthrough in national politics. Several other movements led prominent campaigns in favour of specific social issues, such as Prohibition, pacifism, women's suffrage and nativism. Although all these movements made a significant impact at times, they did not break the mould of American politics; their main effect was to influence the policies and political fortunes of the Republicans and Democrats.

Socialism made great advances in terms of the development of trades unions and campaigns for labour rights and improved working conditions but, unlike in Europe, it did not lead to a mass political party. The talented and widely respected socialist leader, Eugene Debs, ran for president on five occasions between 1904 and 1920 but the 6 per cent of the vote he achieved in 1912 proved the high point. There was no national political organisation and socialism remained on the political margins. The political backing of the trades unions was eventually directed towards support for the Democratic Party, which reduced the chances of a powerful separate socialist party developing.

## Key profile

### Eugene Debs

Eugene Debs (1865–1926) was a Socialist – a railroad worker and trades union activist who played a leading part in the formation of the Industrial Workers of the World (IWW), although he split from the union in 1908. He was sent to jail for his part in the Pullman Strike of 1894. Debs was a brilliant speaker and ran for president five times – in 1900, 1904, 1908, 1912 and finally 1920. He strongly opposed the First World War and was sent to jail again – he was actually in prison while fighting the 1920 election.

Populism had a big influence on the Democratic Party. When William Jennings Bryan emerged as a national figure in the 1890s, many people saw populism as 'swallowing' the Democratic Party; in the end, it was the other way around. Populism was mostly an anti-urban movement hostile to big business and central government. The Populist Party was formed in 1889–90 based on support from farmers in the Great Plains and the south-west, who opposed the dominance of American political and economic life by the banks, big business and the rich east-coast elites. Populist ideas were set out in the Omaha Platform of 1892, with attacks against America's reliance on the gold standard by 'Silverites' – those who campaigned for reform of the financial system, and especially for the mass circulation of silver, because they believed that their economic problems were caused mostly by insufficient money in the economy as there was not enough gold. This idea is also known as 'bimetallism'.

Other populist causes included the campaign against drink and demands to bring in Prohibition; the fight against Darwinism and the teaching of evolution in schools; and anti-imperialism and pacifist opposition to the expansionist foreign policies of McKinley and Theodore Roosevelt. The Populist Party as a separate organisation was overshadowed by William Jennings Bryan and the Democrats. After 1908 it virtually went out of existence.

Progressivism was massively influential between 1890 and 1920 and seemed likely to become a national political force in its own right. As president, Theodore Roosevelt's policies were often influenced by progressive ideas. Robert La Follette and the progressive 'insurgents' within the Republican Party gained considerable support and this caused a growing split with William Howard Taft and the conservative 'stalwarts'. As well as the politicians, Progressives included several influential journalists.

## Key profile

### Robert La Follette

Robert La Follette (1855–1925) was governor of Wisconsin from 1901 until he became senator in 1906. He was a leader of the progressive 'insurgent' Republicans, campaigning for the rights of ordinary voters and consumers against big business. He hoped to run for president in 1912 but was overshadowed by Theodore Roosevelt. He was a notable opponent of US involvement in the First World War.

## Exploring the detail

### 'Bull Moose' progressivism

'Bull Moose' progressivism derived its name from a typically colourful statement by Theodore Roosevelt. In answer to a journalist's question in 1912, Roosevelt declared himself 'as fit and strong as a bull moose'. The name stuck and is always associated with Roosevelt's run for the presidency in 1912.

## Key chronology

### Landmarks in the development of progressivism

**1901** 'Trust-busting' policies are carried out by President Theodore Roosevelt.

**1904** Jane Addams emerges as a supporter of the women's suffrage movement.

**1909** Progressivism emerges in Wisconsin under Senator Robert La Follette.

**1912** 'Bull Moose' Progressive Party is formed, led by Theodore Roosevelt.

**1916** Progressive wing of Republican Party is defeated.

## Key term

**'Trust-busting'**: refers to government activities designed to break up trusts or monopolies.

## Activity

### Group activity

Assume you are political advisers to one of the candidates fighting the 1912 election on behalf of the Progressive Party. Working in two groups, draw up two lists: one giving the negative points that should be included to attack the other parties, and the other giving the policies that the Progressive Party will bring in if it is elected.

Progressives believed in government intervention. Strong central authority was needed to bring about reforms and to ensure efficiency. Progressives wanted to protect people's rights against corruption and to fight against the evils of industrialisation, but without going as far as socialism. They appealed for 'social justice', including causes such as women's suffrage, direct elections to the Senate and protection of the environment by better conservation. Some Progressives were pacifists and anti-imperialists but most were strongly nationalist.

In 1912, a separate 'Bull Moose' Progressive Party was formed as a vehicle for Theodore Roosevelt to run for the presidency against President William Howard Taft and the traditional conservative Republicans. Roosevelt was defeated but the Progressive Party continued to exist as a separate force until 1916. Progressivism also appealed to sections in the Democratic Party. In 1912, Woodrow Wilson adopted many progressive ideas during his election campaign and later in his policies as president.

The growth of mass newspapers and the rise of 'muckraking journalism' also played a big part in strengthening the influence of progressivism. Writers such as S. S. McClure and Lincoln Steffens, and the novelist Upton Sinclair, used mass-circulation magazines to highlight 'the shame of the cities' and to campaign for government intervention and reform. In areas like conservation, **trust-busting**, workers' compensation schemes and protection of child labour, they increased the pressure on politicians to be seen to be doing right.

> To destroy this invisible government, to dissolve the unholy alliance between corrupt business and corrupt politics is the first task of statesmanship today.

**3**     *Platform of the Progressive Party, 1912, attributed to Theodore Roosevelt*

## Key profile

### Jane Addams

Jane Addams (1860–1935) was a peace campaigner who won the Nobel peace prize. She was the leader of the settlement house movement and a committed supporter of the campaign for Prohibition. She was also a feminist and became vice-president of the National American Women's Suffrage Association in 1911.

### The political parties and the situation of African-Americans

One great reform movement – the campaign to advance rights and freedoms for African-Americans – made little progress during this period. A number of prominent reformers, led by Booker T. Washington and William Du Bois, achieved prominence with their campaigns for greater equality and access to legal rights and education. Washington established links with white politicians, including President Roosevelt, and with rich northern philanthropists who donated money to improve education.

In 1906, Du Bois founded the radical Niagara movement, which merged in 1909 with other groups to become the National Association for the Advancement of Colored People (NAACP). However, despite the commitment and idealism of these reformers, discrimination was not overcome. Between 1890 and 1920, the reality was exclusion not equality – this was the worst period of discrimination against

African-Americans since the abolition of slavery. **Disfranchisement** occurred all over the South. Many people migrated northwards in search of casual labour in the cities.

In addition to bending the law to take away the vote, there was also institutionalised segregation, the system widely known as '**Jim Crow**'. Laws were passed to segregate the races in railway carriages, hotels, restaurants and even law courts. Organised violence by white racists was widespread, with frequent lynchings. The worst of many cases of racial violence was a riot in Atlanta in 1906, when 11 black people were killed and dozens of homes and businesses were burned down.

Whites outside the South supported segregation. A key decision of the Supreme Court in 1896 (*Plessy* v. *Ferguson*) ruled by eight votes to one in favour of the principle of segregation and completely undermined the Fourteenth Amendment of the Constitution, which granted citizenship to and protected the rights of freed slaves. Leading segregationists, such as 'Pitchfork' Ben Tillman of South Carolina and James Vardaman, the 'White Chief' of Mississippi, were important allies of William Jennings Bryan in the Democratic Party. The 'Solid South' was one of the main pillars of electoral support for the Democrats. Both major parties were content to appeal to the white vote and to accept segregation and disfranchisement. In 1920, far fewer black people in the South were eligible to vote than in 1890.

Despite all the rapid economic and social changes between 1890 and 1920, the American political system and the role of the president remained intact. Reform movements had considerable impact on many aspects of society, but only when they were able to win support from the political mainstream. The stranglehold of the two main parties remained intact, and the political power and prestige of the presidency was strengthened.

## The role of the president

**Table 1** *The presidency, 1892–1920*

| Year | President | Political party | Vice-president | Defeated candidate |
|---|---|---|---|---|
| 1892 | Grover Cleveland | Democratic | Adlai Stevenson | Benjamin Harrison |
| 1896 | William McKinley | Republican | Garret A. Hobart | William J. Bryan |
| 1900 | William McKinley | Republican | Theodore Roosevelt | William J. Bryan |
| 1904 | Theodore Roosevelt | Republican | Charles W. Fairbanks | Henry Davis |
| 1908 | William Howard Taft | Republican | James S. Sherman | William J. Bryan |
| 1912 | Woodrow Wilson | Democratic | T. R. Marshall | William Howard Taft |
| 1916 | Woodrow Wilson | Democratic | T. R. Marshall | Charles Evans Hughes |
| 1920 | Warren G. Harding | Republican | Calvin Coolidge | James M. Cox |

Grover Cleveland was in many ways a traditional Democrat. His power base was northern New York state, where he was mayor of Buffalo before becoming governor of New York in 1882 and then president in 1884. Cleveland was anti-imperialist, pro-**free trade** and hostile to big business interests. Having been defeated in 1888, he made a comeback in 1892.

The re-election of Grover Cleveland reflected a key difference between politics then and now – the long careers of major politicians. In the modern media-driven age, political careers are short and rarely survive an electoral defeat. The trend was different in the years between 1890 and 1920. William Jennings Bryan, for example, was the defeated Democrat

### Key terms

**Disfranchisement:** removing the right to vote.

**'Jim Crow':** the racial system that operated in southern and border states between 1877 and 1965. Jim Crow laws discriminated against African-Americans with regard to attendance in schools and the use of facilities such as restaurants, theatres, hotels, cinemas and public baths. Trains and buses were also segregated and in many states marriage between whites and African-Americans was forbidden.

**Free trade:** the idea of open markets and minimum trade barriers between nations.

### Activity

Write a letter to be sent to Washington on behalf of African-Americans living in the Deep South in the 1890s, outlining their grievances and appealing for help from politicians at a national level.

candidate for the presidency in 1896 and 1900, but he remained prominent in national politics. He ran for president again in 1908 and then served as secretary of state to Woodrow Wilson from 1912. Similarly, Theodore Roosevelt's career did not end after his two terms as president from 1901 to 1908; he ran again in 1912 and remained a key player in Republican politics until 1920.

Grover Cleveland was generally successful in his second term but lost a lot of support from the trades unions when he was accused of 'betraying' the railroad workers by using government agencies to assist the railroad companies in putting down the 1894 Pullman Strike. At the National Convention in Chicago in 1896, the nomination went to the charismatic moral crusader, William Jennings Bryan. It was Bryan's bad luck that the height of his career coincided with a long period of Republican political dominance after the 'turning point' election of 1896; he lost three presidential election campaigns and the Democrats were in opposition for 16 years.

### Republican dominance

The presidential election of 1896 changed the face of American politics for a generation. The Republicans held a dominant position until 1912 and would almost certainly have won again then but for internal party divisions and personality clashes. This period of political dominance was based on the backing of big business and on the political skills of Mark Hanna, a clever political strategist from Cleveland, Ohio. From 1896 William McKinley was able to rely on a strong position in the country and in Congress. In 1900, with Theodore Roosevelt as his new running mate, McKinley was re-elected with an increased majority, partly as a result of the popularity gained through success in the Spanish–American War. The political power of the presidency increased significantly.

The assassination of President McKinley in 1901 brought Theodore Roosevelt to the presidency. 'TR' was a controversial politician, both because of his larger-than-life personality and because of his support for several progressive causes, including attacks on corruption and support for anti-trust actions. This alienated sections of the Republican Party, notably Mark Hanna and other conservative supporters of big business, and intensified the ideological divisions within the party between progressive 'insurgents' and traditional conservatives who called themselves 'stalwarts'.

Theodore Roosevelt was generally able to overcome opposition from elements in his own party because he was so successful, both at home and abroad. He easily won re-election in 1904 and even after his term in office ended in 1908 he remained a key player in national politics. Roosevelt virtually chose his successor, William Howard Taft, and the Republican domination over the Democrats carried on for four more years.

Roosevelt supposedly retired to the sidelines after 1908 but made a significant return to party politics in 1910. Deep ideological differences turned Taft and Roosevelt into bitter rivals and did much to undermine Taft's presidency. In the 1912 election, these party divisions brought about the defeat of Taft and handed power back to the Democrats. Theodore Roosevelt made a bid for the presidency in 1912, running on

**Fig. 5** *The assassination of President McKinley, 1901*

behalf of the newly founded Progressive Party. He won 4 million votes – almost a million more than President Taft – and in the process ensured victory for Woodrow Wilson.

The splits in the Republican Party continued after 1912, until the nomination of a moderate candidate, Charles Evans Hughes, enabled a show of unity in the 1916 election. Hughes lost narrowly, by less than 1 million votes. During the war, President Wilson's prestige rose enormously and there seemed little chance of any significant Republican revival.

After long years in the political wilderness, Democrat fortunes revived in 1912 with the election of Woodrow Wilson. This revival was brought about partly by the internal divisions in the Republican Party, weakening President Taft's chances of re-election, and partly by the political skills of the new leader of the Democrats. Wilson was a reformer and an intellectual, having made his name running Princeton University, and a moral idealist. He was also an organised and skilful politician, capable of dominating national politics and winning re-election by a convincing margin in 1916.

At the start of his second presidential term, Wilson seemed to be building a powerful base for further Democrat successes in the future. It was the adverse impact of foreign affairs, not any failings in domestic politics, which undermined Woodrow Wilson and caused the Democrats to lose the presidential election in 1920.

## Mass immigration and its impact on society and politics

### A nation of immigrants

Although there were already 9 million foreign-born Americans by 1890, mass immigration had not yet reached its peak. American society had already been transformed by the earlier generations of immigrants, such as the Irish in Boston, Scandinavians in the Great Lakes region and Chinese labourers brought in to help build the transcontinental railways. A bewildering mix of peoples and cultures settled in the great metropolitan cities like Chicago and New York.

**Fig. 6** *An idealised image of immigrants arriving in New York in about 1890*

I was especially curious about my grandfather, Martin Feeney. I found out from the record office that Martin's father, Thomas Feeney, had lived with his wife, Mary, and their children in the small town of Lettercalla in Ireland in the 1870s. Also living in the same house was Martin's brother, Patrick, and his famil – 14 people in a one-room cottage. Times were hard, the stony soil unyielding. Thomas and his family left for America. Patrick stayed behind.

*Margaret Feeney, researching the experiences of her family leaving Ireland for America*

## Activity

### Statistical analysis

Study Tables 2 to 5.

**1** Which was the fastest-growing city in 1890?

**2** What was the rate of increase in Italian immigration between 1880 and 1890?

**Table 5** *Place of birth of the foreign-born population of the USA, 1890*

| Place | Population (millions) |
|---|---|
| Europe | 8.10 |
| Asia | 0.01 |
| Latin America | 0.02 |
| Canada | 0.90 |
| *Total* | *9.03* |

Between 1890 and 1914 an even greater flood of immigrants arrived. Most of the earlier waves of immigration had come from northern Europe: Britain, Ireland, Germany and Scandinavia. After 1900 there was a surge of immigrants from southern and eastern Europe: Jews from the Russian Empire; peasants from southern Italy, Spain and Portugal; and millions from south-east Europe. The influx of these millions accelerated the transformation of the USA, with rapid economic growth fuelled by a population explosion.

**Table 2** *European immigration to the USA, 1880–1919*

| Period | Number of people |
|---|---|
| 1880–1889 | 5,248,568 |
| 1890–1899 | 3,694,294 |
| 1900–1909 | 8,202,388 |
| 1910–1919 | 6,347,380 |

**Table 3** *Italian immigration to the USA, 1871–1910*

| Period | Number of people |
|---|---|
| 1871–1880 | 55,759 |
| 1881–1890 | 307,326 |
| 1891–1900 | 655,899 |
| 1901–1910 | 1,927,102 |

**Table 4** *Population growth of selected cities in the USA, 1870–1910*

| City | 1870 (thousands) | 1890 (thousands) | 1910 (thousands) |
|---|---|---|---|
| New York | 942 | 2,507 | 4,766 |
| Philadelphia | 674 | 1,043 | 1,549 |
| St Louis | 319 | 452 | 687 |
| Chicago | 299 | 1,099 | 2,191 |
| Boston | 251 | 426 | 671 |

In the years after 1890, the flood of immigrants reached its peak, motivated by both 'push' and 'pull' factors. Many immigrants were lured to America by a positive dream of improving their lives – what would nowadays be called economic migrants. Huge numbers of other immigrants would be more accurately described as having been uprooted – people forced to leave by political or religious persecution, such as many Russian Jews, or by economic collapse and the fear of starvation, such as many from southern Italy.

As a boy, I experienced a thrill every time one of the men from our village returned home from America. Listening to them, at only eight or nine years old, I was already playing with the idea of going to America. My notion of the United States then was of a great, amazing, somewhat fantastic place – a sort of Paradise – huge beyond conception, thousands of miles across the ocean, a place full of movement and excitement. In America everything was possible. There, even the common people were 'citizens' not 'subjects' as they were in the Austrian Empire and most other European countries.

**5** *A young Slovenian boy's impressions of America*

**Fig. 7** *East European female immigrants arriving at Ellis Island, New York*

My great-grandfather, David, came to America in the mid-19th century. He died when my father was 12. I knew that he had died in Chicago, so I looked for information there. It turned out he had actually lived in New York and was buried there. I searched the New York City directories. In the 1890 directory, I found several Woodles: Bernhard, a peddler [pedlar]; Leopold, a stenographer; and Morris, a capmaker. Later, I found evidence that David Woodle (then spelled Wudl) and his brothers, Moses and Simon, had emigrated from the village of Ckyne in Bohemia. Most of the Jews who carried on living in Ckyne later died in the Holocaust.

**6**

*Alex Woodle, researching the history of his Jewish family from Bohemia*

**Activity**

**Revision exercise**

Using evidence in this chapter, outline in order of importance the main motives for European immigrants coming to the USA in the late 19th century.

## The impact of immigration on society

The traditional view of this process of assimilating new citizens has been described as a 'melting pot', forging a new nation from 'wretched and huddled masses' seeking a better life in the New World. It is a view of American society symbolised by the Statue of Liberty looking down at the immigrant ships arriving in New York. It might be more accurate to describe it as a 'mosaic' because immigrants often clung together in localised communities. Almost every city in the east, for example, had its 'Little Italy'. Catholic Irish and Polish immigrants were prominent in cities like Boston and Chicago. Jews from tsarist Russia dominated the garment industry in New York until it was later taken over by Italians. Other immigrant communities included Greeks, Hungarians and South Slavs.

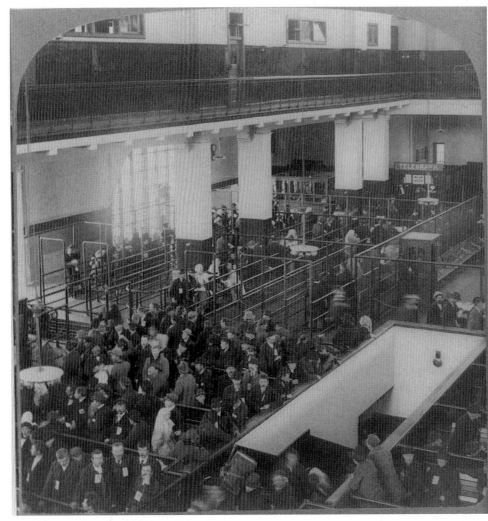

**Fig. 8** *The immigration reception centre at Ellis Island*

After 1890, mass immigration led to fundamental changes in American society and politics. Although many of the earlier immigrants settled in rural areas, their greatest impact was in the cities. By 1900, the population of the USA had grown to 76 million. There were 38 cities with a population of 100,000 or more. The birth rate was actually declining compared with earlier in the 19th century but the death rate, at 16.5 per thousand, was the lowest in the world. After 1900, the increase in the urban population was dramatic.

This tide of immigration brought with it tensions and sources of discrimination and conflict. There were many cases of friction between newly arrived immigrants and those who had settled earlier. Such friction was often made worse by matters of religion. The majority of those who had arrived from northern Europe in the 19th century were Protestants; those who came after 1900 were mostly Catholics or Jews.

Political power remained chiefly in the hands of WASPs – white Anglo-Saxon Protestants – and there were many instances of anti-Catholic prejudices holding back the political aspirations of immigrant communities. There were also rivalries between different ethnic groups as they competed for things such as jobs and housing. Irish-Americans provide one notable example of an ethnic community sticking together and maximising its political influence.

 A closer look

### Tammany Hall

Irish-Americans were already well established in cities such as Boston, New York and Chicago when the surge of mass immigration from southern and eastern Europe began in the 1890s. Irish-Americans were keen to strengthen their position in the labour unions and in politics. They wanted to fight against discrimination from those above them in the pecking order and to maintain superiority over the newer arrivals. The role of the Irish in politics was symbolised by Tammany Hall.

Tammany Hall was built on East 14th Street in New York City in 1830. The hall, and the Tammany Society that used it, had existed well before the time of mass immigration but it developed into a powerful local political machine that always supported the Democratic Party and relied on immigrants, and above all the Irish, to provide its electoral base. From the 1870s onwards, the political boss of Tammany Hall was Irish; Charles F. Murphy held control there from 1902 to 1924. Tammany Hall had a powerful influence within the Democratic Party because of its ability to 'get out the vote'.

Tammany's system was based on patronage. Tammany provided immigrants with a social safety net, assisting immigrants with jobs, social integration and a sort of welfare network. Tammany got to control businesses, influence the police and certain labour unions, and 'look after' the immigrant community in return for its voting support. It was regularly accused of corruption but was able to keep political control in New York almost continuously because of its strong immigrant support and because the Democratic Party relied on it at election time.

One of the most important social issues affected by the impact of immigration was the battle over Prohibition. This was not specifically an immigrant issue but it reflected the impact of immigration on American society. It showed the gulf between small-town America and the new booming cities. It had religious overtones because not only the Irish but also many in the new wave of immigrants after 1890 were Catholic. Most of the new arrivals came from a cultural background in which social drinking, especially by men, was a central part of social life.

The fight by the **temperance movement** to outlaw alcohol was not new in the 1890s – there was a long tradition of campaigns against drink, especially from the small-town, Protestant elements in American society – but it gained more support in reaction against the rapid rise of the big cities and their immigrant populations. The battle lines were drawn between the **'Wets'** and the **'Drys'**, led by influential pressure groups such as the Prohibition Party, the Woman's Christian Temperance Union (WCTU) and the Anti-Saloon League.

### A closer look

#### Carrie Nation and the WCTU

The organisation and political skill of the Anti-Saloon League made it the leader in the campaign for Prohibition, but the longest-established temperance pressure group was the Woman's Christian Temperance Union (WCTU), which was founded in 1874. The WCTU was militantly Protestant, crusading against alcohol, drunkenness and domestic violence. WCTU branches were set up in many locations and the movement gained widespread support from churches, newspapers and local politicians.

The most notorious campaigner against the 'demon drink' was Carrie Amelia Nation (1846–1911), a believer in direct action

### Key terms

**Temperance:** the watchword of campaigners against the 'demon drink', the word literally means moderation. Actually, what most people in the temperance movement wanted was not moderation but a total ban on alcohol.

**Temperance movement:** the origins of the temperance movement went back to the middle of the 19th century, but the campaign became much more vocal and effective from the 1880s. Many in the movement were women, some of whom were also involved in the campaign for women to get the right to vote.

**'Wets':** those opposed to Prohibition. They were more likely to live in less affluent areas of the community and represent the working class. Many belonged to the Catholic and Lutheran Churches and were of Russian and German backgrounds.

**'Drys':** those in favour of Prohibition. Loyal Prohibitionists were more likely to be native-born, that is, born in America.

**Fig. 9** *Carrie Nation campaigns for Prohibition, 1902*

and proud of her nickname, the 'Kansas Bar Room Smasher'. Nation was exceptionally tall and had a gift for attracting publicity. Her extreme views probably arose from the fact that her first husband had been an alcoholic, but she was also intensely religious. Her favourite saying about herself was 'I'm just a bulldog running about at the feet of Jesus, barking at what He doesn't like.'

She first smashed up a bar with a hail of large stones but then developed her own trademark style of what she called 'hatchetations' – smashing mirrors and bar fittings with an axe. She was often arrested and fined, so she had to be an efficient fundraiser through her lecture tours and the sale of replica 'Carrie Nation axes'. Although she was seen by many as an extremist, she did a lot to publicise and promote the temperance ideal up until her death in 1911.

The cultural conflict over Prohibition overlapped with other reactions against immigration. The ideas of nativism and the movement to limit or stop the inflow of immigrants grew stronger, especially after 1910. One aspect of this was the revival of the Ku Klux Klan (KKK) during and after the First World War.

Immigration was not only from Europe. Two million African-Americans migrated northwards between 1900 and 1910 in search of economic opportunity. They were met with hostility and discrimination much like that in the South and the migration had little impact on social attitudes or politics. It is sometimes said that the First World War paved the way for change through the experiences of African-American soldiers. In reality, African-American soldiers almost always served in segregated units, and there were many instances of discrimination and racial conflict within the armed forces. It would be another generation, after another world war, before long-term trends finally opened the door for the civil rights movement of the 1950s and 1960s.

The anti-immigration movement had several strands. There were local acts of violence, such as the lynching of 11 Italian-Americans in New Orleans in 1891. The trades unions, most of whose members were immigrants or sons of immigrants, were opposed to continued mass immigration because it would keep pay levels low. Small-town America worried about 'alien' influences undermining traditional moral and religious values. Such ideas gained widespread support during the first years of the 20th century, when immigration levels peaked.

The issue gained national prominence in the 1912 election but did not have much effect because all three main candidates – Wilson, Taft and Theodore Roosevelt – were opposed to the idea of setting quotas to control immigration. Even so, the subject remained an emotive one, especially when war broke out in Europe in 1914; one of the factors behind the policy of neutrality between 1914 and 1917 was anxiety about stirring up nationalistic tensions among Germans, the Irish or those whose origins had been in Austria-Hungary.

After the USA entered the war in 1917, persistent fears about the possible disloyalty of immigrant groups became even more intense. By the end of the war the political and social mood of the nation had changed. Both the drive to place strict limits on inward migration and the campaign for a legal ban on the consumption of alcohol had gained a strong political momentum.

## The rise of big business and its impact on the economy and politics

The USA was already a booming industrial power by 1890. At about this time, Germany was becoming Europe's 'superpower', overtaking Britain as the leading producer of steel and leading the way in key new industries such as electrical engineering, chemicals and armaments. However, America's productive capacity was already far greater than Germany's and the USA possessed almost unlimited natural resources in both the energy and raw materials for industry and in the huge potential for agriculture. In the years after 1890, the process of industrialisation rushed ahead even faster.

The expansion of the US economy was fuelled by several key factors:

- The huge increases in manpower and markets that came with mass immigration so that the labour force was always growing and the construction industry was always booming.
- The impact of technology enabled the rapid development of transatlantic steamship companies and the mechanisation of industry. The invention of the steel plough, the refrigerated ship and the expansion of the railways led to a massive expansion of meat production for both the domestic economy and exports abroad.
- The opening up of the Great Plains enabled the cultivation of fertile virgin lands and the production of huge surpluses of cereals.

Perhaps above all, the expansion of the American economy was marked by the rise of big business and the emergence of huge industrial companies such as Bethlehem Steel, the Carnegie Steel Company and John D. Rockefeller's Standard Oil Company. Many of these companies merged to make vast combined enterprises linking manufacturing, railroads and shipping. Men like Cornelius Vanderbilt and Samuel Cunard built up massive transportation empires. There was also rapid expansion of banking and finance. J. Pierpont Morgan was the most famous of the new breed of big financiers who provided the capital for industrialisation.

### Activity

**Revision exercise**

Study the text on mass immigration and Tables 2 to 5.

**1** Make a list of reasons why mass immigration benefited the US economy during this period.

**2** Make a list of reasons why the impact of mass immigration led to social and political divisions.

### Exploring the detail

**The Bethlehem Steel Corporation**

The Bethlehem Steel Corporation was formed in 1857 at Bethlehem, Pennsylvania. It became the second largest steel producer in the USA after Pittsburgh's US Steel. The company was one of the largest shipbuilding organisations in the world and a powerful symbol of US industrial manufacturing leadership. It rose to great prominence in American industry, producing the first wide-flange structural shapes to be made in the USA. These shapes were largely responsible for ushering in the age of the skyscraper and establishing Bethlehem Steel as the leading supplier of steel to the building industry.

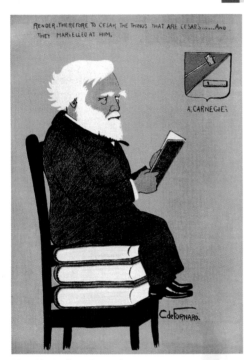

**Fig. 10** *Andrew Carnegie*

## Key profiles

### Andrew Carnegie

Andrew Carnegie (1835–1919) was founder of the Pittsburgh-based Carnegie Steel Company, forerunner of US Steel, and one of the richest and most powerful of the big industrialists. He sold out to J. Pierpont Morgan in 1901 and spent his final years as a philanthropist, spending his huge fortune on good causes.

### John D. Rockefeller

John D. Rockefeller (1839–1937) founded the Standard Oil Company in 1870, becoming the world's richest man and the first US dollar billionaire.

### Cornelius Vanderbilt

Cornelius Vanderbilt (1794–1877) was a transport pioneer who founded many early ferries and railroads. By the time of his death, Vanderbilt controlled 16 major railroad companies including the New York Central.

### J. Pierpont Morgan

J. Pierpont Morgan (1837–1913) was a banker and financier who made his fortune reorganising American railroad companies. In 1891, he masterminded the mergers that led to the formation of General Electric.

## Exploring the detail

### The Sherman Antitrust Act

The Sherman Antitrust Act of July 1890 was aimed at preventing price-fixing and unfair competition by big monopolies. It gave the federal government powers to break up such monopolies into smaller units to ensure genuine competition.

The act put responsibility on government attorneys and district courts to pursue and investigate trusts, companies and organisations suspected of violating the act. President Theodore Roosevelt used the act extensively in his antitrust campaign, which included dividing the Northern Securities Company. President William Howard Taft used the act to split the American Tobacco Company.

The size and scale of American wealth and the relatively new and unregulated financial system meant that great entrepreneurs (often referred to as 'robber barons') could use ruthless methods to defeat their competitors. In 1890, Congress passed the Sherman Antitrust Act in an attempt to limit the power of the big new monopolies such as Rockefeller's Standard Oil Company, but the impact of the act was patchy and monopolies continued to grow. The great entrepreneurs could also wield massive political influence, especially in the Republican Party. In the 1890s the foundations were in place for the future American domination of the world economy.

**Table 6** *Iron ore, coal and population figures, 1870–1913*

| Country | 1870 | 1890 | 1913 |
|---|---|---|---|
| **Iron ore production (millions of tonnes)** | | | |
| France | 1.2 | 2.0 | 5.2 |
| Germany | 1.4 | 1.7 | 16.7 |
| Britain | 6.0 | 8.0 | 10.4 |
| USA | 1.7 | 9.5 | 31.6 |
| **Coal production (millions of tonnes)** | | | |
| France | 17 | 26 | 41 |
| Germany | 33 | 64 | 154 |
| Britain | 112 | 185 | 292 |
| USA | 40 | 143 | 517 |
| **Population (millions)** | | | |
| France | 37.6 | 38.4 | 39.6 |
| Germany | 48.4 | 52.6 | 65.1 |
| Britain | 28.4 | 36.9 | 42.8 |
| USA | 38.7 | 62.6 | 100.4 |

## Activity

### Statistical analysis

Study Table 6. Write a paragraph to explain the speed and size of American economic expansion after 1890.

## Big business and American politics

**Fig. 11** 'All freight … MUST pass here and pay any tolls we demand.'
A contemporary cartoon attacking Cornelius Vanderbilt and the 'railroad
barons'

The rise of big business had a massive political impact.
Industrialisation made the USA into a more urban society and created
a powerful new elite of wealthy industrial 'barons'. These men were
able to gain direct political influence, especially within the Republican
Party and over the emerging mass newspapers. At the same time,
the growth of big business created a strong backlash against it. The
emergence of a new mass labour force led to the spread of socialist
ideas and the organisation of labour into trades unions.

There were problems caused by the volatile 'boom-and-bust' nature
of industrial and financial growth. Sudden downturns in the economy
led to hard conditions for farmers, small businesses and workers.
The financial Panic of 1893, for example, led to a sharp drop in
gold reserves and put pressure on the government to bring in a high
**protective tariff**.

### Key term

**Protective tariff:** in economic hard
times, producers often ask for a
protective tariff to be imposed on
imported goods in order to make
them more expensive to buy,
thereby 'protecting' the home
market by reducing competition.

Both Populists and Progressives were quick to blame big business for these evils and to campaign for 'trust-busting' by the federal government to restrict the power of railroad companies and big industrial conglomerates. However, the protest movements rarely achieved lasting success; big business kept its economic power and political influence. This was shown during the election of 1896, which has been described as 'the struggle of the robbers against the robbed'.

From 1896 the political influence of big business remained a key factor in politics. Big business contributed to the political dominance of the Republican Party until 1912. Many of the new mass newspapers promoted the ideas of their rich proprietors and helped to ensure that efforts to bring about reforms against the interests of rich businessmen were frustrated.

> A great change came over capitalism about 1880 or 1890. Formerly characterised by a very large number of small businesses run by individuals, it was increasingly taken over by large corporations. The first modern corporations emerged from the railroad companies. They became the usual form of organisation for industry and commerce. And as corporations grew in size and number, so the influence and importance of banking grew. In commerce, large department stores started to appear about 1890. At around the same time, huge industrial organisations merged into even bigger ones, especially in the production of steel.

**7**     *The rise of capitalism in the United States. By American historian R. R. Palmer in **History of the Modern World**, 1971*

## Industrialisation and the rise of American socialism

**Fig. 12** *Workers in a Chicago meat processing factory*

Industrialisation and the rise of big business inevitably aroused opposition and protest from those groups in society who were adversely affected. Industrial expansion meant the emergence of mass labour in the new factories – the breeding ground for socialism. Business leaders were afraid of organised labour; one of the surprising features of American history is the failure to produce a mass socialist political movement similar to those that developed in Europe at this time.

The rise of organised labour did succeed in terms of the growing strength of trades unions, but there was no breakthrough for socialism as a political party. This would have seemed surprising in the 1890s, when trades union power was rapidly increasing and the expansion of big factories and the influx of immigrants from Europe seemed certain to strengthen American socialism.

> Friends, we meet here in Louisville today to celebrate the idea that on May the first 1890 the wage-workers of America and the world will lay down their tools to establish the principle that workers should have eight hours of labour, eight hours of sleep, and eight hours for anything they wish. We are living in the late 19th century, in the age of electricity and steam that has increased wealth a hundred fold. We insist that this wealth has been brought about by the intelligence and energy of working men.

**8**  *Extract from 'What does the working man want?', a speech by the trades union leader Samuel Gompers in 1890*

In the late 19th century, trades union membership increased rapidly and there were a number of high-profile strikes that caused alarm among conservatives and big business. In 1886, the American Federation of Labor (AFL) was founded under the leadership of Samuel Gompers, who remained its president until his death in 1924. The membership of the AFL grew quickly to more than 300,000, gaining most support from skilled workers. In 1890, the United Mine Workers of America (UMWA) was formed in Ohio.

Under Samuel Gompers, the AFL concentrated on improving working conditions rather than radical socialist politics. Gompers did not align himself with the socialist leader Eugene Debs – the differences between them were accentuated during the First World War, when Gompers was strongly pro-war whereas Debs was a pacifist. In 1907, the AFL established strong links with the Democratic Party at national, state and local level. The link between the Democrats and the AFL became one of the key features of American politics for generations.

The AFL was perceived by many workers as too moderate and having little concern for the unskilled. This led to the formation of the more radical Industrial Workers of the World (IWW) in 1905, led by 'Big Bill' Haywood and Eugene Debs (although Debs broke away from the organisation in 1908). By 1912, membership was above 50,000. The IWW, popularly known as the 'Wobblies', advocated openly socialist ideas and saw no room for compromise between workers and employers; there were strong links between the IWW and anarchists such as Emma Goldman. These links accentuated the divisions in the IWW between those who wanted political action as opposed to those who wanted direct action through strikes and boycotts.

### Cross-reference

To recap on **Eugene Debs**, see page 17.

## Key chronology

### The rise of American socialism

**1886** Formation of the AFL.

**1890** Formation of the UMWA.

**1894** Pullman Strike against railroad companies.

**1901** Formation of the Socialist Party of America.

**1905** Formation of the IWW.

**1907** Alliance between the AFL and the Democratic Party.

**1912** Eugene Debs achieves highest-ever vote for a socialist presidential candidate.

## Cross-reference

The **'Red Scare'** is covered in more detail on pages 60–64.

## Activity

### Talking point

Marshal the arguments for and against the proposition that 'Ordinary people suffered badly from the consequences of rapid economic growth in the USA by 1890.'

## Cross-reference

For more on **Robert La Follette**, see page 17.

## Key profile

### Emma Goldman

Emma Goldman (1869–1940) was a Russian Jewish immigrant who believed in the ideas of anarchism and overthrowing the State. She was also a radical feminist who was eventually deported from the USA at the time of the 'Red Scare'.

Big business and conservatives regarded the IWW as dangerously revolutionary, especially during a wave of strikes that were often accompanied by violence such as the McKees Rocks strike of 1912 and the Wheatland Hop Riot of 1913. Employers frequently used the courts to suppress the 'socialist threat', with legal injunctions against strikes and many prosecutions of socialist leaders. During the First World War, the IWW was attacked for being unpatriotic. In 1919 and 1920, it was a major target of the 'Red Scare'.

The rise of political socialism never matched the strength of the trades unions. Although the socialist leader Eugene Debs was talented and respected, he could never break the mould of two-party politics.

The increasing power of big business caused other important reactions apart from socialism, above all from populism and progressivism. Partly because of the influence of populism, the electoral map began to show more clearly the division between support for the Democratic Party from a coalition of blue-collar workers, western voters and the 'Solid South', with support for the Republicans concentrated in the East and Middle West. Even more so than populism, progressivism was a direct response to the power of big business. It was strongest within the Republican Party but also influenced Democrats.

One prominent Progressive was Robert La Follette, who served three terms in the House of Representatives in the 1880s and was governor of Wisconsin from 1901 to 1906, when he was elected to the Senate. From the early 1890s, La Follette was a leading figure of the 'insurgents' in the Republican Party, opposed by the anti-reform 'stalwarts'. When Theodore Roosevelt became president in 1901, he gave his support to the Progressives on many issues, especially on corruption and enforcing anti-trust actions.

From 1908, the divisions within the Republican Party worsened. This led to the formation of a separate 'Bull Moose' Progressive Party to fight the 1912 election, led by Theodore Roosevelt. It is difficult to measure support for the Progressive Party in and after 1912 because of the dominant personality of its presidential candidate, Theodore Roosevelt. Many of the votes cast for Roosevelt were based on loyalty to him personally, not to the Progressive Party. The progressive wing reunited with mainstream Republicans in 1916. Progressivism achieved little as a separate party but its influence on American politics was important. Woodrow Wilson, the victorious Democratic candidate in 1912, supported many progressive ideas in his campaign.

The rise of big business did much to shape American society and politics, both directly and indirectly, between 1890 and 1920. Directly, big business transformed the USA into a modern economic superpower and had a dominant influence over politics and public opinion. Indirectly, the rise of big business had an equally important impact in provoking various forms of opposition and social mobilisation from those who felt threatened by the consequences of industrialisation and the raw power of capitalism.

### Summary questions

1 Explain why the Democratic Party was overshadowed by the Republicans between 1896 and 1912.

2 Explain why the American economy expanded so much and so fast between 1890 and 1920.

# The USA and the world

*In this chapter you will learn about:*

■ why the USA was traditionally an anti-imperialist nation

■ the impact of Theodore Roosevelt on American foreign policy

■ why the USA entered the First World War in 1917

■ why American political and public opinion rejected Wilson's post-war peace.

Any nation that has trained itself to a career of unwarlike ease and isolation is bound in the end to go down before other nations which have not lost the manly and adventurous qualities. If we Americans are to be a really great power we must strive to play a great part in the world. If we shrink from the hard contests, then bolder and stronger peoples will pass us by and win for themselves the domination of the world.

**1**         *Theodore Roosevelt speaking in 1899, a year before his election as vice-president*

## ■ The objectives of US foreign policy from 1890

For the United States to acquire colonies would be to place a false construction upon the foundation stones quarried by our revolutionary patriots from the mountains of eternal truth. It is far better for us to remain a republic standing erect while empires are bowed beneath the weight of their own armaments. It is far better for the United States to be a republic whose flag is loved, where other flags are only feared.

**2**         *William Jennings Bryan's campaign speech in the 1900 presidential election*

### ■ Cross-reference

There is a lot of material about the political careers of **Theodore Roosevelt** and **William Jennings Bryan** in Chapter 1. On pages 39–42 there is more information and an assessment of **Theodore Roosevelt's impact on US foreign policy**.

**Fig. 1** *Theodore Roosevelt*

Theodore Roosevelt and William Jennings Bryan had major impacts on American foreign policy. Roosevelt, the expansionist, came to prominence by his well-publicised actions in the Spanish–American War of 1898 and went on to become a president who followed ambitious and interventionist policies abroad. Bryan, the pacifist, spent much of his long career in politics attacking people like Roosevelt for being immoral and for betraying the ideals of George Washington and the Founding Fathers. This debate about America's rightful place in world affairs lasted long after both men had died.

The USA was far from being a world power before the 1890s. Its foreign policy stance was essentially defensive, seeking to keep the New World of the Americas free of wars and diplomatic tangles. Most Americans were hostile to the ideas of **imperialism** and wished to steer clear of international alliances. However, the events of the 1890s pushed the USA into rapid naval expansion, a war against Spain and the annexation of territories in the Pacific Ocean, far from the USA.

Several of the motives behind this shift in foreign policy were openly expansionist. The rapid growth of the American economy seemed to prove that the USA needed to control new markets overseas. This idea increased the influence of the theorists and politicians who believed in the importance of sea power and in the need for the size and strength of the new American nation to be reflected by greater prestige and influence in the world.

The 1890s was the great age of European imperialism. Many Americans were influenced by the imperialist **ideologies** of the time, including notions of racial and cultural superiority and the need for the USA to accept its 'civilising mission' to raise up non-white societies from their 'backwardness'.

Men such as Senator Henry Cabot Lodge of Massachusetts, Theodore Roosevelt and the naval theorist Alfred Thayer Mahan were influential in promoting expansionism and a more 'forward' American foreign policy based on modern sea power.

## Key profile

### Alfred Thayer Mahan

Alfred Thayer Mahan (1840–1914) was a naval officer who developed new theories about the role and importance of sea power. His career as a naval commander was undistinguished (the one ship he captained sank after a collision) but he wrote a series of influential books and articles recommending American naval expansion. Mahan's most famous book was *The Influence of Sea Power upon History* (1890). He had a close friendship with Theodore Roosevelt, who was assistant secretary for the navy in the 1890s before the Spanish–American War.

Whether they want it or not, Americans must now begin to look outward. Command of the seas is the chief element in the power and prosperity of nations. It is imperative to take possession of such maritime bases as can be righteously obtained. Hawaii occupies a position of unique importance powerfully influencing the commercial and naval control of the Pacific.

**3**                           *Naval theorist Alfred Thayer Mahan, writing in **Atlantic Monthly** in 1890*

On the other hand, many politicians had ideas on American foreign policy that were more traditional and defensive. One such defensive impulse was the Monroe Doctrine and the traditional American hostility to European 'interference'. The Monroe Doctrine had been formulated in 1823 when the USA was a much smaller and weaker country. Although it was based on a defensive mindset, it had always carried with it a presumption that the republics of Latin America would be receptive to American influence, if not

### Key terms

**Imperialism:** refers to a country's desire to extend its power and control over foreign lands, either through diplomacy, economic means or outright military force. Before 1890, the USA had traditionally regarded itself as an anti-imperialist nation, morally superior to the European colonial powers.

**Ideology:** a concept that means more than just ideas – it means ideas organised into a system of principles and beliefs, into a programme for action.

### Question

What were the reasons that made people like Mahan believe that the possession of sea power was especially important for the USA?

### Cross-reference

For more on the **Monroe Doctrine**, see page 1.

## ■ Key chronology

### Landmarks in the development of US expansion

**1890** Publication of Mahan's *The Influence of Sea Power Upon History*.

**1895** Revolt in Cuba headed by Jose Marti, with unofficial American backing.

**1898** Destruction of USS *Maine* and outbreak of the Spanish–American War; Spanish forces defeated in Cuba; annexation of Hawaii, Guam and the Philippines.

**1899** Start of the Filipino Revolt against American rule.

**1900** America participates in the international armed intervention in China.

**1901** The Platt Amendment is passed.

**1903** Settlement of the Alaska Boundary Dispute in favour of the USA; secession of Panama from Colombia; start of the Panama Canal project.

**1904** Roosevelt Corollary is issued to the Monroe Doctrine.

**1905** American mediation in the peace settlement ends the Russian–Japanese War.

**1908** William Howard Taft elected as president and commits to the Dollar Diplomacy.

**1912** Woodrow Wilson elected as president.

domination. It is no accident that the first move by the USA towards an expansionist foreign policy was prompted by concerns about Cuba, a Spanish colony situated only 145 km (90 miles) away from the American mainland.

Another key factor was American perception of events on the other side of the Pacific Ocean. Instability in China led to greater American involvement in the Far East, both for commercial and strategic reasons. The startlingly fast modernisation of Japan after 1868 was seen as a threat to American interests in the Pacific. These worries about Asia and the 'Yellow Peril' were intensified by growing social tensions in the western states in the 1890s caused by fears of the extent of Chinese and Japanese immigration.

All these factors help to explain why the USA adopted a more active foreign policy after 1890, first in Cuba from 1895, then war against Spain in 1898, then the American annexation of Hawaii, Guam and the Philippines, and finally the American participation in the international armed intervention in China in 1900. Slowly, perhaps mostly by accident, the USA began its rise to world power, but this rise was far from straightforward and would not be completed until 1945, after reluctant involvement in two world wars.

> Is America a weakling, to shrink away from the work of the great powers? No! The young giant of the West stands on a continent and has the crest of an ocean on either hand. Our nation, glorious in youth and strength, looks into the future with eager eyes. It rejoices, just as a strong man rejoices to run a race.

**4**  *Theodore Roosevelt in a letter dated 1897 to John Hay, the US ambassador in London*

## The Spanish–American War

The Spanish–American War was recognised at the time as a turning point in US history. Both supporters and opponents of expansionism understood that, for better or worse, relationships between the USA and the outside world were being fundamentally changed.

The origins of the war were in Cuba, which was at that time still part of Spain's American empire. Cuba's economy was already dependent

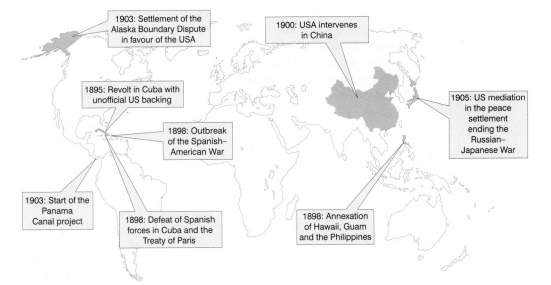

**Fig. 2** *American expansion, 1898–1905*

1903: Settlement of the Alaska Boundary Dispute in favour of the USA

1900: USA intervenes in China

1895: Revolt in Cuba with unofficial US backing

1905: US mediation in the peace settlement ending the Russian–Japanese War

1898: Outbreak of the Spanish–American War

1903: Start of the Panama Canal project

1898: Defeat of Spanish forces in Cuba and the Treaty of Paris

1898: Annexation of Hawaii, Guam and the Philippines

on exporting tobacco and sugar to American markets. When Cuban **Nationalists**, led by Jose Marti, began a revolt against Spanish rule in 1895, they received significant backing from American sympathisers based in New York. The Spanish army crushed the 1895 revolt but their harsh methods were strongly criticised in the USA, where there was strong support for American intervention in Cuba.

Those seeking intervention gained an ideal pretext in February 1898, when an American warship, the USS *Maine*, blew up while stationed in the harbour at Havana. All the evidence suggested that the ship had been destroyed by an internal explosion, but the event was seized on as a Spanish provocation and an excuse for war. A hysterical newspaper campaign was waged by the popular press (often referred to as the 'Yellow Press', especially those newspapers owned by the press baron William Randolph Hearst). The press campaign was encouraged by business interests and politicians, led by Theodore Roosevelt, the assistant secretary of the navy.

Peace could easily have been negotiated but war was the preferred solution. American forces invaded Cuba and gained a swift victory with minimum casualties. This victory helped to make a national hero out of Theodore Roosevelt, who resigned his position in the government and led a volunteer force, the Rough Riders, in the siege of Havana, making sure in the process that there was lavish newspaper coverage of his heroic actions. Spain made peace at the Treaty of Paris and Cuba remained under American military rule until 1902, when it became an American **protectorate**.

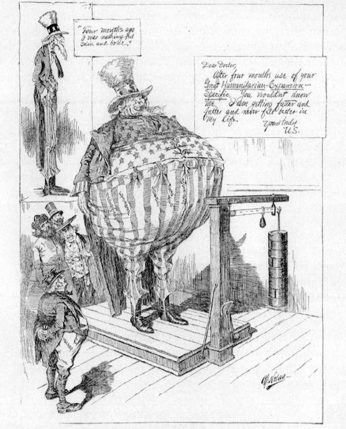

BEFORE AND AFTER TAKING. UNCLE SAM FREELY TELLS HIS PHYSICIAN THAT HIS TREATMENT HAS BEEN A SUCCESS.

**Fig. 3** *'I am getting fatter and fatter and never felt better in my life.'*
*A contemporary cartoon satirising Uncle Sam's (i.e. the US's) expansion after the Spanish–American war*

## Key terms

**Nationalist:** someone who seeks to defend and protect the rights and independence of his or her own nation, and usually a person who puts the interests of the own nation above those of other countries.

**Protectorate:** a state or territory partly controlled by (but not in the possession of) a stronger state. Protectorates are autonomous in internal affairs.

## Exploring the detail

### The 'Yellow Press'

The Yellow Press was a term of abuse directed at the style of journalism in the newspapers and magazines owned by William Randolph Hearst (one of the popular features in Hearst's newspapers was a series called 'The Yellow Kid'). Many people criticised the rabble-rousing tone of the Yellow Press, but it made a lot of money for Hearst's newspaper empire. In 1898, it was claimed that Hearst's nationalist press campaign had actually been a main cause of the Spanish–American War, but most historians now reject this theory.

## Activity

### Revision exercise

Study the key chronology showing US expansion overseas on page 36. Make a list of the five events that you consider to be the key turning points shaping US policy. Rank them in order of importance and add a brief reason for your choices.

## Activity

### Thinking point

1 Using the information in this chapter, create a spider diagram to summarise the main reasons put forward by supporters of an expansionist foreign policy.

2 Which reasons do you believe were the most effective in persuading Americans to believe in such a policy?

If the war of 1898 had been only about Cuba, it might have been seen as an exercise in defending the principles of the Monroe Doctrine. However, the war with Spain included the annexation of other Spanish possessions in the Caribbean and the Pacific; Puerto Rico, Guam and the Philippine Islands became virtual American colonies. The previously independent islands of Hawaii were annexed at the same time because of their significance as a naval base.

The seizure of the Pacific islands was achieved using sea power. Admiral Dewey's Pacific squadron sailed into Manila Bay and destroyed the outdated Spanish fleet. Soon afterwards, American land forces arrived to establish military control. There was a wave of imperialist triumphalism in the American press and among politicians.

Although American officials had gained the support of nationalist rebels, led by Emilio Aguinaldo, by seeming to promise independence for the Filipinos, it soon became clear that this was not going to happen. A Filipino Revolt broke out in 1899, which was only suppressed in 1902 after extensive American military action.

### Key profile

#### Emilio Aguinaldo

Emilio Aguinaldo (1869–1964) was a leader of the campaign for Filipino independence from Spain. In 1898, he organised a rebel force and cooperated with Admiral Dewey in the liberation of the islands. In February 1899, convinced that the Americans had broken their promises to him, Aguinaldo launched the Filipino Revolt against American occupation. The revolt failed but Aguinaldo became the first president of the Philippines soon afterwards. Despite his efforts, the Philippines did not achieve full independence.

The American conquest of the Philippines caused controversy within the USA. For many, it was a betrayal of the principles of freedom and equality. Critics of the new imperialist policy, such as the Anti-Imperialist League, attacked the government for deserting the anti-colonial traditions of the Founding Fathers, and for the violence, paternalism and racial prejudice that had been shown by Americans in their treatment of their 'little brown brothers' as they established control.

> Mine eyes have seen the orgy of the launching of the Sword;
> He is searching out the hoardings where the stranger's wealth is stored;
> He hath loosed his fateful lightnings, and with woe and death has scored;
> His lust is marching on.
>
> I have read his bandit gospel writ in burnished rows of steel:
> 'As ye deal with my pretensions, so with you my wrath shall deal;
> Let the faithless son of Freedom crush the patriot with his heel;
> Lo, Greed is marching on!'

 **5**   *Extract from 'The Battle Hymn of the Republic, Updated' written by Mark Twain in 1901 as a mocking parody of American imperialism*

### Activity

#### Source analysis

Study Source 5. Write a paragraph to explain:

1. What 'message' Twain is trying to get across.
2. The methods he is using to persuade opinion.
3. How effectively he does this.

Political leaders, including President McKinley, protested that they had not been motivated by greedy imperialism but by a 'civilising mission' to aid the development of less advanced peoples. However, public pronouncements about these more idealistic motives were very different from the blatant comments made privately behind the scenes. There is no doubt that events in Cuba and the Philippines were deliberately manipulated to bring about American domination and to stir up popular support for interventionist policies.

## Theodore Roosevelt and US foreign policy

After the Spanish–American War of 1898, issues in the Pacific Ocean, China and Japan became much more important for American policymakers. The Far East was seen as a vital area for the expansion of American trade. The extent of European interference in China was a threat to American interests. There was also concern about the rapid rise of the Japanese Empire.

The main policy of the USA was the Open Door policy set out by John Hay. This was aimed at keeping China free of colonial control and preserving free trade, but the collapse of imperial rule in China led to instability and extensive foreign interference. The USA was keen to see free trade in China and to avoid China being carved up by European powers because American trade would benefit.

In 1900, when the Boxer Rebellion led to foreign embassies in Beijing being besieged, the USA joined the international force that was sent to break the siege and restore order in China. With the defeat of the rebellion, it seemed certain that China would be partitioned between the European powers. The USA saw this as a threat to American trade interests. The result was the Open Door policy, set out by Secretary of State John Hay, to prevent China being carved up and to keep the principle of free trade in China.

At the 1900 election President McKinley was re-elected, with Theodore Roosevelt as his vice-president. When McKinley was assassinated in 1901, Roosevelt became president in his own right. American foreign policy was in the hands of the most committed imperialist in the country. Although American foreign policies were not all down to one man, Roosevelt's ideas and personality did much to shape American policy over the next decade.

In 1901, Congress passed the **Platt Amendment** authorising extensive American intervention in the international and domestic affairs of Cuba. The amendment was incorporated into the Cuban–American Treaty of 1903. Consenting to this showed that Cuba was not really independent but virtually an American protectorate. Later, the Platt Amendment was used to justify American intervention in other parts of Latin America. Its passing in 1901 was a significant departure from the Monroe Doctrine and reflected the new expansionist approach of American foreign policy at that time.

> ARTICLE III. The government of Cuba consents that the United States may exercise the right to intervene for the preservation of Cuban independence, the maintenance of a government adequate for the protection of life, property and individual liberty.

**6**         *Extract from the Cuban–American Treaty, 1903*

In 1903, the Alaska Boundary Dispute took place with Canada and Britain. There had been long-standing disagreement over the exact line of the southern border of Alaska. In tough negotiations, Roosevelt obtained

**Activity**

**Talking point**

Using the information in this chapter, assemble appropriate evidence to support a debating position to be used during the 1900 presidential election, for and against the proposition that 'Current American foreign policy is a betrayal of our nation's principles of freedom and equality.'

**Key term**

**Platt Amendment:** passed by Congress on 2 March 1901, this was claimed to protect Cuba's independence from foreign intervention. It permitted extensive American involvement in Cuban international and domestic affairs and was eventually repealed in 1934.

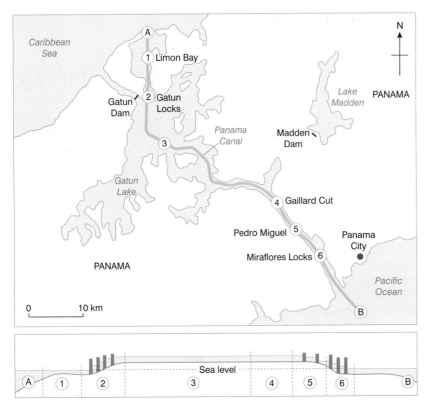

**Fig. 4** *The Panama Canal*

**Fig. 5** *Construction work on the Panama Canal*

a border settlement in favour of American rights. The issue was not important in itself but was typical of Roosevelt's assertive approach.

In the same year, Roosevelt pushed through perhaps his most significant achievement, the Panama Canal project. The idea of a canal through Central America, linking the Atlantic and the Pacific, was not new. A massive French scheme had been launched in the 1880s, but it had collapsed because of technical and financial problems. Roosevelt took up this project and carried it through on terms very favourable to the USA.

This involved bringing a new country into existence. When the government of Colombia proved difficult to negotiate with, Roosevelt sponsored a national uprising of Panamanian separatists and forced Colombia to accept the creation of an independent republic of Panama – virtually a puppet state under American direction. This new state of Panama negotiated the terms for building the canal, including an extensive Panama Canal Zone totally dominated by American regulation. The canal was not finally completed until 1914 but intervention in Panama was a personal triumph for Roosevelt.

In 1904, he turned his actions into a theory. He set out the Roosevelt Corollary to the Monroe Doctrine, stating the principle that the USA had the right to 'exercise international police power' in Latin America if there were 'flagrant cases of wrongdoing or impotence'. It was all part of showing the world that the USA was a power to be reckoned with and that American policy would fully control its own 'back yard' in Latin America. The Roosevelt Corollary was an important shift in American policy – virtually an amendment to the Monroe Doctrine formulated in the 1820s. Roosevelt asserted the new principles in 1904 to justify his interventionist policy in forcing through the independence of Panama in order to secure American control over the Panama Canal.

All that this country desires is to see the neighbouring countries stable, orderly and prosperous. Any country whose people conduct themselves well can count upon our hearty friendship. If a nation shows that it knows how to act with reasonable efficiency and decency in social and political matters, if it keeps order and pays its obligations, it need fear no interference from the United States. Chronic wrongdoing, or an impotence which results in a general loosening of the ties of civilised society, may in America, as elsewhere, ultimately require intervention by some civilised nation, and in the Western Hemisphere the adherence of the United States to the Monroe Doctrine may force the United States, however reluctantly, in flagrant cases of such wrongdoing or impotence, to the exercise of an international police power.

**7**                                          *The Roosevelt Corollary, 1904*

### Activity

**Revision exercise**

One of Roosevelt's most famous sayings was that, in foreign policy, he liked to 'speak softly and carry a big stick'. Make a list of his successes and failures in foreign affairs and decide how highly you rate his achievements.

**Fig. 6** *The inauguration of President Taft, 1909*

Roosevelt's determination to have the USA recognised as a world power was shown again in 1905. First, he took a leading role in the international response to the Morocco crisis, an involvement in European diplomacy that would have been unthinkable even a few years before. Second, he offered American mediation to end the Russian–Japanese War. This was carried through successfully at the Treaty of Portsmouth, New Hampshire in October 1905. At the same time, Roosevelt achieved great international prestige and ensured that Japan would not make excessive gains from military victory over Russia. The rise of Japanese power was already seen as a serious threat to American interests in the Pacific.

Even after William Howard Taft had won the Republican nomination in 1908, Roosevelt continued to have a massive influence on American foreign policy, both through his own actions and because the next president was very much Roosevelt's choice as successor. Taft continued to support interventionist policies, although he favoured avoiding direct colonialism. Taft became famous for the policy of Dollar Diplomacy, using American financial power to secure economic domination in Latin America and China.

## Activity

### Revision exercise

Summarise the key stages of American expansion overseas between 1890 and 1914.

## A closer look

### Dollar Diplomacy

In one sense Dollar Diplomacy began when Theodore Roosevelt forced through the building of the Panama Canal and ensured it would be under the control of the USA. From 1909, President Taft tried to avoid direct interventions, using American financial power instead. In 1909, he bought up the financial debts of Honduras to establish American financial control there. In the Caribbean state of Haiti, American banks took over Haiti's national debt and virtually ran the economy. In 1912, Taft used American bankers to provide loans to the new government of Nicaragua in order to control the economy and to benefit American mining interests. Dollar Diplomacy did not quite work out as intended in Nicaragua. The American-backed government faced internal revolts and in 1914 American troops had to be sent in, exactly the kind of action Taft's policy had been supposed to avoid.

The policy of Dollar Diplomacy was also used in the Far East. In 1911, Taft got American financiers led by J. Pierpont Morgan to join a big European consortium that was backing railroad projects in China. Shortly afterwards, American bankers tried to buy another railway scheme – the South Manchurian – partly to try to block Russian and Japanese influence in China. These schemes had only limited success. When Woodrow Wilson was elected president in 1912, one of his first steps was to renounce Dollar Diplomacy in favour of a more ethical policy. Even so, American interests in Latin America continued to be important; Wilson sent troops to occupy the Mexican port of Vera Cruz in 1914.

There was no major shift in the policy of American imperialism until the Republicans lost power and Woodrow Wilson was elected president in 1912.

### Woodrow Wilson and US foreign policy

The Democrats' election victory in 1912 and the arrival of Woodrow Wilson as president marked a big change in attitudes towards American foreign policy. Wilson emphasised the need for a peaceful and ethical approach to foreign affairs. He appointed William Jennings Bryan as his secretary of state, the leader of Democratic anti-imperialist opposition to the policies of Theodore Roosevelt and William Howard Taft. One of Bryan's most famous public lectures was called 'The Prince of Peace' – arguing that almost all wars in history had been wrong and that disputes between nations should be settled peacefully. Both Wilson and Bryan took their Christian principles seriously.

The new approach to policy showed itself in the Far East in 1913. Wilson's government turned away from Taft's Dollar Diplomacy in China and gave his support to the Open Door policy. Wilson gave diplomatic recognition to the new regime in China that had gained power after the 1911 revolution. One side effect of this was to worsen US relations with Japan.

On the other hand, Wilson followed an interventionist policy in Mexico. The Mexican Revolution of 1910–11 had produced violence and instability in Mexico, threatening American business interests there including oil. In April 1914, Wilson sent American marines to occupy the port of Vera Cruz and 'restore order' there. One of the reasons for doing this was the hope that it might help to overthrow the regime of the military dictator Victoriano Huerta, but the American occupation actually strengthened Huerta's position. Wilson was criticised by

**Fig. 7** *Woodrow Wilson at Princeton University*

anti-imperialists for intervening at all, whereas Theodore Roosevelt and Henry Cabot Lodge attacked him for not being tough enough.

In 1916, Wilson intervened again in Mexico, sending a large military force under General John Pershing to pursue the guerrilla leader Pancho Villa, who had carried out attacks on American travellers in Mexico and crossed the American border to raid the town of Columbus in New Mexico. Pershing's 'punitive expedition' spent many months chasing Pancho Villa without success before the force was pulled out in 1917. The instability in Mexico remained an important problem for the USA. In 1917, it was fear of German interference in Mexico that triggered the decision to enter the First World War.

### Key profile

#### General John Pershing

General John 'Black Jack' Pershing (1860–1948) became the highest-ranked general in American history apart from George Washington. His career covered the period from 1890 to 1920. He fought in the last Indian wars and was present at the Battle of Wounded Knee Creek in 1890. He fought in Cuba in 1898 and served in the Philippines from 1899 to 1903. He was a military adviser at the Treaty of Portsmouth in 1905. The 'punitive expedition' he led into Mexico chasing after Pancho Villa was a total failure but it did not damage his career. Later in 1917, he led the American Expeditionary Force to France and continued in command until the end of the First World War. In 1920, he was close to being nominated as the Republican candidate for the presidency, but the party eventually chose Warren G. Harding instead.

## The reasons for US entry into the First World War

When the First World War began in Europe in August 1914, Wilson's response was to proclaim American neutrality. 'We Americans must be neutral in fact as well as in name,' he said. 'We must be impartial in thought as well as in action.' There was no prospect at that time of American involvement in the war in Europe – a war seen by most Americans as a faraway conflict fought for reasons they did not understand or care about. By 1919, the USA would become a world power as a direct result of involvement in the war, but when the war began the one thing most Americans agreed about was that they should stay out of it.

Many factors pushed the USA towards neutrality and isolationism:

- Traditional attitudes of neutrality going back to George Washington that all 'foreign entanglements' except trade should be avoided.
- The USA had no tradition of a **standing army**. The American tradition was for volunteer militias to be called out when there was an emergency. There was deep-rooted resistance against the idea of a large national army.
- Anti-imperialist ideas, advocated by people like Secretary of State Bryan (who believed that wars could only be fought if morally justified) and many pacifist organisations (which believed that all wars were morally unacceptable). Such people wanted the USA to be peacemaker, representing higher moral values.
- Anti-colonial ideas reflecting the origins of the USA in a revolution against British colonial rule.

### Key term

**Standing army:** a permanent army in peacetime.

### Activity

#### Talking point

In small groups, discuss the list of factors in American reluctance to become involved in the First World War. Which factors do you consider to be the most important? Can you think of any others that might be added?

- Resentment of the British naval blockade, cutting off the USA from Germany by intercepting neutral ships on the high seas. This caused financial losses to American enterprises, such as cotton exports.
- Dislike of the European powers among immigrant communities. Many people from central Europe had reasons to hate Austria-Hungary. Many of the 8 million German-Americans and the 4.5 million Irish-Americans were hostile to Britain.

The powerful reasons why the USA did not wish to be involved in the First World War make it important to understand why Wilson led the nation into war in 1917. In searching for these reasons, historians must evaluate the influence of people, events and historical forces.

Many key personalities influenced the decision to go to war, above all Woodrow Wilson himself. It is important to explain why Wilson changed his mind. There were other key personalities, too. William Jennings Bryan was a noted orator with strong support in the country for his pacifist views – when he resigned as secretary of state in 1915 it weakened the anti-war elements in the government. Those urging the USA to have a world role, led by Theodore Roosevelt and Henry Cabot Lodge, were obviously influential – it is necessary to balance their effect on American opinion against other factors. Businessmen and bankers such as J. Pierpont Morgan profited hugely from increased trade with the Allies during the war. Some people felt at the time that there was a conspiracy led by these powerful interests to trick the American people into something they did not want to do.

> Two thousand millions of dollars in trade is the prize which world conditions have set before the American people. Europe's tragic crisis provides America's golden opportunity.

**8**         *Editorial in the **New York American** newspaper a few days after the war began in 1914*

Between August 1914 and the final decision to enter the war, American attitudes were strongly influenced by dramatic events. The German invasion of Belgium in 1914 led to emotive reports of atrocities against the people of 'plucky little Belgium' and increased anti-German feeling. In 1915, the sinking of the RMS *Lusitania* en route from New York to Liverpool caused a storm of protest against Germany. Despite these reactions, there was still no willingness from the USA to enter the war, although Germany suspended its use of unrestricted submarine warfare for fear of provoking direct intervention.

> The example of America must be a special example because peace is the healing and elevating influence in the world and war is not. There is such a thing as a man being too proud to fight. There is such a thing as a nation being so right that it does not need to convince others by force that it is right.

**9**         *Wilson's speech in Philadelphia, soon after the sinking of the **Lusitania***

Other key events were pushing the USA towards involvement in the war. In December 1916, a secret report to the British government warned that the British war effort was bankrupt and the nation could not carry on the war unless the USA joined the struggle. In February 1917, the Russian Revolution and the downfall of the Tsar meant joining the Allies would

**Fig. 8** *An illustration in a British newspaper depicting the sinking of the* Lusitania *in 1915*

be a 'fight for democracy'. American policy was, of course, influenced by the impact of events such as these, but not sufficiently to drag the USA away from neutrality.

The decisive event was the interception of the Zimmermann Telegram. By the end of 1916, Germany's economic position was so desperate that it decided to launch unrestricted submarine warfare in the Atlantic, even though this might provoke the USA into joining the war. Hoping to keep the USA distracted by problems nearer home, the German foreign minister, Alois Zimmermann, secretly proposed an alliance between Germany and Mexico. The Zimmermann Telegram, promising German support for Mexico against the USA, was intercepted by British intelligence and passed to Washington. It was the German decision to let loose the submarines, and to tempt Mexico into the war, that led directly to the USA declaring war on Germany in April 1917.

> We intend to begin unrestricted submarine warfare on 1 February. We shall endeavour in spite of this to keep the United States neutral. In the event of this not succeeding, we propose to Mexico an alliance on the following basis: make war together, make peace together – with generous financial support and an understanding on our part that Mexico is to get back the lost territory in Texas, New Mexico and Arizona.

**10** *The Zimmermann Telegram, decoded in February 1917*

Beyond all the events, and the influence of key individuals, there were deep impersonal forces pushing the USA towards a world role. Economic and geographical factors meant that America was bound to become a major player in the Pacific after 1890. American policy could not ignore what was happening in China or the rise of Japan. American strategic interests in the Pacific made it inevitable that, whoever was shaping American policies, there would be growing rivalry between the USA and Japan.

■ **Key term**

**Central Powers:** Germany and its allies: Austria-Hungary, Bulgaria and the Ottoman Empire.

■ **Activity**

**Revision exercise**

'The USA entered the First World War in 1917 against the wishes of the majority of the American people.' Create a two-column table. In the left-hand column, outline the main reasons for agreeing with the statement. In the right-hand column, outline the reasons for arguing that the statement is wrong. Which list do you find the more convincing?

In the same way, trade issues brought the USA closer to Britain and its allies and further away from the **Central Powers**. American trade with Britain and France increased by four times between 1914 and 1916. In contrast, by the end of 1916 American trade with Germany was only 10 per cent of what it had been before the war. However much the USA wished to remain neutral and impartial, massive American and financial support for the Allies meant taking sides. The policy of 'avoiding all foreign entanglements except trade' was, in the end, illogical. The trade links led in the direction of a strategic alliance even if many politicians and ordinary citizens did not wish it.

## The USA and the First World War

American intervention in the First World War fundamentally changed the course of the conflict. What had been an unbreakable deadlock at the end of 1916 – a war that nobody knew how to win but nobody knew how to stop – was turned into a decisive victory for the Allies by November 1918. The war also changed the USA, both at home and abroad. For the first time, American troops fought overseas as part of an alliance with other powers. The USA also had a mass conscript army. Many attitudes changed and social changes were brought about or speeded up.

It took a long time before American forces were able to make a major contribution to the war in Europe. The process of calling up, training and equipping the new army was time-consuming. For most of 1917, the flow of American combat troops into France was only a trickle. However, from January 1918 onwards American troops were arriving at a rate of 250,000 a month.

Once the arrival of American troops had reached this level, the defeat of the Central Powers was only a matter of time. General Ludendorff organised one last-gasp German offensive in the west but this was eventually blocked, partly as a result of fresh American reinforcements. After the failure of the Ludendorff Offensive, events moved rapidly. The Ottoman Empire collapsed, Austria-Hungary disintegrated and Bulgaria surrendered. On 9 November 1918 the Kaiser abdicated. The armistice came two days later.

American intervention had produced a decisive military outcome to a struggle that had been hopelessly deadlocked in 1917. The power and prestige of the USA was greatly enhanced. As the war ended, it was clear that America would take the leading role in shaping the post-war peace. In January 1918, Woodrow Wilson had set the agenda for shaping this post-war peace by issuing his Fourteen Points, based on the principles of self-determination and collective security.

**Fig. 9** *Soldiers home from the war, 1919*

## A closer look

### Wilson's Fourteen Points

The Fourteen Points were principles to provide the basis for peace after the First World War. Woodrow Wilson set out the Fourteen Points in January 1918 following the advice of a team of 150 experts. They were intended to provide the basis for the peace settlement when the war was won.

1 Open covenants of peace, openly arrived at (no secret treaties).

2 Absolute freedom of navigation of the seas (bound to infuriate Britain, which relied heavily on the naval blockade to win the war).

3 The removal of trade barriers and the establishment of equality in international trade.

4 National armaments to be reduced to the lowest level consistent with internal security.

5 Free and impartial adjustment of all colonial claims (bound to concern Britain, France and Italy).

6 The evacuation of all foreign troops from Russia. A sincere welcome for Russia into the society of free nations.

7 Belgium to be restored to full independence and all German troops withdrawn.

8 The return of Alsace-Lorraine to France.

9 Re-adjustment of the borders of Italy according to nationality (giving Italy territories previously ruled by Austria).

10 Self-determination for the peoples in the Austro-Hungarian Empire.

11 Romania, Serbia and Montenegro to be evacuated and Serbia to be given access to the sea.

12 Self-determination for the non-Turkish peoples of the Ottoman Empire.

13 A new independent Polish nation to be formed, containing all indisputably Polish populations. Poland to have access to the sea and Polish territorial integrity to be guaranteed by international covenant.

14 A general association of nations to be formed for the purpose of guaranteeing the political independence and territorial integrity of great and small states alike (the League of Nations).

## The role of the USA in the post-war peace settlement

At the beginning of 1918, Woodrow Wilson was by far the most famous man in the world. The USA was seen as a beacon of hope for war-torn Europe, offering idealistic and democratic principles instead of the power politics of the 'Old Europe'. When Wilson sailed to France, he was greeted with hysterical enthusiasm. The crowds lining the track as his train crawled slowly from Cherbourg to Paris were so huge and excited that numerous observers likened Wilson's arrival to Jesus Christ entering Jerusalem on Palm Sunday.

## Activity

### Thinking point

Study Wilson's Fourteen Points. Which points do you feel were likely to produce the greatest difficulties for the peacemakers after the war was over and negotiations for the post-war peace had begun?

## Key chronology

### The USA and the First World War

| | |
|---|---|
| **1914 August** | Start of the First World War in Europe. |
| **1915 May** | The sinking of the RMS *Lusitania*. |
| **1916 December** | Secret report to the British government on the need for US help. |
| **1917 February** | German order to begin unrestricted submarine warfare; American protests to Germany after the Zimmermann Telegram. |
| **1917 April** | Announcement of American entry into the war. |
| **1917 August** | Departure of American Expeditionary Force to France under General Pershing. |
| **1918 January** | Proclamation of the Fourteen Points by President Wilson; start of mass American troop arrivals in France. |
| **1918 November** | German acceptance of an armistice. |
| **1919 January** | Start of the Paris Peace Conference. |
| **1919 June** | Signing of the Treaty of Versailles. |
| **1920 June** | Final rejection of the League of Nations by Congress. |
| **1920 November** | Defeat of Woodrow Wilson in the presidential election. |

Like Jesus Christ, President Wilson brings good news above all to the small and the weak. To the humiliated and the insulted he gives the idea of equality. The European powers are none too enthusiastic about Wilsonism. They are already trying to work out how to exploit his ideals for their own purposes. But the ordinary masses believe one hundred per cent in Wilson. They see him as their chief ally and greatest hope.

**11**  *By a young Croatian in 1919*

There were understandable reasons for the incredibly high hopes placed on Wilson and the USA as the peace conference began in Paris. The USA had not suffered years of exhaustion; its enormous economic and military potential put the nation first among the great powers. The fact that American involvement began only in 1917 meant that there was no question of American guilt for starting the war. The position of the USA as a republican democracy with an anti-colonial history emphasised the idea of 'clean hands' and moral superiority.

Woodrow Wilson's distinctive personality strengthened this sense of idealism and moral purpose. His Fourteen Points laid the foundations for a just peace. The Fourteen Points were an expression of 'Wilsonian idealism'. The future peace settlement should be based on self-determination, allowing peoples and smaller nations to decide their own destinies outside the control of the old empires, and on collective security, with peace protected by international agreements not by national armies and wars. One of Wilson's key proposals was for a League of Nations to make collective security safe.

**Fig. 10** *A painting of President Wilson at the Paris Peace Conference*

### The post-war peace settlement

The peace settlement did not turn out that way. Wilson quickly became bogged down in complex negotiations with the other members of the 'Big Four': Clemenceau (prime minister of France), Lloyd George (prime minister of Britain) and Orlando (prime minister of Italy). These leaders, especially Clemenceau, had different priorities from Wilson, less focused on self-determination and 'Wilsonian idealism' and more concerned with issues like extending their empires and extracting reparations from defeated Germany.

What ignorance he had of Europe and how difficult it was to work with him! He believed you could do everything with formulas and his Fourteen Points. Even God himself was content with Ten Commandments. Wilson modestly inflicted upon us Fourteen Points of empty theory!

**12** *The recollections of Georges Clemenceau, French prime minister in 1919*

Dealing with the question of Germany was hard enough but that was only a small part of Wilson's problems. It was also immensely difficult to cope with the emerging new nations asserting their independence from the old empires. American diplomats became frustrated and angry trying to mediate bitter disputes like the one between the Poles and the Czechs over the territory of Teschen. There was the problem of post-revolutionary Russia and the consequences of the collapse of the

Ottoman Empire. Wilson promised support for the independence of the Armenian and Kurdish peoples. Neither promise could be fulfilled because other powers wanted control.

What Wilson wanted most of all was to get ahead with plans for general disarmament and setting up the League of Nations. Nevertheless, for much of 1919 and 1920, the peacemakers were distracted by the long business of finalising the treaties with the five defeated powers: Germany, Austria, Bulgaria, Turkey and Hungary. However, the peace settlement was not a complete failure. In many ways the Allies did a decent job in difficult circumstances, but there was widespread disillusionment everywhere, among both winners and losers.

Although the USA signed the peace treaties, they were not accepted or approved by Congress until August 1921. This reflected the growing political difficulties Wilson faced at home. Within the USA, the glow of victory did not last long. The demobilisation of the US army was not carried out smoothly and there were several instances of inter-racial violence between army units. There were economic problems at home, especially inflation. Many people began to feel that the rewards of the war were not worth the costs. Almost 50,000 American soldiers had been killed in action. Even more had been killed by disease. In 1918 and 1919, the terrible 'Spanish flu' pandemic took the lives of millions of people across Europe and the world. The numbers of American casualties were small in comparison with the mass casualties of other nations, which totalled some 21 million, but they were enough to turn people against 'Europe's war'.

Looking back, it is easy to see that the expectations of what Wilson would achieve were completely unrealistic and bound to end in disillusionment. However, it is important to remember just how high those hopes were at the beginning of 1919 and how deeply Wilson's ideas influenced the peacemakers in Paris – and the history of the rest of the 20th century.

## The retreat to isolationism

When Wilson returned from Paris to the USA, he found a different national mood. He campaigned hard for acceptance of the League of Nations but ran into opposition. He clung firmly to his idealistic principles about the league, but the longer ratification of the peace treaty was delayed, the less likely it was to happen.

> The stage is set, our destiny is revealed. This destiny has come about by no plan of our conceiving but by the hand of God. We cannot turn back. The light streams down on the path ahead, and nowhere else.

 *Extract from Woodrow Wilson's speech to Congress, July 1919*

Some of the public opposition to Wilson was due to a natural reaction of war-weariness. In the USA, as in all countries, the long months of diplomatic wrangling in Paris had turned people away from the enthusiasm they had felt in 1919. Domestic political issues began to take people's attention. Those who had always opposed American entanglements abroad had the chance to make themselves heard again. Some of the opposition came from committed isolationists such as Senator William Borah of Idaho, leader of a group of Republican senators known as the 'Irreconcilables'. His speech in November 1919 was

**The post-war peace treaties**

| | |
|---|---|
| **1919 June** | Treaty of Versailles (dealing with Germany and establishing the League of Nations). |
| **1919 September** | Treaty of St Germain (dealing with Austria). |
| **1919 November** | Treaty of Neuilly (dealing with Bulgaria). |
| **1920 June** | Treaty of Trianon (dealing with Hungary). |
| **1920 August** | Treaty of Sèvres (dealing with the Ottoman Empire). |

considered at the time to have played an important part in convincing the Senate to vote against the League of Nations. Some of the opposition was caused by Wilson's own stubbornness.

> We have entangled ourselves with all European concerns and are dabbling in their affairs. In other words, we have surrendered, once and for all, the great policy of 'no entangling alliances' upon which this Republic has been founded for 150 years. Acting in accordance with decisions taken by the League of Nations is in conflict with the right of our people to govern themselves, free of any restraint by foreign powers. A real republic cannot get mixed up with the discordant and destructive forces of the Old World. You cannot yoke a government of liberty to a government whose first law is the law of force.

**14**        *Senator Borah attacks the Treaty of Versailles and the League of Nations in the Senate debate, November 1919*

### Activity

**Source analysis**

Study Source 14.

**1** Make a list of Senator Borah's key arguments.

**2** Try to explain why his speech was thought to be devastatingly effective by those who heard it at the time.

Key personalities also influenced the national debate, especially the clash between Woodrow Wilson and Henry Cabot Lodge. Senator Lodge was not an isolationist – far from it. For years, he had urged the USA to act like a world power, but he was not willing to see American power merged into a supranational organisation outside national control. Wilson stubbornly insisted that the League of Nations was the way forward. The clash between Lodge and Wilson became a conflict of personalities as well as a policy disagreement. Many groups in Congress and the country opposed the league for a wide variety of reasons.

> The independence of the United States is more precious to us than any single possession. In making this treaty, all we do is in a spirit of unselfishness and in a desire for the good of mankind. But it is well to remember that we are dealing with nations every one of which has a direct individual interest of their own. There is grave danger in an unshared idealism. You may call me selfish if you like, but an American I was born, and an American I have remained all my life. I have always loved one flag and I cannot share that flag with a mongrel banner created for a League of Nations. The United States is the world's best hope, but if you chain her to the interests and quarrels of other nations, if you tangle her in the intrigues of Europe, you will destroy her power to do good and you will endanger her very existence.

**15**        *Henry Cabot Lodge's speech in Washington, DC, August 1919*

Wilson's personality suffered from the effects of illness and exhaustion. Many commentators remarked on how obstinate he had become – much less skilful and much less consensual in his political methods. He alienated many former allies and may well have missed the chance to make a reasonable compromise with Henry Cabot Lodge and the opposition from the Senate. Despite his illness, Wilson insisted on lengthy and exhausting campaigning across the country, even though he was warned that he faced a humiliating defeat. In September 1919, after a speech in Pueblo Colorado, Wilson suffered a serious stroke and collapsed. After this, he was paralysed on his left side and blind in his left eye, although the public never realised how badly he had been affected until after his death in 1924.

**Fig. 11** *'Another effort to reform him.' An isolationist cartoon from the Chicago Tribune in 1940 warning Americans against repeating the mistake of fighting a war on behalf of Britain*

Woodrow Wilson's ideals and policies were decisively rejected in 1920. Despite all his campaigning, the ratification of the League of Nations was finally voted down by Congress. The Democratic Party suffered a catastrophic defeat in the presidential election. The Republicans achieved domination of both the House and the Senate. The new president, a little-known mid-westerner called Warren G. Harding, had little interest in or knowledge of foreign affairs. He assured the American people that his policy would be one of **'normalcy'**, avoiding excessive government intervention at home and giving international complications low priority. Harding's vice-president, Calvin Coolidge, was also little interested in world affairs. He was fond of saying 'America's business is business'.

> The Members of the League undertake to respect and preserve as against external aggression the territorial integrity and existing political independence of all Members of the League. In case of any such aggression or in case of any threat or danger of such aggression the Council shall advise upon the means by which this obligation shall be fulfilled.

**16**  *Article 10 of the Covenant of the League of Nations*

## Key term

**'Normalcy'**: the term invented by Warren G. Harding in the presidential election campaign. He probably meant to say 'normality' but the word took root and is always used to define the less ambitious foreign policies of the USA after the rejection of Woodrow Wilson and the League of Nations. 'Normalcy' did not mean outright isolationism, just a return to a quiet, sensible approach.

## Did you know?
### 'Normalcy'

'Normalcy' was not a detailed policy, more a general idea. Harding aimed to have less government intervention, both at home and abroad, and to avoid problems rather than try to solve them.

## Activity
### Source analysis

Article 10 of the Covenant of the League of Nations was described by Wilson's opponents as being 'at the heart of the dispute' about American acceptance of the League of Nations. Study Source 16 and suggest reasons why this clause was so controversial in the USA.

*Learning outcomes*

In this section you have looked at the development of the USA during 30 years of dramatic change. At home, this change was marked by the economic effects of industrial expansion and the social effects of mass immigration. Abroad, it was marked by the rise in American power and influence – to the point where the USA held the position of a world power but then, after the war, chose to turn inwards. The situation would be very different after the next world war had ended in 1945.

#  Examination-style questions

(a) Explain why the American people rejected the peace treaties negotiated on their behalf by Woodrow Wilson. *(12 marks)*

Questions like this are testing understanding of chronology and causation. In one way they may seem easy and 'factual', but the answer needs to be more than a list of reasons. A long answer full of detailed information in the right order may not score as well as a shorter answer that is more structured and shows differentiation. A good answer will decide which factors or personalities had the most impact on political and public opinion.

(b) How important were economic factors in shaping US foreign policies between 1890 and 1917? *(24 marks)*

Questions like this need answering on at least two levels. First, there is the issue of balance and relative importance: were economic factors the key to foreign policies? Or were other factors more important? This is the core question – you need to think about what other factors were involved in shaping US policies and then assess which ones mattered most and why. Second, there is the issue of economic motives. How and in what ways did economic issues affect foreign affairs? Remember that the primary task is the first one – depending on your view of its relative importance, you might need just enough evidence about the effects of economic issues before moving on to evidence about other, more significant, factors, or you might go into great detail about economic motives because you feel they were all-important.

# 3 | Post-war America

## Key term

**Sedition:** any actions or words that seek to destabilise or overthrow a government.

## Exploring the detail

### The Espionage Act

The Espionage Act was passed in June 1917, not long after the USA had entered the war. It was motivated by fear of disloyalty from American citizens who had recently immigrated from parts of Europe ruled by the enemy powers (Germany and Austria-Hungary) and by fears of radical Socialists opposed to American participation in the war. The act provided for heavy fines or prison terms of up to 20 years. In 1918 the Sedition Act extended the provisions of the Espionage Act, allowing the government to open and inspect items sent by mail. One of the people arrested under this legislation was the socialist leader Eugene Debs.

From Seattle to Boston, four million Americans marched on picket lines in 1919. Even Boston's policemen, symbols of law and order, joined shipyard workers, meat-packers and steelworkers from across the country to protest against wage cuts and layoffs. Many confrontations turned violent when employers hired strike-breakers. On Wall Street, an anarchist's bomb killed thirty-eight people. Swollen with discharged veterans and unemployed workers, both black and white, cities such as Chicago and St Louis erupted into violence between the races. The Justice Department fuelled a hysterical press by blaming the disorders on communist agents. The federal government arrested thousands of alleged subversives. The Spanish influenza epidemic left hundreds of thousands dead, far more than the losses in the Great War.

**1**         *Michael Parrish, **Anxious Decades: America in Prosperity and Depression, 1920–1941**, 1994*

This description of the USA in 1919–20 paints a dramatic picture of violence and upheaval. It does not fit in easily with the idea that the USA had just been victorious in the First World War and was widely seen in Europe as a shining light among nations or with the fact that, for many Americans, the 1920s were going to be a time of prosperity and social advancement. It is important to analyse the sense of crisis in post-war America – to see how deep it went and to decide whether or not it was more than a temporary blip in America's march onwards and upwards to progress and prosperity.

## ■ US attitudes after the First World War

The USA was greatly changed by the First World War. The impact of the war on the economy, and especially the disruption caused when the war ended and the nation attempted to adjust to peacetime conditions, created many problems for American society. These economic problems were the setting for a period of violence and political upheaval in 1919–20. Attitudes changed – towards immigration, for example, towards social issues like Prohibition and towards America's place in the world.

Several of these changes were not new or directly caused by the war. They were longer-term trends that were intensified by the experiences of the war and by the sense of anxiety and uncertainty that followed it. Wartime attitudes and propaganda stereotypes led to more intense suspicion of foreigners and 'aliens', as shown by the Espionage Act 1917 and the **Sedition** Act 1918. The anti-immigration movement grew stronger and laws were passed restricting immigration, especially from central, eastern and southern Europe.

These anti-foreigner attitudes were also shown by the surge of support for nativism and racial exclusion, with a boom in support for the Ku Klux Klan (KKK) in the early 1920s. This changed national mood worked against

## Exploring the detail

### Republican dominance in the 1920s

After Warren G. Harding had won the 1920 election, the Democrats found it hard to fight their way back. Harding continued in office until he died in 1923 when Calvin Coolidge, his vice-president, took over. Coolidge won the 1924 election easily. When Coolidge decided not to run again in 1928, another experienced Republican politician, Herbert Hoover, became president in what looked an unassailable position, both because of his own high abilities and because the Democratic Party was badly divided.

Fig. 1 *President Warren G. Harding*

## Exploring the detail

### The Teapot Dome scandal

The Teapot Dome scandal tarnished the image of President Harding after his death. It was revealed that officials in the Harding administration had been selling off oil exploration rights on land owned by the federal government at knockdown prices to their cronies. This seemed to confirm the impression that Harding had been surrounded by corruption, although the details did not become public until after he had gone.

Woodrow Wilson's ideals of American prestige and influence in the post-war world and helps to explain why the USA turned its back on the League of Nations and retreated back into isolationism and 'normalcy' in the 1920s.

Politics changed, too. The Democratic Party was badly weakened by the unpopularity of Wilson and the election of Warren G. Harding as president in 1920 marked the beginning of a long period of Republican domination. Attitudes were also changed within the Republican Party. The progressive ideas that had influenced Theodore Roosevelt and split the party in 1912 lost their force. The Republican Party under Harding and Coolidge was strongly conservative and pro-business. The veteran progressive campaigner, Robert La Follette, ran for the presidency against the Coolidge Republicans in 1924 but gained little support outside his home state of Wisconsin.

Politics in the USA became more conservative and more inward, less dominated by big political personalities and with less enthusiasm for government intervention. Warren G. Harding fitted in perfectly with this. He was an amiable political 'fixer' from Ohio whose main interests were said to be 'golf, drink and other men's wives'. His administration was plagued by accusations of corruption against his political cronies, especially the Teapot Dome scandal, but there is no doubt that Harding's approach was what most people wanted at that time.

Fig. 2 *President Calvin Coolidge addresses Congress*

When Harding died in 1923, his vice-president, Calvin Coolidge, succeeded him. Coolidge was not linked to corruption but he was another cautious conservative, with little desire to push through reforms at home or to follow an adventurous policy. He was content to do almost exactly what big business wanted. His time in office coincided with a prolonged economic boom and a constantly rising stock market. The Republicans won the presidency again in 1928 with the election of Herbert Hoover, who had been secretary of commerce under both Harding and Coolidge – and was seen as more energetic and capable than either of them. The economy seemed to be prospering and there appeared to be little prospect of the Democrats making a comeback.

The Democratic Party had little success in the 1920s. There were divisions within the party because delegates from the West and the South, mostly strong supporters of Prohibition, had little sympathy with those from the big cities, who were largely Catholic, immigrant and hostile to Prohibition. Many Progressives voted for La Follette instead of the Democratic candidate in 1924; in 1928, the Democratic nomination went to Al Smith, the governor of New York. Smith was a skilful and experienced politician but he was a divisive candidate because of his Catholicism and because he was an outspoken 'Wet' (strongly opposed to Prohibition).

## Key profile

### Al Smith

Al Smith (1873–1944) is often thought of as the champion of the Irish Catholics, even though his father was actually of Italian-German origin. His mother was Irish. Smith's power base was the Democratic political machine in New York. Those who voted against him in 1928 were not only anti-Catholic but also anti-urban; he did extremely well in the big cities but badly in the South, usually a Democratic stronghold. Al Smith expected to be the Democratic candidate in 1932 but was forced to stand by and watch his former political ally, Franklin Roosevelt, win an election victory Smith thought should rightfully have been his. He never spoke to Roosevelt again afterwards.

Al Smith was easily defeated in the 1928 election; anti-Catholic prejudice played a large part in this. It seemed that no Catholic had any chance of winning the presidency – at least until John F. Kennedy's victory in 1960. Some political commentators suggested that the Democratic Party was finished for ever. The Republicans held the presidency and controlled both the House and the Senate. Their dominance seemed set to continue until the financial crash of 1929 and the onset of the Great Depression undermined Hoover from 1930.

## Activity

**Thinking point**

Write a brief newspaper article about the 1928 election, explaining to readers why Al Smith and the Democrats have no chance of winning.

**Table 1** *The presidency, 1920–45*

| Year | President | Political party | Vice-president | Defeated candidate |
|---|---|---|---|---|
| 1920 | Warren G. Harding | Republican | Calvin Coolidge | James M. Cox |
| 1923 | Calvin Coolidge | Republican | — | — |
| 1924 | Calvin Coolidge | Republican | Charles Dawes | John W. Davis |
| 1928 | Herbert Hoover | Republican | Charles Curtis | Al Smith |
| 1932 | Franklin D. Roosevelt | Democratic | John Gardner | Herbert Hoover |
| 1936 | Franklin D. Roosevelt | Democratic | John Gardner | Alf Landon |
| 1940 | Franklin D. Roosevelt | Democratic | Henry A. Wallace | Wendell Willkie |
| 1944 | Franklin D. Roosevelt | Democratic | Harry S. Truman | Thomas Dewey |
| 1945 | Harry S. Truman | Democratic | | |

## ■ The end of mass immigration

*"What Fools these Mortals be!"*

## Puck

AS TO JAPANESE EXCLUSION.

PERHAPS, IF THEY CAME IN KIMONOS, THE *real* UNDESIRABLES MIGHT ALSO BE KEPT OUT.

**Fig. 3** *An anti-immigration poster*

■ Key term

**Restrictionists:** those who wanted to cut down or stop altogether the flow of immigration.

■ Cross-reference

The **'Red Scare'** is covered in more detail on pages 60–64.

■ Exploring the detail

**The Sedition Act**

This act extended the Espionage Act 1917 so that it covered 'scurrilous or abusive language against the United States form of government'. More than 900 people were imprisoned. In the 'Red Scare' of 1919–20, the powers given to the authorities by these acts were used extensively by Attorney General A. Mitchell Palmer (see pages 62–4).

Immigration to the USA had peaked in the years before the First World War. Between 1900 and 1914, more than 10 million immigrants arrived – almost two-thirds of them from eastern, central and southern Europe. The USA had always been a 'nation of immigrants', but there had frequently been a negative reaction against newcomers from those who had established themselves earlier. For example, in 1882 the Chinese Exclusion Act restricted immigrants from China; in 1907 immigration from Japan was reduced by a diplomatic agreement between the USA and Japan.

In 1907, the Dillingham Commission, set up by Congress, investigated immigration and reported that many immigrants from newer parts of Europe were not finding it easy to assimilate and that this was causing economic and social problems. By this time, there was also pressure from trades unions, especially the American Federation of Labor (AFL), to restrict the inflow of cheap immigrant labour. There were increasing calls to stop or reduce immigration by establishing a literacy test for immigrants, but this had little effect on government policy at first because all the main political parties were opposed to it.

Attitudes changed during the First World War. The flow of immigration was halted during the conflict. The war intensified fear and hostility towards 'aliens', whose loyalty was seen as unreliable. Support for the **restrictionists** increased and in 1917 Congress finally adopted the Literacy Test, which required immigrants to be able to speak English to qualify for entry into the USA. This law also contained clauses deliberately designed to reduce immigration from Asia. Anti-foreigner feeling was also reflected in the Espionage Act 1917 and the Sedition Act 1918, legislation that was strongly influenced by the idea that recently arrived immigrants were a danger to national security. The 'Red Scare' made such views even more popular in 1919–20.

Restrictionists were unhappy when immigration, mostly from western Europe, picked up again after the war, with new arrivals totalling more than 400,000 each year. Strong pressure was placed on Congress. In 1921, the Emergency Quota Act was passed, the first time there had ever been numerical limits on inward migration. Quotas were set at 3 per cent of the numbers of people from any country in the 1910 census. The act aimed at restricting immigration to below 350,000 people per year – half from northern Europe; half from southern and eastern Europe. This kept the numbers arriving from northern Europe unchanged but cut other immigration by 70 per cent.

However, the Emergency Quota Act was not enough to satisfy the restrictionists. In 1924, another act, sometimes known as the National Origins (Quota) Act, changed the rules so that numbers would be calculated at 2 per cent of the 1890 census. This deliberately discriminated against ethnic groups who had had high levels of immigration since 1890, and favoured people from northern and western Europe. The hope was that annual immigration would settle at about 165,000. Despite the legal restrictions, however, immigration continued at fairly high levels. The overall total for the 1920s was more than 4 million. It was not the Emergency Quota Act that finally slowed immigration from Europe to a trickle after 1930 but the impact of the Great Depression.

**Table 2** *Immigration statistics, 1920–9*

| Country or area of origin | Percentage of annual total |
| --- | --- |
| Britain and Ireland | 8 |
| Germany and northern Europe | 9 |
| Central and eastern Europe | 14 |
| Southern Europe | 16 |
| Canada and Latin America | 27 |

*Annual average: 412,000*
*Total during the period: 4.2 million*

Although the total of new immigrants was below 5 million, birth rates in the 1920s meant that the total population increase between 1920 and 1929 was more than 16 million.

## The introduction of Prohibition

The changed social and political situation after the First World War enabled supporters of Prohibition to achieve their goal. The temperance movement had been a prominent feature of local and national politics for more than a generation before the war. In 1919, there was at last a Congressional majority in favour of Prohibition. Between the passing of the Volstead Act in 1919 and the repeal of Prohibition in 1933, a great social experiment began, with profound and sometimes unexpected consequences for the USA.

Prohibition had deep roots. Numerous organisations, especially at local level, had campaigned against the evils of alcohol during the 19th century. The pressure for reform increased in reaction to urbanisation and mass immigration after 1890. The Prohibition movement received strong support from Protestant religious groups and women activists. One of the most vocal organisations was the Woman's Christian Temperance Union (WCTU), but the most effective in terms of political action was the Anti-Saloon League.

The Anti-Saloon League was founded in Ohio in 1893, although its origins went back to 1869. It became a national organisation in 1895. The league's most influential leader, Wayne Wheeler, led an aggressive campaign of grass-roots pressure politics, often known as 'Wheelerism', directed at gaining support from Progressives in the two main political parties rather than working through the Prohibition Party.

The evils of drink    The evils of Prohibition

**Fig. 4** *The evils of drink and Prohibition*

Wheeler's lobbying was decisive in the defeat of Myron Herrick in his attempt to be re-elected as governor of Ohio in 1906. In the following years, Wheeler steadily gained political influence. Between 1917 and 1919, it was Wayne Wheeler who personally drafted the legislation that introduced Prohibition.

> Wayne Wheeler dominated Congress, dictated to two presidents of the United States, directed legislation in most states of the Union, picked the candidates for state and federal elections, and held the balance of power in both the Democratic and Republican parties. He was recognised by friend and foe alike as the most masterful and powerful single individual in the United States.

**2**    *Description of Wayne Wheeler by his publicity secretary*

Wartime conditions aided the campaign for Prohibition because restrictions on drinking seemed important to safeguard war production. Changing social attitudes were also pushing politicians towards Prohibition. Both parties were divided on the issue. When Congress debated the Eighteenth Amendment in 1917, the Democrats had 152 'Drys' against 81 'Wets'; for the Republicans it was 140 against 62. One of the Democrats who opposed the amendment was President Wilson. He later tried to block the Volstead Act using his presidential veto, but there was a big enough majority in Congress for him to be overruled.

> Section 1. After one year from the ratification of this article the manufacture, sale, or transportation of intoxicating liquors [alcohol] within, the importation thereof into, or the exportation thereof from the United States and all territory subject to the jurisdiction thereof for beverage purposes is hereby prohibited.
>
> Section 2. The Congress and the several States shall have concurrent power to enforce this article by appropriate legislation.
>
> Section 3. This article shall be inoperative unless it shall have been ratified as an amendment to the Constitution by the legislatures of the several States, as provided in the Constitution, within seven years from the date of the submission hereof to the States by the Congress.

**3**    *Eighteenth Amendment to the US Constitution, ratified by Congress on 16 January 1919*

The passing of the Eighteenth Amendment was a rare case of a constitutional amendment taking away rights and freedoms rather than protecting them. In 1933, it became the only constitutional amendment ever to be repealed, but in 1917 there was strong national support behind it. In 1919, Congress passed the Volstead Act, enabling the enforcement of Prohibition. This was the beginning of a huge social experiment, using the power of the law to improve the behaviour of all citizens. The effects, however, were different from what the Prohibitionists had had in mind.

Throughout the 1920s, the Volstead Act was widely ignored and illegal drinking continued at a high level. Producing, importing and distributing alcohol was quickly taken over by private individuals and criminal gangs. Enforcement proved impossibly difficult. Far too few law enforcement officers, working on far too small a budget, came up against sophisticated and well-financed networks run by **bootleggers**. For all the political support there had been for Prohibition, millions of ordinary Americans had no intention of obeying this law, and there was massive corruption

## ■ Exploring the detail

### The Volstead Act

The Volstead Act 1919 (officially called the National Prohibition Act) was named after Andrew Volstead, head of the Senate Judiciary Committee. Volstead guided the act through Congress but it was actually drafted by Wayne Wheeler of the Anti-Saloon League.

## ■ Key term

**Bootlegger:** someone who made or sold illegal alcohol.

**Fig. 5** *Resting after doing 'God's work' – destroying illegal booze*

among public officials and the police. Prohibition did more for the rise of organised crime than any other factor.

Opinion continued to be divided throughout the 1920s as to whether Prohibition was a valuable defence against social breakdown or an inefficient and costly failure. Sources 4 and 5, both from the middle years of the decade, illustrate the conflict of opinion.

> We must remember that Prohibition is the greatest effort for human advancement and betterment ever attempted in history, and that while the nearest approach, perhaps, was the destruction of human slavery, let us not forget that that revolutionary policy affected only one section of the nation – whereas the national Prohibition policy called for changing the habits and customs of the people in all sections of the nation.
>
> Therefore, the most gratifying and heartening feature of the situation is that so large a majority of our people respect the Constitution and observe this law, and this in spite of the fact that there is a very considerable number of citizens of influence and position who, by non-observance, are embarrassing the government in the promotion of its great task.
>
> But what has the experience of these seven years taught us? We have learned: (1) size of the task; (2) power of propaganda; (3) inadequacy of our legislation; (4) not enough emphasis on observance; (5) who are the friends and who are the foes, and the real plans of the latter; (6) in spite of all, real progress is being achieved; (7) how to measure progress.

**4**
*Roy Haynes, the first Prohibition commissioner, in a speech delivered to the WCTU, 26 January 1927*

### Exploring the detail

**'Little Chicago'**

Johnson City, located on a railway crossroads in the Appalachian mountains of Tennessee, became a key point in the importation and distribution of illegal alcohol in the 1920s. It was notorious for corrupt public officials and police chiefs and was known as 'Little Chicago', with huge numbers of people involved in bootlegging and gambling. Al Capone was rumoured to have stayed in Johnson City on several occasions.

## Key terms

**Speakeasies:** illicit drinking clubs during Prohibition.

**Moonshine:** homemade alcohol.

**'Red Scares':** Bolshevik revolutionaries in Russia were known as 'Reds' and the name came to be widely used in post-war America as a general term for dangerous radicals and subversives. The term 'Scare' describes the way that fears of revolution were whipped up by the authorities and the press to grab public attention.

**McCarthyism:** the man most associated with the First Red Scare in 1919–20 was Attorney General A. Mitchell Palmer. In the Second Red Scare, the lead role was taken by Senator Joseph McCarthy – hence the term 'McCarthyism'.

## Cross-reference

The **Sedition Act** is covered on page 53.

It is impossible to tell whether Prohibition is a good thing or a bad thing. It has never been enforced. At least a million quarts of liquor are consumed each day in the United States. I believe that the percentage of whisky drinkers in the United States is now greater than in any country in the world. Prohibition is to blame for that. A billion dollars a year is being lost to the federal government and the states in lost customs duties. The money now goes instead into the pockets of the bootleggers and corrupt public officials. I agree that the saloons were odious – but now we have delicatessen stores, pool halls, drug stores and 57 varieties of **speakeasies** selling liquor and flourishing. The Drys are seemingly afraid of the truth. Why not take stock and find out the true facts? Let us have an official survey, and let the American people know what is going on.

*Fiorello LaGuardia, a prominent New York politician, testifying to the Senate Judiciary Committee hearings on Prohibition in 1926*

Prohibition also widened divisions between rich and poor. Poorer people relied on self-help, brewing their own beer or distilling **moonshine** secretly at home. Those with money could easily acquire alcohol through speakeasies or private clubs. The law was widely disrespected and criminals became glamorized. Political and religious divisions over Prohibition remained deep and did not weaken with the passage of time. The demand to repeal the Eighteenth Amendment became a live political question in the early 1930s.

## The 'Red Scare'

There were two great **'Red Scares'** in American history, each one in the aftermath of a world war. The Second Red Scare, often known as **McCarthyism**, dominated politics and public life in the early 1950s and was closely linked with American fears about the communist revolution in China. The First Red Scare, in 1919–20, coincided with the end of the First World War and was linked to other anti-foreigner attitudes and the campaign to limit immigration. The anti-communist hysteria of the Red Scare grew out of genuine American fears about communist revolution spreading from Russia and post-war Europe.

When the Bolshevik revolutionaries seized control of Russia late in 1917, it seemed that they were about to spread Marxist revolution all round the world. In 1918–19, there were communist revolutions in Berlin, Munich and Hungary. Many Americans saw immigrants from southern and eastern Europe as potential spies and subversives. The American Congress passed two acts based on fears of radicals and revolutionaries as an 'enemy within'. The Sedition Act 1918 was an attempt to clamp down on the expression of any anti-government or anti-American ideas.

Whoever, when the United States is at war, shall wilfully make or convey false reports or false statements with intent to interfere with the operation or success of the military or naval forces of the United States, or to promote the success of its enemies, or shall wilfully make or convey false reports, or false statements … or incite insubordination, disloyalty, mutiny, or refusal of duty, in the military or naval forces of the United States, or shall wilfully obstruct … the recruiting or enlistment service of the United States, or … shall wilfully utter, print, write, or publish any disloyal, profane, scurrilous, or abusive language about the form of government of the United States, or the Constitution of the United States, or the military or naval forces of the United States … or shall wilfully display the flag of any foreign enemy, or shall wilfully …

urge, incite, or advocate any curtailment of production … or advocate, teach, defend, or suggest the doing of any of the acts or things in this section enumerated and whoever shall by word or act support or favour the cause of any country with which the United States is at war or by word or act oppose the cause of the United States therein, shall be punished by a fine of not more than $10,000 or imprisonment for not more than twenty years, or both.

| 6 | *Adapted from Section 3 of the Sedition Act 1918* |

The Alien Act, passed by Congress in 1918, followed on from the Sedition Act by giving the US government the power to deport anyone who had been 'a member of any anarchist organisation' – what constituted such an organisation could be the interpretation of the authorities. Taken together, the two acts allowed the US government to clamp down hard on left-wing political thinkers.

Another cause of social upheavals was the migration of African-Americans from the South to northern cities. This resulted in racial tensions and there were more than 20 race riots in 1919, the worst of them in Washington and Chicago. The Chicago race riot resulted in 38 deaths and massive damage to property. There was a wave of lynchings in the South.

The Red Scare was also fuelled by the intense social and industrial problems in the USA after the First World War. There was high inflation, with steeply rising prices making life hard for ordinary people whose wages and salaries went up more slowly. The rapid demobilisation of the armed forces caused serious problems in the job market. There was a wave of industrial unrest and trades union militancy. During 1919, there was a record number of strikes, involving more than 4 million workers. Some 60,000 workers joined a general strike in Seattle organised by the Industrial Workers of the World (IWW); other major strikes were called by the United Mine Workers and the United Steel Workers. The most controversial strike of all was the Boston Police Strike.

**Fig. 6** *The depression in Seattle*

### The Boston Police Strike

In September 1919, 75 per cent of the Boston police force, almost entirely made up of Irish-Americans, went on strike in a dispute over pay and the right to join a trades union, the American Federation of Labor (AFL). The Boston police officers had many complaints about overwork and poor conditions, and their wages were falling badly behind the rate of inflation. The Boston police commissioner took a hard line and refused to allow a police union, but the police officers went ahead anyway.

On 8 September the Boston police force voted by 1,143 to 2 to call a strike. Boston was left without police protection. This led to two nights of lawlessness, with armed gangs roaming the streets in several neighbourhoods. Emotive newspaper reports made the Boston strike into a national sensation. President Wilson, in one of his last acts before suffering a stroke in Colorado, denounced the strike in dramatic fashion as 'a crime against civilisation'.

The Massachusetts state governor, Calvin Coolidge, originally hoped to end the strike by negotiations, but overheated public reaction prompted him to take a tough line. New recruits were sworn in to replace the strikers, the strike was broken and Coolidge became wildly popular. It was the popularity he gained by his response to the Boston Police Strike that played a decisive part in his rise to become vice-president at the Republican convention in 1920.

Kettner for Western Newspaper Association

**Cloudy and unsettled!**

**Fig. 7** *'Cloudy and unsettled!' A cartoon showing the stormy political weather hitting the USA in 1919*

## The Palmer Raids

A few months before the Boston Police Strike, Mayor Hanson of Seattle had gained great popular approval for his tough stance against strike action by the IWW. Other politicians learned lessons from this, including Attorney General A. Mitchell Palmer. Sometimes known as the 'Fighting Quaker', Palmer had been appointed attorney general by President Wilson in March 1919. He became the key figure in the campaign to root out Communists and radicals. Palmer was a reformist Democrat with political ambitions. He had been suggested as a possible Democratic presidential candidate in 1912 and fancied his chances of securing the nomination as Wilson's successor in 1920. He saw the political advantages to be gained by taking a hard line against radicals.

On the other hand, Palmer had a genuine fear of Bolshevism and was shocked by the series of bombings that took place in April and May 1919, soon after he had taken up office. Bombs were sent in packages through the US postal service to several public figures, including Mayor Hanson and Palmer himself. A bomb sent to his home exploded, killing the man who had delivered it – who turned out to be an Italian immigrant. There was a public outcry against anarchists and suspicious foreigners. In the summer of 1919, Palmer opposed Wilson's plan to give an amnesty to all those imprisoned during the war. When the strikes by the coal and steel workers broke out in the autumn, Palmer took an uncompromising position against them.

"COME UNTO ME, YE OPPREST!"

– Alley in the Memphis Commercial Appeal.

**Fig. 8** *'Come unto me, ye opprest!' A cartoon dramatising the danger of terrorism by radical European immigrants at the time of the Red Scare in 1919*

## ▓ Activity

### Source analysis

Study Figures 7 and 8.

1 For each cartoon, answer the following questions.

   a What is the message that the cartoonist is trying to convey?

   b Which features of the cartoon show an attempt to manipulate reaction to the cartoon?

2 Compare the two cartoons. Which image do you consider to more effective? Explain why.

The industrial unrest in autumn 1919 was the background to the Palmer Raids. On 7 November agents under orders from the Justice Department raided the offices of alleged radical organisations in 12 cities across America. Documents were seized and more than 250 suspects rounded up. In December, Palmer deported 199 of them, together with other radicals imprisoned during the war. The Palmer Raids continued into January 1920, with coordinated action in 33 different cities to close down all known communist party offices. Some 4,000 arrests were made. These raids were carried out by the Bureau of Investigation (later the FBI) and made the career of its young assistant director, J. Edgar Hoover.

## ▓ Key profile

### J. Edgar Hoover

J. Edgar Hoover (1895–1972) was the key figure in the FBI for nearly 50 years. He was director of the Bureau under eight different presidents until his death in 1972. Hoover was an efficient organiser and had strongly anti-communist and socially conservative views. The Palmer Raids were in many ways the launching pad for his long career.

The raids in January 1920 encouraged similar actions at state and city level. In New York, elected socialist members of the legislature were banned. Many cities passed 'red flag' laws to prohibit communist banners and insignia. In Washington state and California, there were outbreaks of vigilante violence against the IWW and radical organisations. However, this intensity did not last. During 1920, there was a strong reaction against the violation of people's rights and the Red Scare faded away.

In January 1920, the Supreme Court ruled against the use of evidence seized illegally by raids. The cases against many of those arrested had to be dropped. Some of Palmer's colleagues in the Wilson administration did not support him. The governor of New York, Al Smith, led a powerful campaign to reverse the expulsion of the Socialists from the state legislature. When Palmer tried to whip up a new scare about radical violence, which he predicted would happen on 1 May 1920, no such revolution took place. Public opinion turned sharply against him and his political career ran into the sand. The Red Scare blew itself out in 1920 but it left behind a divisive legacy. The symbol of this legacy was the Sacco and Vanzetti case.

## ▓ A closer look

### The Sacco and Vanzetti case

In May 1920, two Italian immigrants, Nicola Sacco and Bartolomeo Vanzetti, were arrested and charged with murder after a violent robbery in Massachusetts. These men were not harmless innocent citizens; both were carrying guns. They were political activists linked to previous acts of violence, including bombings, carried out by anarchists in Massachusetts. They were duly convicted and sentenced to death.

The trial was not the end of the case, however, only the beginning of a long legal and political controversy that divided the nation. The handling of the trial by Judge Webster Thayer was highly controversial, with many witnesses excluded on ethnic grounds and much contradictory evidence from the witnesses who got to testify. The whole thing was regarded by many liberals as a frame-up.

The trial and legal appeals that followed lasted for years. The case became a national sensation and polarised opinion between liberals and conservatives across America. The legal rights and wrongs almost ceased to matter. Liberals were certainly justified in criticising the flagrant bias of the judge in the original trial; conservatives were justified in their claims that the two men were genuine radicals who had committed crimes, if not the actual one they were convicted of. Sacco and Vanzetti were executed finally in August 1927, but political divisions surrounding their case remained deep.

## The rise of the Ku Klux Klan

A key factor in the changing attitudes within the USA during the years after the First World War was the revival of the Ku Klux Klan (KKK). The organisation was not new. From its formation in December 1865 by ex-soldiers of the Confederate army until 1874, the first Klan carried out a wave of racist violence in the South and at its peak claimed to have half a million members. The driving idea of the Klan was white supremacy – most of the violence was directed against freed slaves but members also hated Republican politicians and the policies of Reconstruction. The Klan was suppressed after the Ku Klux Klan Act 1871 and the use of federal troops, but it left behind a legacy.

Many southern politicians continued to sympathise with the KKK's racist ideas. Intimidation and murders of African-Americans were widespread and rarely punished. Most of the Klan's objectives, including depriving African-Americans of their voting rights, were achieved. 'Jim Crow' dominated the South. When the Klan was reborn in 1915, it could rely on traditional support from white supremacists in the South. It also began to attract many thousands of new supporters outside the South, especially in the mid-west states of Indiana, Ohio and Illinois and in south-west states like Arizona.

The new Klan was founded in Atlanta by a Methodist preacher, William Simmons, who gave the Klan its organisation, insignia and rituals. The image of the Klan was boosted by, and sometimes copied from, the infamous 1915 silent film directed by D. W. Griffith, *The Birth of a Nation*. Griffith's epic glorified the memory of the first Ku Klux Klan and was massively popular with white audiences. The film made everyone familiar with the key images of burning crosses and hooded white costumes.

### Key chronology

**Radicalism in the USA**

| | |
|---|---|
| **1919** February | General strike called in Seattle by the IWW; 60,000 strikers take part. |
| **1919** April/ May | 36 bombs sent through the post to prominent public figures. |
| **1919** September | Strike by the United Steel Workers; Boston Police Strike. |
| **1919** November | Strike by United Mine Worker; launch of the Palmer Raids. |
| **1920** January | Second wave of Palmer Raids; Supreme Court ruling on illegally seized evidence. |
| **1920 May** | Arrest of Sacco and Vanzetti. |
| **1920 June** | Race riot in Washington. |
| **1920 July** | Race riot in Chicago. |

### Cross-reference

For more on **'Jim Crow'**, see page 19.

**Fig. 9** *A theatre poster for* The Awakening

The white men were roused by a mere instinct of self-preservation ... until at last there had sprung into existence a great Ku Klux Klan, a veritable empire of the South, to protect the Southern country.

**7** *Subtitle from the film* **The Birth of a Nation**. *The words were reproduced from Woodrow Wilson's* **A History of the American People**, *1902*

William Simmons set up the organisational structure of the KKK. Meetings of local groups, the Knights of the Ku Klux Klan, were called a klavern, presided over by a kleagle. Regional meetings of several klaverns were called klonklaves, presided over by a grand dragon or grand goblin. Simmons gave himself the title of imperial wizard. These names may seem ridiculous to modern eyes but the Klan was a serious organisation that soon gained mass support. By 1920, it had 4 million members.

The second Ku Klux Klan was much more widely based than the first. In addition to the idea of white supremacy, it was anti-Catholic, anti-Semitic and anti-communist. It claimed to represent a crusade to protect Christian values against immorality and 'alien' influences. The new Klan fitted closely with other groups opposed to immigrants and radicals, especially those in favour of Prohibition. There were strong links between the Klan and the Anti-Saloon League – the Klan was described as the 'extreme militant wing of the temperance movement'.

Between 1917 and 1920, the KKK kept up its attacks on 'enemies' such as German-Americans, Communists, Jewish radicals and African-American soldiers demobilised after the war. From 1920, the Klan increased its membership rapidly through the aggressive marketing methods devised by young public relations agents Edgar Young Clark and Elizabeth Tyler. William Simmons was pushed out and new leaders emerged: Hiram Wesley Evans as imperial wizard and David Stephenson as grand dragon of Indiana. As membership rose, huge amounts of money rolled in. The Klan's own newspaper, the *Fiery Cross*, promoted its ideas nationwide. The KKK, often known at this time as the 'Invisible Empire', seemed unstoppable.

The greatest achievement so far has been to formulate, focus, and gain recognition for an idea – the idea of preserving and developing America first and chiefly for the benefit of the children of the pioneers who made America, and only and definitely along the lines of the purpose and spirit of those pioneers. The Klan cannot claim to have created this idea – it has long been a vague stirring in the souls of the plain people. But the Klan can fairly claim to have given it purpose, method, direction, and a vehicle.

When the Klan first appeared, the nation was in the confusion of sudden awakening from the lovely dream of the melting pot, disorganised and helpless before the invasion of aliens and alien ideas. After 10 years of the Klan it is in arms for defence. This is our great achievement. The second is more selfish; we have won the leadership in the movement for Americanism. Except for a few lonesome voices, almost drowned by the clamour of the alien and the alien-minded 'Liberal', the Klan alone faces the invader.

**8** *Hiram Evans,* **North American Review**, *1926*

## Lynching

The word 'lynch' has its origin in the figure of Charles Lynch (1736–96), a hard-line justice of the peace from the state of Virginia. The term came to refer to the killing of African-Americans by white mobs without any legal process. Lynching was mostly but not entirely confined to the American South. It could apply to all races and peoples but African-Americans formed the bulk of the targets. Victims could be lynched for theft, murder or trivial charges such as 'looking at a white woman without respect'. The killings, often conducted under the approval of local law enforcement officers, frequently included torture or burnings but hanging was the principal method of execution. Huge crowds would gather to view the events and photographs of the killings were sold openly.

In 1901, former slave and Congressman George Henry White put forward a bill to the House of Representatives that proposed making lynching a federal crime, but this bill was defeated. Lynchings subsided a little in the first decade of the 20th century, but in the aftermath of the First World War they rose again, often directed at black servicemen returning from the war in Europe. Between 1919 and 1922, a total of 239 African-Americans were lynched according to 'official records' – many unrecorded killings occurred away from public view.

Repeated attempts to pass anti-lynching legislation were foiled in the US Congress, although the passing of the Civil Rights Act in 1964 went some way to protecting the rights of African-Americans. Nonetheless, lynchings continued throughout the 1960s and 1970s, almost always without the suspect being tried. There was even open support for lynchings from elected politicians. Perhaps the most notorious racist was 'Pitchfork Ben' Tillman, the governor (and later senator) of South Carolina. 'Pitchfork Ben' both encouraged and participated in the lynchings of black people. It was a lynch mob fired up by Tillman that hunted down and burned to death a schoolteacher named Frazier Baker.

Three thousand, seven hundred and twenty-four people were lynched in the United States from 1889 through to 1930. Over four-fifths of these were Negroes, less than one-sixth of whom were accused of rape. Practically all of the lynchers were native whites. The fact that a number of the victims were tortured, mutilated, dragged, or burned suggests the presence of sadistic tendencies among the lynchers. Of the tens of thousands of lynchers and onlookers, only 49 were indicted and only 4 have been sentenced.

**9**     *Arthur Raper, Southern Commission on the Study of Lynching, 1933*

In 2004, the US Senate finally issued a public apology for the fact that nothing had been done to halt the lynching of nearly 5,000 African-Americans. However, in South Carolina the Confederate flag still flies from the State House and in the grounds below there remains a statue in memory of Benjamin Ryan Tillman, 'erected by the Legislature, the Democratic Party and the Private Citizens of South Carolina'.

■ **Activity**

### Preparing a presentation

Working in small groups, prepare a 10-minute presentation to be given to the class, explaining the main reasons for the sudden rise in support for the KKK between 1915 and 1925.

■ **Activity**

### Revision exercise

Summarise the reasons for the collapse in support for the KKK after 1925.

In the early 1920s, the Klan was no longer seen just as a terrorist organisation. It gained respectability and considerable political influence. The KKK influenced the outcome of many local elections and engineered the passing of numerous local laws on issues like the language used in schools. It controlled many judges, sheriffs and police officials. Klan sympathisers reached very high positions, including both Georgia senators and the governors of Colorado and Oklahoma.

After 1925, the Klan went into a sudden and dramatic decline. This was due to a number of factors:

- David Stephenson, the grand dragon of Indiana, was sentenced to 25 five years for rape and manslaughter. The scandal spoiled the KKK's image as defenders of womanhood and moral purity. Several cases of bribery and fraud concerning Klan connections with disgraced public officials had a similar effect.
- Publicity and marketing were less effective after the death of Elizabeth Tyler in 1924.
- There were divisions about tactics among Klan leaders and Hiram Evans lost a lot of his credibility as leader.
- Some of the grievances that had fuelled mass support for the KKK lost their force. Anti-immigrant feeling was reduced by the success of the campaign to limit immigration and the passing of the National Origins (Quota) Act in 1924; hatred for big business was weakened by rising prosperity in the USA after this time.
- Many politicians who were happy to have links with the KKK when it was on the rise were simply opportunistic; they were just as quick to dissociate themselves when public opinion began to turn the other way.

The sudden decline of the Ku Klux Klan did not mean that its ideas and attitudes had disappeared. Discrimination against African-Americans continued throughout the South. Resentful feelings among small-town Protestants remained strong. One feature of this was the popularity of evangelical preachers like the Reverend Billy Sunday and Aimee Semple McPherson. They drew huge audiences to their live rallies and radio shows.

■ **Key profile**

### Aimee Semple McPherson

Aimee Semple McPherson (1890–1944) was a fundamentalist preacher like Billy Sunday. She specialised in glamour mixed with faith healing and a showbusiness style. She used the methods of modern advertising but blamed all the vices of modern big-city America on a lack of old-fashioned religion.

Billy Sunday's preaching style was aggressively fundamentalist. He appealed to many of those who had backed the Klan. He told his audiences that he wanted to see radicals shot by firing squad. He had no time for free speech or emancipated women wearing new fashions. He claimed only fundamentalist religion could save the nation from immorality. His revival meetings were attended by thousands and his popularity was typical of the cultural backlash of the 1920s. So were the events in Dayton, Tennessee in 1925, which led to the 'Monkey Trial' – a national sensation.

## A closer look

### The 'Monkey Trial' (Scopes Trial)

The Scopes Trial was both a local and a national sensation. It took place in the packed courthouse of Dayton, Tennessee, in suffocating heat. It was attended by scores of journalists reporting to local and national newspapers. Later, the trial was turned into a Hollywood feature film *Inherit the Wind*, with Spencer Tracy starring as Clarence Darrow. Above all, the trial was a clash of values, symbolised by the two star witnesses: Clarence Darrow, the brilliant, atheist, 'Wet' northern lawyer from Chicago, against William Jennings Bryan, the 'Dry' fundamentalist, the hero of Populists in the West and the South.

Tennessee was the battleground because the state had passed the Butler Act, outlawing the teaching of evolution or any other theory that contradicted the literal version of the Creation story as described in Genesis – and thus could be seen as suggesting that humans were descended from monkeys in the chain of evolution. John Scopes, a local schoolteacher, volunteered to challenge the new state anti-evolution law by teaching evolution in his science lessons.

The Scopes Trial, and the courtroom debate between Darrow and Bryan, has often been misrepresented. To northern liberals and journalists, the performance of William Jennings Bryan as chief witness for the prosecution made him look old-fashioned and ridiculous. Clarence Darrow cross-examined him, always trying to poke fun at Bryan's literal belief in the more fanciful Bible stories such as Jonah being swallowed by a whale. Bryan died a few days after the trial. Many people who completely disagreed with his views regarded the Scopes Trial as a sad end to Bryan's long and distinguished career.

However, that was not how the trial was perceived by Bryan's fundamentalist followers. For them, the Scopes Trial was a vindication not a defeat. Scopes was found guilty, although the state government made sure he never actually went to jail. The Butler Act remained in force for another 40 years, until 1967. Even after the act was repealed, few teachers were brave enough to teach evolution in the South and school textbooks just avoided controversy by not mentioning evolution at all. Anti-Darwinism remained deeply entrenched.

The 'Monkey Trial' showed once again the gulf in American society between big-city modernism and small-town traditionalists. That gulf continued to exist long after 1925.

### Questions

How far does the evidence in this chapter suggest that America in the 1920s was marked by a 'backlash against modernity'?

## The return to 'normalcy' in foreign policy

The more negative and inward-looking attitudes in the USA in the years after the First World War were reflected in US foreign policy. At the beginning of 1919, Woodrow Wilson was the most prestigious political leader in the world and many Americans shared his ideals. However, peacemaking proved to be long, difficult and frustrating. The peace talks in Paris got bogged down in endless disputes. At home, the nation was concerned with issues like Prohibition, immigration and hunting down radicals and Communists. A wide gulf opened up between Wilson and Congress in their view of America's relationship with the outside world. The League of Nations became a symbolic issue.

**Fig. 10** *A contemporary cartoon attacking Woodrow Wilson's obsession with the League of Nations*

Wilson's stubborn refusal to compromise over the league strengthened his opponents, both Republicans and Democrats. It also strengthened isolationism by dividing the internationalists. Many of those who were against Wilson over the league, like Theodore Roosevelt and Henry Cabot Lodge, agreed with him about the importance of the USA having an outward-looking foreign policy. By 1920, Wilson was steadily losing his political authority. This tends to happen anyway to a president approaching the end of his second term. With Wilson the loss of authority was severe because he had serious health problems after suffering a stroke. These were made worse by the strain of long journeys around the country campaigning for ratification of the Treaty of Versailles and for the USA to join the League of Nations.

All this made the Democratic Party weaker in 1920. It was difficult for the party to focus on selecting a new presidential candidate while Wilson was ill but would not let anyone else take over. By the end of 1920, two things were clear. The next president was almost certain to be a Republican; and, whoever was president, the national mood was moving towards isolationism and fear of foreign entanglements.

The Republican candidate who emerged as the surprise choice at the 1920 convention was Warren G. Harding, a politician from Ohio with little interest in or knowledge of foreign affairs. It was Harding who invented the famous, not-very-grammatical term 'normalcy' as his motto

**Cross-reference**

See pages 47–52 for further coverage of the **rejection of Wilson and the League of Nations** in 1919.

for American foreign policy. However, the idea of 'normalcy' was popular with many Americans and helped Harding to win the presidential election. Many people felt that the war had been a European affair and the USA should be careful to avoid the same mistake in future. The post-war treaties had been a failure because of devious and selfish Europeans. Problems at home were more important. The USA should get on with its own, superior, way of life.

> America's present need is not heroics but normalcy; not revolution but restoration; not internationality but nationality. It is one thing to battle successfully against world domination by a military autocracy, but it is quite another thing to try to revise human nature. My best judgement of America's needs is to steady down, to get squarely on our feet, to make sure of the right path.

**10**
*Election speech by Warren G. Harding, May 1920*

In reality, American foreign policies under Harding and Coolidge in the 1920s were not completely isolationist. The USA was the world's greatest economic power and overseas trade was expanding. This necessitated numerous agreements with other nations. American diplomats and financiers played a big part, for example, in restructuring Germany's reparations payments through the Dawes Plan of 1924 and the Young Plan of 1929. In 1928, the American secretary of state, Frank B. Kellogg, played an important role in trying to get international support for the Kellogg-Briand Pact, an idealistic agreement intended to renounce war and aggression. So there was considerable diplomatic activity during the 1920s, not rigid isolationism.

**Fig. 11** *Calvin Coolidge signs the Veterans' Bill, 1921*

## ■ Key chronology

### The USA and foreign affairs

**1920** Appeal for 'normalcy' by Warren G. Harding; final rejection of the League of Nations by Congress; victory of Warren G. Harding in the presidential election.

**1921** Start of the Washington Naval Conference.

**1924** Loans to Weimar Germany agreed through the Dawes Plan.

**1925** Intervention in Nicaragua by US troops.

**1928** Launch of the Kellogg-Briand Pact; American protests to Japan about military action in China.

The USA continued to be interventionist in Latin America. American troops were sent into Nicaragua in 1924, as had happened before in 1912–14. There were a series of disputes with the government of Mexico over its failures to protect American citizens; there was pressure from American oil companies for the US government to back its claims. A compromise agreement was made in 1923 but two years later the new president of Mexico, Plutarco Calles, took a tough line against British and American oil companies. By 1927, it looked as if relations between Mexico and the USA might break down completely. The crisis was smoothed over in the end but it showed that Calvin Coolidge was just as ready as his predecessors had been to intervene in Latin America.

There was also concern about developments in the Far East. The USA was still committed to the Open Door policy in China and attempted to block Japanese expansion into China in the late 1920s. Worries about Japanese naval expansion were part of the reason why the American secretary of state, Charles Evans Hughes, organised and hosted the Washington Naval Conference in 1921–2. The conference led to the Four Power Pact and the Five Power Naval Limitation Treaty, agreeing a 10-year 'holiday' in battleship building to avoid the dangers of a naval arms race. Therefore, 'normalcy' did not mean ignoring the outside world altogether, but the general tone and direction of American policy was to keep out of European affairs, to limit defence spending and to put domestic interests, especially business interests, first.

### ■ Summary questions

**1** Explain why there was widespread social unrest in the USA in the years following the First World War.

**2** How important was the contribution of Calvin Coolidge to the political dominance of the Republican Party in the 1920s?

# 4    Prosperity in the 1920s

In this chapter you will learn about:

- the reasons for the boom in prosperity for most Americans during the 1920s

- the social developments of the decade and who was affected by them

- the problems that persisted in agriculture and some parts of the economy

- the growth of organised crime and its effects on society.

Flappers are we
Flappers are we
Flappers and fly and free.
Never too slow
All on the go
Petting parties with the smarties.
Dizzy with dangerous glee
Puritans knock us
Because the way we're clad
Preachers all mock us
Because we're not all that bad
Most flippant young flappers are we!

**1**  *From the song **Tea for Two** in the popular 1925 stage musical **No, No, Nanette***

**Fig. 1** *A 'flapper'*

It beats rugs gently; sweeps as no broom can; and thoroughly air cleans – *electrically!* Its brand new air-cleaning tools dust – *dustlessly!* It keeps your home immaculate; saves time, strength, health; makes rugs wear years *longer*. Certainly, it's a Hoover. Delivered to any home upon payment of only $6.25 down! Your authorised Hoover dealer will explain our easy purchase plan. The Hoover – it beats, as it sweeps, as it cleans!

**2**  *1924 advertisement for a Hoover vacuum cleaner*

Nearly half the population were still counted as part of the rural population in 1930. Fifty million Americans still moved between birth and death to the rhythms of the sun and the seasons. More than forty-five million of them had no indoor plumbing, and almost none had electricity. They relieved themselves in chamber pots and outdoor latrines. For cooking and for heating they used wood stoves and lit their smoky houses with oil lamps. In the roadless Ozark mountains, the mother of the future governor, Orval Faubus, could not do the family laundry until she had first boiled the guts of a freshly butchered hog to make lye soap.

**3** *David M. Kennedy, **Freedom From Fear**, 1999*

### Key term

**Real wages:** the value of wages after inflation has been taken into account.

Giving an impression of a decade is always difficult, even in a smaller and less diverse country than the USA. Sources 1, 2 and 3 give tiny glimpses of a time of social change. It was an age of the New Woman, with political liberation to the right to vote, economic liberation to jobs and household appliances, and social liberation to fashion and new norms of behaviour symbolised by 'flappers'. It was an age of leisure, prosperity and brand-name consumer goods: the radio, the vacuum cleaner, the cheap motor car.

However, it was also an age when prosperity was not evenly divided. There were losers as well as winners. The 'Roaring Twenties' roared only in urban America, not in the struggling country districts.

## The reasons for the economic boom of the 1920s

From 1920, after a brief period of painful adjustment from the wartime economy to peacetime conditions, the USA experienced a decade of prosperity, often referred to as the Great Boom. Most Americans did well out of the boom years, benefiting from steady work, low prices, higher **real wages** and access to a vast range of new consumer goods. Some economic historians have claimed that the full employment and low inflation of the 1920s was the best economic performance of any decade in the history of the USA.

Much of this was due to the strength of industry and big business in the USA. The war years had stimulated industrial production and innovation. Throughout the 1920s, big business knew it could rely on favourable, pro-business policies being followed by the Republican presidents, especially Calvin Coolidge, and by the long-serving secretary of the treasury, Andrew Mellon, who was especially committed to cutting government intervention and keeping taxes low.

### Key profile

#### Andrew Mellon

Andrew Mellon (1855–1937) was a conservative financier, industrialist and multi-millionaire who served as secretary to the treasury from 1921 to 1932. The Mellon Plan of 1923 recommended reducing national debt and keeping taxes low, especially for the rich. His conservative ideas on finance and taxation were put forward in his 1924 book *Taxation: The People's Business*. He became unpopular during the Great Depression.

Society was also changed after 1918 by modernisation and technological innovation. More and more Americans lived in urban areas. Factories were increasingly taken over by mass production and the modern methods of industrial management that had been pioneered before the war by Frederick Winslow Taylor. Henry Ford used these methods to introduce the Model T, the first cheap, mass-produced car. The drive of manufacturing industry to expand production and increase profits went hand in hand with a booming demand for consumer goods. The result was a social revolution. The symbol of the social revolution was the Model T Ford.

**Fig. 2** *Chevrolet cars come off the production line*

## Key profile

### Frederick Winslow Taylor

Frederick Winslow Taylor (1856–1915) was an engineer and management expert who set out his ideas in *The Principles of Scientific Management* published in 1911. 'Taylorism' emphasised the importance of systematic work schedules and worker cooperation, strictly enforced by management. Taylor's ideas continued to influence others after his death, including Henry Ford in the USA and the new communist regime in the Soviet Union.

## A closer look

### The Model T Ford

The Model T Ford represents a turning point in American industry, the taking of mobility to the masses in a way that had never before been considered possible. Before the Model T, cars had been novel items only available for those with plenty of money to spend on luxury goods. The mass population continued as before, travelling by foot, by public transport and, in rural areas, by horse. Henry Ford had started his motor company back in 1903, but his early models met with only limited success. However, Ford had a dream of producing a car that was simple to use and within the budget of most of families

**Fig. 3** *The American future*

in America. He set his team of engineers working to fulfil this dream and the result was the Model T, with production beginning in 1908.

The Model T was designed for mass production. It was simple, sturdy and had nothing elaborate about it – its sole purpose was to get the driver and passengers from A to B. Between 1914 and 1925, the only colour of vehicle was black, a fact that led to one of Ford's most famous expressions: 'You can paint it any colour, so long as it's black.' (There is no specific evidence to indicate that Ford actually said this, but it became part of the Ford legend anyway.) Ford also pioneered new methods of assembly-line production. Instead of a team of men working on individual cars until completion, each worker focused his efforts on a specific part, and these parts were assembled as they travelled along a moving production line to produce the final car. The result was that cars could be turned out at an incredible pace; by 1914, one car could be made every 93 minutes, and over 19 years Ford produced 15 million Model T cars. All the parts were completely interchangeable, meaning that the cars were easy to maintain and repair as the owner did not need unique parts to be made. By 1917, the Model T was so successful that Ford stopped spending on advertising – he simply did not need to create any publicity.

The Model T illustrates how industry was transforming the lives of Americans in the early years of the 20th century. When first released it cost only $850, whereas most other cars cost about $2,000 or $3,000, but the price had dropped to less than $400 by 1914. This was about four months' wages for an average worker and the availability of new credit deals (where you pay by instalments) meant that the Model T truly 'put America on wheels'.

It has been asserted that machine production kills the creative ability of the craftsman. This is not true. The machine demands that man be its master; it compels mastery more than the old methods did. The number of skilled craftsmen in proportion to the working population has greatly increased under the conditions brought about by the machine. They get better wages and more leisure in which to exercise their creative faculties.

There are two ways of making money – one at the expense of others, the other by service to others. The first method does not 'make' money, does not create anything; it only 'gets' money – and does not always succeed in that. In the last analysis, the so-called gainer loses. The second way pays twice – to maker and user, to seller and buyer. It receives by creating, and receives only a just share, because no one is entitled to all. Nature and humanity supply too many necessary partners for that. True riches make wealthier the country as a whole.

4

*Henry Ford in* **Forum** *magazine, October 1928*

Other pre-war technologies grew into nationwide mass trends. Radio spread rapidly, bringing news, sport, light entertainment and advertising into every home. From the outset it was also realised that radio could be an important political tool. The first licensed American public commercial radio broadcast was made by the KDKA company in Pittsburgh on 2 November 1920 (although experimental and unauthorised radio broadcasts had been made before this date). Its first transmission broadcast the results for the Warren G. Harding/James M. Cox presidential election, this information being received by a tiny audience of only 1,000 listeners – few people had radios and the radio transmitter had little power. Nevertheless, KDKA started to sell radio sets via newspaper advertisements and the medium quickly spread throughout the population, spawning more radio broadcasts.

The 1920s was the golden age of silent cinema, with the emergence of Hollywood as the 'dream factory' of the world and a new obsession with film stars as celebrities. It was also the decade of the New Woman. The long fight for women's suffrage ended in success when Congress ratified the Nineteenth Amendment on 18 August 1920, giving women the right to vote (Source 5).

As well as the right to vote, women (at least those in urban areas) gained new social freedoms. Fashion, advertising and the growth of the retail industry had a big impact on the image and roles of women. New household appliances began to change the face of domestic life for millions of women. Previously, those women who were unable to afford domestic staff had to perform most household chores by hand, such as cleaning clothes or washing dishes. Yet the increasing availability of electrical appliances such as washing machines, electric irons, electric water heaters and dishwashers promised to liberate millions of women from lives of drudgery. Advertisements often depicted women out enjoying themselves golfing or meeting friends while their appliances did all their housework for them. Many homes also received central heating, increasing the comfort of domestic life.

For many women, however, the benefits of all these appliances were balanced out by the creation of more jobs elsewhere. As the need for domestic service staff disappeared, for example, the housewife suddenly had to take responsibility for running the entire household.

The image of the 'Roaring Twenties' is partly a myth, but there is no doubt that many people at the time, at least in urban America, saw the 1920s as an era of prosperity, more freedom and opportunity for ordinary people.

Section 1. The right of citizens of the United States to vote shall not be denied or abridged by the United States or by any state on account of sex.

Section 2. Congress shall have power to enforce this article by appropriate legislation.

**5**    *Nineteenth Amendment to the US Constitution, ratified by Congress on 18 August 1920*

**Fig. 4** *The New Woman?*

■ **Key term**

**Gross domestic product (GDP):** a measurement of the total national output of goods and services.

Between 1922 and 1929, the annual unemployment figure never rose above 4 per cent. **Gross domestic product (GDP)** grew at a steady rate of 2 per cent a year – double the average increase in prices. Americans knew they were better off than their parents had been, even though prosperity and living standards had increased rapidly in the generation before the war. They knew that the American economy was racing far ahead of Europe's.

Most Americans earned more pay for fewer hours of work. Between 1909 and 1919, per capita annual income was $517. During the 1920s, this rose to $612. Real wages went up by 30 per cent. The result was that people ate better, lived longer and had much more money to spend. This increase in spending power led to a consumer boom, with a rush to buy cars, radios, fashionable clothes and household appliances. It is no coincidence that the 1920s was a golden age for advertising.

The mass ownership of cars that followed Henry Ford's launch of the Model T was the biggest single symbol (and also in itself a cause) of the 1920s consumer boom, but it was not the only one. As personal incomes went up, there was a vast range of new things to spend money on. Many of these new goods were powered by electricity, which became more widely available as technology advanced.

The sense of prosperity and individual advancement during the Great Boom was not only based on economic factors. There was also a powerful 'feel-good factor' reflecting the rise of leisure opportunities and mass entertainment in the Jazz Age. There was mass interest in popular music on the radio, in jazz clubs and in dance halls. Cinema had been growing steadily before 1918 but really took off in the 1920s with the great age of silent films and the development of 'talking pictures' from 1927. Sport became a national obsession, with new national heroes such as 'Babe' Ruth in baseball, 'Red' Grange in American football and Jack Dempsey in boxing.

### Factors underpinning the 1920s boom

There were many factors that created the conditions for the Great Boom. Some were political. The Republican presidents between 1921 and 1929, Harding and Coolidge, favoured big business to an even greater extent than their Republican predecessors like McKinley and Taft. Business could rely on low taxes and on the minimum of regulation or anti-trust actions. The commerce secretary, Herbert Hoover, was highly capable and well respected by business leaders.

There were also important structural factors:

■ There was already massive growth of the American economy before the First World War, based on immense natural resources, the role of big business and the economic benefits resulting from millions of immigrants. The American economy was already outstripping European competitors before 1914. The 1920s was simply the continuation of these trends.

■ The mobilisation of the wartime economy had increased efficiencies and stimulated both manufacturing and agriculture. The wartime boom in agricultural production fell away but the stimulus to industry carried on into the 1920s with factories working at full capacity. The USA also gained because the damage and dislocation of the war was much deeper in Europe – the American economy was able to recover much more quickly.

Management methods were modernised, often following the principles laid down by the 'time-and-motion' expert Frederick Taylor. Although Taylor had promoted his ideas before the war (he died in 1915) it was in the 1920s that these principles were widely applied. The most famous example of this was Henry Ford's development of the assembly line to produce cars.

Technological advances assisted the development of new industries:

New oilfields were developed after 1920 in Oklahoma, Louisiana and Texas. The flow of oil was vital to the growth of the motor industry.

Oil enabled a huge expansion of the electricity supply. Electricity was already big business before the war – Samuel Insull was famous as the man who built up a giant monopoly of utilities in Chicago – but it was in the 1920s that Insull's methods of running and financing the energy industry really took off. By 1929, 16 holding companies controlled most American electricity production.

**Fig. 5** *Oil wells in the USA*

## Key profile

### Samuel Insull

Samuel Insull (1859–1938) was a business investor who emigrated from London in 1881 and took a leading role in building up General Electric. He bought up many enterprises in electric power, trams and railroads in Chicago and the mid-West.

Perhaps the most notable aspect of the Great Boom was the expansion of banking, credit and the stock market. The rapid growth of corporate enterprises was matched by the rapid rise in value of stocks and shares. The **Great Bull Market** of the later 1920s was partly a symptom and partly a cause of rising prosperity. The stock market was used to finance economic expansion, often with too little **securitisation** or regulation. Many companies and individuals built up paper fortunes on the constant rise of stock market shares.

## Key terms

**Great Bull Market:** on the American stock market, a rising market (a good thing) is known as a bull market. A falling market (a bad thing) is a bear market. The rise in share values in the late 1920s was so unusually sustained that it acquired the name Great Bull Market.

**Securitisation:** securing a loan means having something to back it up as security. Some homeowners, for example, take out loans secured against the value of their home. An unsecured loan is a risky business.

By the end of 1927, the share index of the *New York Times* stood at 245. It rose to 331 by October 1928 and 452 by September 1929. It is clear in hindsight that this steep rise was not based on sound economic foundations and that it could never have been sustained without a drastic correction downwards. At the time, however, it was all part of the boom mentality. When Herbert Hoover was inaugurated as president in 1929, the rising stock market was taken for granted as proof of the unstoppable prosperity and economic power of the USA. Few people realised that a financial and economic disaster was waiting to happen.

**Fig. 6** *A well-stocked store during the 1920s*

**A closer look**

### Easy credit

The stock market crash followed a period of wild financial speculation. The stock market did not stay in step with business growth but shot ahead on its own, jumping upwards in leaps and bounds. This frenzy of speculation was partly caused by psychological factors – by a kind of infectious belief that the Great Bull Market would last indefinitely – but it was also fuelled by easy credit. Money was cheap and borrowing easy. In the months before the Great Crash, there was a tide of easy credit.

Some of the money came from private investors, although more came from big corporations looking to invest their cash reserves. Above all, the banks were awash with money and ready to lend freely. A lot of the money lent by banks for buying stocks was financed by what was known as **call loans**. These enabled borrowers to buy stocks without putting up more than a small amount of their own money. In effect, the ability of the borrower to repay the loan depended almost entirely on the value of the stocks bought with the loan. By the end of 1928, outstanding call loans were worth $8 billion. If and when the paper value of stocks collapsed, as it did from October 1929, it was the inability to repay these call loans that meant financial ruin for investors.

**Key terms**

**Call loans:** loans used to finance the purchase of securities and which may be terminated ('called') at the discretion of the borrower or the lender on demand.

# Continuing problems in agriculture and other parts of the economy

The 1920s were not boom years for all Americans. Affluence was not evenly shared. Many of the older, staple industries such as railways, timber, wool and cotton textiles, shoemaking and coalmining experienced slowdowns and depressed conditions because they faced foreign competition and were undercut by the expansion of new growth industries such as oil, rayon (artificial textiles) and concrete.

The growth of mechanisation and 'scientific' management methods reduced the demand for skilled labour and ensured that wages rose more slowly than productivity and profits. Labour unions were weakened by the anti-union policies prevalent among business leaders and by the mismanagement and internal divisions within the unions themselves. For many unskilled workers, mechanisation meant lower rates of pay and hard living conditions. The experience of one worker and his family gives a glimpse of what life could be like at the bottom of the heap in 1920s America.

> There was this guy, Alex Pavlowski. He'd been laid off from the coalmines in Pennsylvania and came to Chicago with his family, wife and four children, looking for work. He couldn't read or write. And could only get part-time jobs loading trucks and shovelling snow. The little money that came in had to be spent on food, and this was of poor quality. The children were all sick and had heavy colds. There was no coal and the house was cold and damp. The gas had been shut off. Added to this, they were about to be evicted and they had no money for rent, old or new.

**6**  *Report by a social worker in Chicago, 1927*

The situation in agriculture was much worse. For millions of American farmers, there was no Great Boom. The USA was becoming an urban country; the 1920 census showed, for the first time, that less than half the people were living in rural areas. Wealth was shifting away from staple crops towards consumer industries and the urban middle class. One symbol of the way in which farmers were left behind was in public utilities; most farmers lived without electricity in a world that went dark and silent at nightfall.

The problems in agriculture seemed dramatic in the 1920s because the situation before and during the First World War was so good for American farmers. From 1890, despite some sharp ups and downs, agricultural prices were generally high. From 1913 to 1918, prices rocketed upwards to meet the demand created by the loss of production in war-torn Europe. The need for food, together with the requirements of the munitions industry, meant that farmers could sell everything they produced at top prices. Many borrowed large sums of money for machinery and to bring new land under cultivation. Farm incomes more than doubled during the war years.

This wartime boom was suddenly cut off in 1920. As soon as the US government and the Allies stopped ordering wheat, its price dropped from $2.50 a bushel to less than $1. The price of wool dropped to one-third of its wartime price. There were similar falls in the price of livestock, cotton, corn and other staple products. There was some recovery from these low prices after 1922 onwards, but agriculture remained depressed throughout the 1920s.

It seems clear that it was not only the dislocation after the war that caused this decline, there were long-term structural factors as well. One proof of this is that there were depressed conditions for agriculture in Europe in the later 1920s; small farmers in Germany, for example, were struggling badly.

**Fig. 7** 'Farm for sale'

The biggest single problem was overproduction. Mechanisation and new techniques meant that far more could be produced by fewer farmers working smaller areas of land. By 1929, the agricultural workforce had been reduced by 5 per cent. Some 13 million acres (5.2 million hectares) were taken out of production. More was actually being produced due to fertilisers, pesticides and the easy availability of tractors. Prices were kept low by all these efficiencies, but the investment costs for machinery and for paying back debts stayed the same. Many farmers became dependent on loans to cover their annual losses.

The situation was worst for the people at the bottom of the agricultural economy such as sharecroppers and wage labourers. Bigger farms could pay their way more easily. Nevertheless, there were urgent demands for government intervention to help agriculture out. In 1922, the Fordney-McCumber Tariff raised the protective tariff against foreign imports. In 1923, the federal government brought in the Agricultural Credits Act to make low-interest loans available. Other attempts to pass laws helping agriculture were blocked by President Coolidge. Huge farm surpluses, and the low prices that resulted from them, continued to exist. When the Great Depression hit in 1929, American farmers were hopelessly vulnerable to its effects.

We'd only get $12 per bale of cotton, and we'd have to pick hard to have money to buy food after the picking season ended. If we had a rainy week we couldn't pick at all. We would have to go and get food on credit.

**7**      *David Jordan recounts the problems of sharecroppers in the South*

## The growth of organised crime and its effects on society

The growth of organised crime in the 1920s was not a new phenomenon. Criminal gangs were already powerful in the USA before the First World War. Wherever there was urbanisation, crime bosses would fight to control the profits to be made from gambling, prostitution and protection rackets. In cities such as New York and Chicago, large criminal networks were established, often linked by ethnic loyalties to particular immigrant groups such as Italians or Irish-Americans. These connections between immigrant communities and organised crime played a big part in the anti-immigration movement and the campaign for Prohibition.

However, there is no doubt that organised crime entered a new phase after 1920. A huge industry was opened up to illegal monopolies. Prohibition was the key factor in making organised crime organised. It provided the ideal conditions for organised crime to grow bigger and gain

### Activity

**Revision exercise**

Outline in order of importance the reasons why people working in agriculture faced difficult economic conditions in the 1920s.

some kind of respectability and acceptance in the eyes of otherwise law-abiding people:

- The production, distribution and selling of alcohol handed criminals the opportunity to control a huge multi-million dollar industry.
- Alcohol was closely linked to other enterprises already controlled by criminal gangs, such as gambling and prostitution.
- Effective enforcement was impossible. The budget for law enforcement officers was tiny compared with the spending power of organised crime, and the sheer length of the US borders made stopping the importation and transportation of alcohol a hopeless task.
- Because so many otherwise decent people opposed Prohibition and were willing to see the law broken, there were willing consumers, and many policemen and public officials were ready to accept payoffs.

The first of the big new criminal organisations to seize the business opportunities provided by the Volstead Act was the Torrio–Capone gang ('the Chicago Outfit') of Chicago. Johnny Torrio grabbed control of the mob previously controlled by his partner 'Big Jim' Colosimo and set about building up a huge bootlegging operation. Because men like Torrio could not rely on the police or the courts to protect his business dealings, they needed their own enforcers to fight off rival gangs and to intimidate the operators of hotels and speakeasies. Torrio brought in extra gunmen, mostly from New York and Brooklyn. The most

**Fig. 8** *Destroying the 'demon drink'*

efficient of these enforcers was Alphonse Capone. After Torrio was badly wounded in 1925, Capone became the driving force of the gang.

It took until 1929 for the Torrio–Capone gang to win the 'beer wars' and secure their monopoly in Chicago. Gang-related killings became a weekly occurrence, usually leading to lurid newspaper coverage. In November 1924, the most powerful rival gang leader, Dion O'Banion, was shot dead. This sparked a long power struggle between the Torrio–Capone Italians and the O'Banion Irish gang. In 1926, the O'Banions sent eight armoured cars to attack Capone's hotel in the Chicago suburb of Cicero. In 1929, the gang war between the Italian South Side and the North Side Irish/German resulted in the St Valentine's Day Massacre.

Cross-reference

See page 58 for more information on the **Volstead Act**.

## The St Valentine's Day Massacre

The word 'massacre' is an exaggeration. A total of seven people died, one of them a car mechanic who was an innocent bystander. The other six were members of the North Side gang, led by George 'Bugs' Moran. They were victims of a carefully planned ambush set by Al Capone, although Capone himself was clever enough to be away in Florida at the time. Moran was a target because of previous murders committed by the North Side gang and because Capone saw him as a main rival for control of bootlegging operations in Chicago. The gang wars also reflected the ethnic tensions between different immigrant societies, with Irish and Germans on one side and Italians on the other.

The Capone plan was to lure the Moran gang to the garage of a transport warehouse to collect a consignment of bootleg whisky. Four of Capone's men, two disguised as police officers, went into the garage to carry out the killings. The North Side gang members did not fight back because they thought they were being arrested by real policemen. The plan failed in one key respect because Moran was not present at the time. His gang was badly weakened and he never recovered his grip on the Chicago crime world.

It did not really do much good for Capone either. The event was so sensational that it forced the police and the authorities into taking action. Two of the gunmen involved in the killings were charged with murder, although they were eventually killed by rival gangs not sentenced by the courts. As for Capone himself, the St Valentine's Day massacre caused federal investigators to step up their campaign to nail him. Two years later, they did.

---

If people didn't want beer and wouldn't drink it, a fellow would be crazy to go around trying to sell it. I never saw a man point a gun at someone and make him drink or go into a gambling house. I regard it as a public benefaction if people are given decent liquor to drink and square games to bet on.

**8**  *Al Capone's view of Prohibition*

By 1929, Al Capone was the dominant figure in the world of organised crime, in Chicago and beyond. Supply lines ran from Canada, the Atlantic coast and the Caribbean, as well as from illegal producers within the USA. His business empire not only covered alcohol, prostitution, slot machines, betting and loan-sharking, it also included property, highway construction and rubbish collection. Thousands of people were involved: boat operators, car dealers, railway porters, hotel staff, restaurant owners, runners collecting bets and touts finding customers for 10,000 speakeasies.

Al Capone achieved celebrity status, always in the news and often seen as some kind of working-class folk hero. The natural fascination with this key personality tends to obscure two important facts. The first is the sheer nastiness of the violence and corruption that was involved. The second is that there was much more to organised crime than guns and gang warfare in Chicago. Organised crime was big business and it set up operations in almost all major cities such as Detroit, St Louis, Philadelphia, Newark and New York. The Purple Gang, for example, controlled organised crime in Detroit. Most of the gang's leaders were Jewish, with a terrible reputation for violence. In New Jersey, the Sicilians were dominant. In Boston, there was intense rivalry between Irish and Italian gangs. New York was a major centre for organised crime, with competition between Irish, Jewish and Sicilian mobs. In the African-American community of Harlem, a separate Black Mafia developed, which controlled gambling. Gangs in these cities were often able to rely on help from corrupt local government officers. Two city mayors infamous for corruption were Frank Hague in Newark and Jimmy Walker in New York.

2    DAILY TIMES, CHICAGO, TUESDAY, FEBRUARY 10, 1931

**Fig. 9** 'Public Enemy No. 1.' The writing on the wall for Al Capone in the Chicago Daily News, 1931

It is often claimed that it was in New York that the Jewish bootlegger, Arnold Rothstein, first pioneered the 'bureaucratisation' of crime, using systematic business methods. Rothstein's nickname was 'The Brain'. He was known as the man responsible for the baseball bribery scandal of 1919, when players of the Chicago White Sox deliberately lost the world series. He became the real-life model for fictional representations – in Scott Fitzgerald's novel *The Great Gatsby* and in the stories of Damon Runyon. Rothstein was murdered in 1928, but he had lasting influence on the world of organised crime.

Arnold Rothstein's businesslike approach appealed to many of the 'Young Turks', the new generation of gang leaders such as 'Lucky' Luciano and Meyer Lansky, who wanted to modernise crime operations and seize power for themselves. At the end of the 1920s, this power struggle led to a sustained wave of gang killings known as the Castellammarese War. Luciano and Lansky were the winners. They ousted the old-style 'capo', Salvatore Maranzano, in 1931.

By the end of the 1920s, organised crime was very different from the early days of the bootleggers.

## The effects of crime on US society

Organised crime at the end of the 1920s was big business. It operated nationwide and provided countless job opportunities. Bootlegging was still the core business but organised crime increasingly diversified into all kinds of activities, many of them legitimate. The impact of organised crime on American society was significant because it blurred the boundaries between crime and decent society. Huge numbers of law-abiding people continued to drink illegally. The poorer classes made do with home-produced beer or moonshine; the more wealthy could go to speakeasies. Either way, respect for the law was lessened.

**Activity**

**Revision exercise**

Outline the main reasons why organised crime was able to grow in size and influence in the 1920s.

The sensational reporting of crime in newspapers often made gangsters and bootleggers appear as larger-than-life celebrities. This trend was boosted by the popularity of feature films about gangsters as the rise of 'talking pictures' from 1927 dominated mass entertainment. Moralists saw the explosion of gangland violence as proof that alcohol was indeed the source of all wickedness and that Prohibition was more necessary than ever. Others took the opposite view – that Prohibition had failed to reform American society and so should be repealed.

*Learning outcomes*

In this section you have looked at some of the issues affecting the problems of post-war America and the prosperity of the 'Roaring Twenties'. You have seen how the aftermath of the First World War led to social unrest and a shift in attitudes, towards both American society and the relationships between the USA and the world outside. You have seen how the prosperity and opportunities of the 1920s were unevenly shared between 'winners' and 'losers', and how social and economic trends had stored up potential problems for the future.

# AQA Examination-style questions

(a) Explain why the Wall Street Crash led to the Great Depression. *(12 marks)*

Questions like this are testing understanding of chronology and narrative. In one way they may seem very easy and 'factual', but the answer needs to be more than a list of reasons. A long answer full of detailed information in the right order may not score as well as a shorter answer that is more structured and shows differentiation. A good answer will decide which events were really 'stages' in a process – important turning points that were more significant than other events. It is also necessary to decide exactly when the Great Depression began: do you think it followed on directly from the Wall Street Crash or do you agree with those historians who say that it only became the Great Depression much later in 1931 or 1932?

(b) 'How important was the impact of the Volstead Act in influencing American society in the 1920s? *(24 marks)*

The real focus of this question is not Prohibition; it is on what happened to American society in the 1920s. You will first need to decide what the overall trends were and then look at the Volstead Act alongside a range of other factors. Obviously, there are many different ways in which Prohibition can be seen as important, including the rise of organised crime, but Prohibition can also be linked to other issues such as the KKK or religious fundamentalism. So, differentiate and be selective. In which specific ways did Prohibition make the biggest difference? Of the many other factors, which ones mattered most?

## 5 The Wall Street Crash and the Great Depression

Fig. 1 *Stock brokers on Wall Street, October 1929*

*In this chapter you will learn about:*

- the causes and immediate impact of the Wall Street Crash

- the reasons why the crash was followed later by the Great Depression

- how Herbert Hoover's government responded and its failures

- the aims and promises of the man who defeated Hoover, Franklin D. Roosevelt.

## The most disastrous decline in the biggest and broadest stock market of history rocked the financial district yesterday

It carried down with it speculators, big and little, in every part of the country, wiping out thousands of accounts. It is probable that if the stockholders of the country's foremost corporations had not been calmed by the attitude of leading bankers and the subsequent rally, the business of the country would have been seriously affected. Doubtless business will feel the effects of the drastic stock shake-out, and this is expected to hit the luxuries most severely.

The total losses cannot be accurately calculated, because of the large number of markets and the thousands of securities not listed on any exchange. However, they were staggering, running into billions of dollars. Fear struck the big speculators and little ones, big investors and little ones. Thousands of them threw their holdings into the whirling Stock Exchange pit for what they would bring. Losses were tremendous and thousands of prosperous brokerage and bank accounts, sound and healthy a week ago, were completely wrecked in the strange debacle, due to a combination of circumstances, but accelerated into a crash by fear.

1

*Adapted from the New York Times, 25 October 1929*

The Wall Street Crash was one of the turning points of the 20th century, both for the USA and for the world. Source 1 gives a glimpse of the surprise and shock people experienced in October 1929. However, the Wall Street Crash was merely a sensational event that affected the stock market and caused ruin for many speculators. The real questions about the crash go much wider, especially to the later consequences. The crash is much less historically important than the long years of economic depression that followed. It is because of those consequences – the mass unemployment and economic stagnation of the 1930s – that it is so important to determine what actually *caused* the Wall Street Crash in the first place.

## The reasons for the stock market crash and the subsequent depression

> The value of your stocks has changed somewhat in the last 24 hours.

**Fig. 2** *The end of the boom*

### Key chronology

#### The Wall Street Crash

| | |
|---|---|
| 1929 September | Sudden fall in stock prices, followed by recovery. |
| 1929 23 October | Stock market panic; $4 billion lost in paper values. |
| 1929 24 October | 'Black Thursday': $9 billion lost. |
| 1929 29 October | 'Black Tuesday': panic selling with 16.4 million transactions. |
| 1929 mid-November | Stock market losses total $26 billion, one-third of the September total. |
| 1930 April | Stock market recovery wipes out 20 per cent of autumn 1929 losses. |

The background to the stock market crash is straightforward. The financial boom and the availability of easy credit led to a Great Bull Market – the doubling of stock prices between 1926 and 1929. In September 1929, there was a sharp fall in prices but no real financial panic. Then prices tumbled through the floor in the Great Crash – first on 24 October ('Black Thursday') and then five days later on 29 October ('Black Tuesday'). The paper value of stocks lost some $26 billion. In 1930 the Great Depression began in both the USA and across western Europe.

Finding an adequate explanation for all this is not straightforward. The first problem for historians is that the stock market crash of 1929 was not all that exceptional. There had been many previous financial panics in the USA since 1873 and this one did not seem notably worse. There was no rush of bank failures, for example, which seems to show that the financial system was able to cope with the crisis. The huge losses in 1929 could be seen as simply correcting an overvalued market back down to realistic levels.

The second problem is that the Wall Street Crash is widely regarded as the trigger for the global depression of the 1930s, but few economic experts agree that it was the main cause. In April 1930, average industrial stock prices were roughly at the same levels as they had been at the start of 1929. The Great Crash looked as if had been a sudden dramatic event, after which the system was getting back to normal. Therefore, it is important to avoid traditional assumptions about 1929 and instead to examine the reasons for the crash and why it was followed by the Great Depression.

The main cause of the Wall Street Crash was simple. In the late 1920s, the buying of stocks and shares went out of control. The value of shares ran far higher than the real worth of the economy. Too many shares were bought 'on the margin' (bought with loans covering up to 75 per cent of the purchase price). The iron rule of economics is that what goes up can always come down; investors forgot this and assumed that the Great Bull Market would go on for ever. The Wall Street Crash brutally corrected the inflated stock market.

Explaining exactly why this was allowed to happen is not quite so simple. Only a few people at the time saw the crash coming. One explanation is that there was relatively little government regulation. This was the decade of pro-business, laissez-faire policies under Harding, Coolidge and Andrew Mellon – policies that assumed that the best thing to do was to interfere as little as possible with the markets. This may explain why the government did not intervene more to prevent the stock market boom going over the top.

Another factor was the impact of policies to maintain the **gold standard**, which tied currencies to a fixed value backed by gold reserves. The key currency in international finance was the British pound sterling. In 1925, the head of the Federal Reserve Board, Benjamin Strong, gave his support to Britain's plan to return to the gold standard. In order to help strengthen the pound, Strong kept interest rates in the USA low. In 1927, with the British economy still struggling, Strong lowered US interest rates again. Some experts claim that this is what led to the disastrous increase in speculation in the USA, because 'cheap money' made borrowing too easy.

### Key profile

#### Benjamin Strong

Benjamin Strong (1872–1928) was governor of the Federal Reserve Bank of New York, the most important of the 12 regional reserve banks in the Federal Reserve Board, the central banking system of the USA.

The rate of speculation and borrowing meant that loans could not be covered if there was a rush of selling. Many seemingly rich people had little real money, only the paper value of their stocks and shares. Many investors relied on call loans, which were liable to be repaid instantly on demand.

Perhaps the most important factors were psychological – what economists call 'confidence'. The boom of the 1920s seemed unstoppable: the boom in exports after the war, the boom in construction and the motor industry, and then the low interest rates from 1925. In June 1929, a new scheme, the Young Plan, seemed to have sorted out the problems of German reparations payments and Allied war debts. The feeling of prosperity and confidence in the rising market drowned out the few warning voices suggesting that something should be done to cool down

### Key term

**Gold standard:** the system of tying a currency to fixed gold reserves.

### Cross-reference

To recap on **call loans**, see page 80.

For more on **Andrew Mellon**, look back at page 74.

By the end of 1928, the Federal Reserve System had barely 200 million dollars of government securities – 'real' money, backed by gold. This was tiny compared to the nearly 8 billion dollars of call loans outstanding. Mere money was not at the root of the evil soon to befall Wall Street; men were – men (and women) whose lust for a fast buck had loosened all restraints of financial prudence or common sense.

2    *David M. Kennedy, **Freedom From Fear**, 1999*

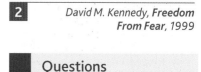

### Questions

1  Why did the Wall Street Crash happen?

2  Why was the financial system taken by surprise?

the speculation. Benjamin Strong's successor at the Federal Reserve pushed for higher interest rates and there was a 1 per cent increase in August 1929. However, by then it was too late. The speculative bubble burst a few weeks later and, in late October, Wall Street crashed.

## The origins of the Great Depression

The symbol of the Great Depression was mass unemployment. As industrial investment and consumer spending slumped, workers were laid off. Unemployment soared – from 3 per cent in 1929 to almost 25 per cent in 1933. The figures dipped slightly from 1934 onwards but remained high until the Second World War brought full employment after 1941.

However, there was more to the Great Depression than industrial stagnation and mass unemployment. The USA was hit by a banking and credit crisis, by the collapse of world trade, and by an absolute disaster for American agriculture. Tables 1 to 6 give some idea of the scale and severity of the Great Depression.

**Table 1** *Unemployment, 1929–33*

| Year | Annual average (percentage of total population) |
|------|------|
| 1929 | 3.2 |
| 1930 | 8.8 |
| 1931 | 15.1 |
| 1932 | 23.6 |
| 1933 | 24.9 |

**Table 2** *Bank failures, 1929–33*

| Year | Number of failures |
|------|------|
| 1929 | 599 |
| 1930 | 1,215 |
| 1931 | 2,344 |
| 1932 | 1,384 |
| 1933 | 3,927 |

**Table 3** *The Dow Jones average, 1927–33*

| Year | End-of-year stock market index |
|------|------|
| 1927 | 154 |
| 1928 | 202 |
| 1929 | 300 |
| 1930 | 248 |
| 1931 | 161 |
| 1932 | 81 |
| 1933 | 56 |

**Table 4** *Economic growth, 1929–36*

| Year | Growth measured by gross domestic product (GDP) (%) |
|------|------|
| 1929 | Base year = 0 |
| 1930 | −8.5 |
| 1931 | −7.8 |
| 1932 | −13.3 |
| 1933 | −2.0 |
| 1934 | +7.7 |
| 1935 | +7.9 |
| 1936 | +14.5 |

**Table 5** *Index of world trade, 1929–33*

| Year | Index of total value |
|------|------|
| 1929 | 3,000 |
| 1930 | 2,740 |
| 1931 | 1,840 |
| 1932 | 1,210 |
| 1933 | 990 |

**Table 6** *Wheat prices, 1920–34*

| Year | Price per bushel ($) |
|------|------|
| 1920 | 2.45 |
| 1928 | 1.36 |
| 1930 | 1.02 |
| 1932 | 0.39 |
| 1934 | 0.62 |

### Key terms

**Dow Jones average:** the average value of stocks and shares traded on Wall Street.

**Deflation:** policies to reduce the money supply and keep prices down.

The causes of the depression were numerous and complicated. Many of these causes were structural: long-term problems that already existed by 1929 and were suddenly worsened by the economic crisis. Some were due to the special circumstances of 1929–30. It is also necessary to look for the reasons why the depression got steadily worse from 1930 onwards. Many people argue that this was due to the mistaken policies of the Hoover administration and that the worst of the depression, in 1932–3, could have been avoided by different policies resulting in less **deflation** in 1929–30.

## Activity

1. Understanding economic history is much less complicated than many A-level students think. It is important to be confident in the use of statistical tables, so practise turning tables into explanatory paragraphs or paragraphs into statistical tables.

2. It is also helpful to master some basic terms, such as the following:
   - Deflation: policies to reduce the money supply and keep prices down.
   - Dow Jones average: the average value of stocks and shares traded on Wall Street.
   - Gold standard: the system of tying a currency to fixed gold reserves.
   - Gross domestic product (GDP): a measurement of the total national output of goods and services.
   - Protective tariff: high import duty to protect home goods from cheaper foreign products.
   - Real wages: the value of wages after inflation has been taken into account.

Many of the structural problems in the American economy dated back to the First World War or before. This was especially true in agriculture, which had experienced a Golden Age from 1900 to 1920. From this peak, long-term decline set in. Farm prices dropped: wheat prices in 1929 were less than half the exceptionally high price of 1920. The trend was consistently downward, even without the Great Crash. The number of the American people working in agriculture fell in every decade of the 20th century. In 1900 it was 40 per cent; by 1945 it was down to 15 per cent. The value of farmland fell by more than 30 per cent between 1920 and 1929. Annual per capita income for farm workers in 1929 was $273; nationwide, it was $750.

Several staple industries faced long-term difficulties in the 1920s. Coalmining, shipbuilding, railroads, shoemaking and wool and cotton textiles were all stagnating or in decline. This trend did not only apply in the USA. Staple industries were in trouble in Britain and Europe at the same time. The weakness of the older industrial sector also undermined the trades unions. The United Mine Workers had 5 million members in 1920 but only 75,000 by 1928. The American Federation of Labor (AFL) lost 1.7 million members, one-third of the total, from 1920 to 1929. A lot of this was due to 'technological unemployment' – the impact of mechanisation which took away about 2 million jobs each year.

There were also short-term factors that created special problems for the economy by 1929–30:

- The construction boom of the 1920s came to end in 1928. This had a knock-on effect, slowing down spending and investment.
- The great boom in car ownership slowed sharply. By 1929, most Americans who could afford a car already had one.
- Industrial production fell in the two months before the Wall Street Crash. There was also a fall in wholesale prices.

Although all these causes played an important part, the impact of the Wall Street Crash was obviously a key cause in itself. The crash caused problems for industries and the banking sector. It affected business confidence, slowing down consumer spending and damaging production. However, although there was a depression from 1929, it did not become the 'Great Depression' until the middle of 1931. It is important to look for the causes of the severity of the Great Depression in the actions taken (or not taken) after the Wall Street Crash by Herbert Hoover's government.

## Activity

**Revision exercise**

Make a list, in order of importance, of the main reasons why the economic situation in the USA got so much worse in 1931–2.

The *New York Times* averages for fifty leading stocks had been almost cut in half, falling from a high of 311.90 in September to a low of 164.43 on November 13th; and the *Times* averages for twenty-five leading industrials had fared still worse, diving from 469.49 to 220.95. The Big Bull Market was dead. Billions of dollars of profits – and paper profits – had disappeared. The grocer, the window-cleaner and the seamstress had lost their capital. In every town there were families which had suddenly dropped from showy affluence into debt. Investors who had dreamed of retiring to live on their fortunes now found themselves back once more at the very beginning of the long road to riches. Day by day the newspapers printed the grim reports of suicides.

**3**                                                            *Frederick Lewis Allen, Only Yesterday, 1931*

## ■ Responses to the Great Depression under Herbert Hoover

Herbert Hoover was a capable politician with an impressive record in public life. He had earned great praise for his work in organising emergency relief schemes during and after the First World War. From 1921, he was an effective and well-respected secretary of commerce. When he became president in 1929, all the expectations were that he would be a great success. However, Hoover spent virtually all his time in office grappling with the crisis of the Great Depression. His career ended in failure and disillusionment when he and the Republicans in Congress were heavily defeated in the 1932 election.

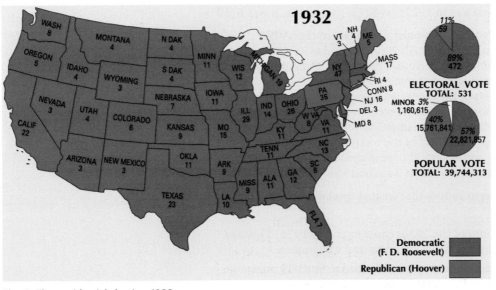

Fig. 3 *The presidential election, 1932*

The main causes of this failure had little to do with Herbert Hoover. The problems of the Great Depression went so deep that all democratic governments in power before 1929 were swept away. Ramsay MacDonald's Labour government in Britain collapsed in 1931. In 1932 and 1933, democracy itself collapsed in Weimar Germany. Whoever had been president of the USA from 1929 would almost certainly have gone down to defeat as Hoover did in 1932. It is important to consider this when assessing Hoover's response to the Great Depression.

People at the time made up their minds about Hoover very quickly. By 1932, he was widely ridiculed and his name became a term of abuse: 'Hoover blankets' were the newspapers that homeless people covered themselves with; 'Hoovervilles' the shanty towns of the unemployed. These negative perceptions of Herbert Hoover lasted for a long time, beyond the New Deal and the liberal era in post-war America. Since the 1980s, however, historians have reassessed Hoover's role, partly because conservative economic ideas came back into fashion with Ronald Reagan and partly because historians have been influenced by new interpretations of the role of government intervention.

There are good reasons to sympathise with Hoover's position. The journalist William Allen White wrote: 'Hoover was the greatest innocent bystander in history, a brave man fighting valiantly but futilely to the end.' Hoover himself claimed in 1931 that 'the major forces of the depression now lie outside the USA'. By mid-1931, the whole system for the payments of reparations and war debts had collapsed. Major European banks started to collapse, first with the Creditanstalt Bank in Austria and then spreading to Germany. Also in 1931, Britain was forced to come off the gold standard. So, Hoover was clearly unlucky, but he was still responsible for the decisions taken by his government in response to the economic crisis. What did Hoover do and how far did these decisions help to cause the Great Depression?

> The primary cause of the Great Depression was the war of 1914–18.
>
> **4** *First sentence of Hoover's memoirs*

The first responses of the Hoover administration were mostly passive. The traditional conservative approach was to leave business to sort itself out. The treasury secretary, Andrew Mellon, was very influential; his view was that the crash would have a beneficial effect in weeding out weak elements. 'Purge the rottenness out of the system,' he said. 'Enterprising people will pick up the wreckage from the less competent people.'

Orthodox economists like Mellon and Hoover thought that deflation was the right answer. They did not believe in the idea promoted by J. M. Keynes that governments should use deficit spending to counteract a recession. It should also be said again here that there was no immediate economic collapse in 1930. Later, in 1931–32, Hoover changed his mind and carried through a lot of interventionist policies. He has often been criticised for doing too little, too late, but in 1930 he did not take drastic action because he and many others were not convinced that this was necessary.

**Cross-reference**

**Andrew Mellon** is introduced on page 74.

## Key profile

### John Maynard Keynes

John Maynard Keynes (1883–1946) was a brilliant British economist who became famous as a key economic adviser at the Paris Peace Conference. In 1919, he wrote a book, *The Economic Consequences of the Peace*, which criticised the orthodox economic thinking of the time. His ideas became known as Keynesian economics, emphasising the importance of government intervention to maintain economic stability. These ideas were summed up in his 1936 book, *General Theory of Economics*. One of the key theories of Keynesianism is 'deficit financing' – using government spending in times of recession to prevent markets from drying up, a bit like injecting a patient. It used to be thought that Franklin D. Roosevelt followed Keynesian principles in his New Deal, but this is not really true, at least not to any great extent.

**Fig. 4** *A soup kitchen in New York, 1930*

One important example of Hoover's thinking was the issue of bank failures. The crisis in banking was a key element of the Great Depression that eventually became so serious that the whole banking system had to be suspended by a **banking holiday**. However, the banking panics in 1930 and 1931 were not seen as exceptional. American banks were often small, local operations and bank failures were a regular occurrence, even in good times. On average, about 600 banks failed every year in the 1920s. This rate doubled in 1930–1 but it was only in 1932–3 that it shot up to more than 5,000.

The area in which the Hoover administration did see an urgent crisis in 1929–30 was agriculture. His 1928 election campaign had promised action to help the struggling rural economy and, in April 1929, Hoover called a special session of Congress to discuss farming. He was against giving farmers direct subsidies as these were expensive and would alienate Europe, but he passed the Agricultural Marketing Act. This set up a Federal Farm Board providing loans to help farmers' cooperatives and support the stabilisation of prices.

> For years it has been an article of faith with the normal American that America, somehow, was different from the rest of the world. The smash of 1929 did not, of itself, shake this serene conviction. It looked, at the time, just because it was so spectacular and catastrophic, like a shooting star disconnected with the fundamental facts. So the plain citizen, no matter how hard hit, believed. His dreams were shattered; but after all they had been only dreams; he could settle back to hard work and win out.
>
> Then he found his daily facts reeling and swimming about him, in a nightmare of continuous disappointment. The bottom had fallen out of the market, for good. And that market had a horrid connection with his bread and butter, his automobile, and his instalment purchases. Worst of all, unemployment became a hideous fact, and one that lacerated and tore at self-respect.
>
> That is the trouble that lies at the back of the American mind. If America really is not 'different', then its troubles, the same as those of Old Europe, will not be cured automatically. Something will have to be done – but what?

**5**                           *M. A. Hamilton, **In America Today**, 1932*

Although the Farm Board was well intended, it could not solve the basic problem that international food prices were going down because producers in the USA, Argentina and Canada were producing massive

### Key term

**Banking holiday:** a complete freeze on bank activity applied by Franklin D. Roosevelt soon after he became president in 1933.

### Cross-reference

**Banking holidays** are covered in more detail on page 102.

surpluses. The Grain Stabilisation Corporation, set up in 1930, tried to guarantee fair prices for farmers by buying up wheat so that it could be stored until the price went back up again, but the price plunged down to less than 40 cents a bushel. The Farm Board was a futile failure and many farmers went broke.

The situation of farmers was also harmed by protectionism. Congress passed the Hawley-Smoot Tariff Act in June 1930, pushing import duties up to extremely high levels. This tariff was supposed to apply only to agriculture, but protectionists in Congress made sure it applied across industry as well. The Hawley-Smoot law did little to help farmers and had a harmful effect on international trade. Hoover's advisers strongly urged him to stop the law by using his presidential veto. Not doing this is reckoned by many historians to be Hoover's biggest single mistake.

The agricultural situation continued to get worse. In 1930–1, farmers across the mid-West were hit by terrible heat waves and drought. This was the first sign of the 'dust bowl' conditions caused by drought and soil erosion ruining crop production. The drought conditions continued throughout most of the 1930s and reached their absolute worst by **'Black Sunday'** in 1935. Hoover's reaction to the crisis was seen as inadequate. At this time, he was still following the idea of **voluntarism** rather than large-scale government intervention. The $47 million in federal loans to farmers was far too little to rescue them from the emergency. By 1932, 25 per cent of farmers had lost their land.

### Key terms

**'Black Sunday':** the dust bowl got its name after Black Sunday, which took place on 14 April 1935. There had been weeks of dust storms, but 20 dust blizzards occurred that day, causing widespread damage.

**Voluntarism:** the use of or reliance on voluntary action to maintain an institution, carry out a policy or achieve an end.

**Fig. 5** *Dust bowl days*

The situation of industry and business also worsened in 1931. Hoover's policy was still to rely on voluntarism and to try to balance the budget by reducing federal spending, which is why he was opposed to relief schemes demanded by Congress. By the second half of 1931, however, the full scale of the Great Depression was becoming plain to see. In addition to the agricultural crisis, there was mass unemployment: 7 million people out of work and rising steadily (it reached 11 million in 1932). Industry was at a standstill. Hoover began to change his thinking and accepted the need for much more government action to provide public works schemes and to help banks and businesses. The charge against Hoover is that he took too long to realise the need for this and that even then he did not do enough.

**Fig. 6** *A 'Hooverville' in 1932*

In January 1932, he pushed through the Reconstruction Finance Corporation (RFC) offering hundreds of millions of dollars in emergency loans to banks and corporations. Later in 1932, this was followed by the Glass-Steagall Act to provide community loans and the Federal Home Loan Bank Act to get banks to provide more mortgages. The Emergency Relief and Construction Act 1932 provided federal funding for states to run public works schemes to create more jobs, similar to later schemes in Roosevelt's New Deal. However, these steps were not enough to bring any immediate success and Hoover's other actions in 1932 increased his unpopularity.

Hoover's Revenue Act 1932 sharply increased taxes on businesses and corporations. This did not aid recovery because it slowed down consumer spending. To be fair to Hoover, almost everyone in Congress agreed with the idea of a balanced budget, but the policy made life harder, not easier, for struggling farmers and the unemployed.

Also in 1932, Hoover's image suffered badly when he came into conflict with army veterans. In May, some 15,000 ex-soldiers, calling themselves the Bonus Expeditionary Force, came to Washington, DC to demand an increase in the bonus payments veterans had been receiving since 1925. The 'Bonus Army' established a tented camp on Anacostia flats. Hoover refused to meet them and offered no concessions except money to go home. On 28 July, there was a violent clash between the Bonus Army and federal troops sent to evict them. Newsreel pictures of the event made Hoover look heartless and 'un-American'.

### ■ Exploring the detail

**The Revenue Act**

The Revenue Act was intended to balance the budget by raising taxes across the board, with the rate on top incomes rising from 25 per cent to 63 per cent. The estate tax was doubled and corporate taxes were raised by almost 15 per cent. At that time, Herbert Hoover believed it was vital to keep interest rates low.

During 1932, the Great Depression was reaching almost its lowest depths. All the economic indicators – mass unemployment, bank and business failures, farm bankruptcies and living standards – were bad and getting worse. The public mood was low, too – a mixture of shock, pessimism and anger. As the 1932 presidential election approached, it was obvious that the Democrats were in position to win it. Whoever gained the nomination at the Democratic convention was all but certain to become the next president.

> There is not a garbage dump in Chicago which is not diligently haunted by the hungry. Last summer in the hot weather when the smell was sickening and the flies were thick, there were a hundred people a day coming to one of the dumps. A widow who used to do housework and laundry, but now had no work at all, fed herself and her fourteen-year-old son on garbage. Before she picked up the meat, she would always take off her glasses so that she couldn't see the maggots.

**6**                            *Edmund Wilson,* **The New Republic**, *1933*

**Fig. 7** *Homeless people sleeping rough in New York*

## Roosevelt and the aims and objectives of the New Deal

Franklin D. Roosevelt's comprehensive victory in the 1932 election began the longest presidency in the history of the USA. He won three more elections, in 1936, 1940 and 1944, before his death in 1945. From 1933 to 1941, Roosevelt's main achievement was to carry through the domestic policies known as the New Deal to cope with the crisis of the

> **Activity**
>
> **Preparing a presentation**
>
> Plan a 10-minute presentation to be given in class, arguing the following case: 'Herbert Hoover has been unfairly criticised for his failure to prevent America from sliding into the Great Depression.'

Great Depression. From 1941 to 1945, he led the USA through to victory in the Second World War. At the beginning of 1933, however, nobody could know how Roosevelt's presidency would work out or even exactly what policies he would pursue. Roosevelt probably did not know himself.

Franklin D. Roosevelt had already had a notable political career. There were many parallels with his distant cousin, Theodore Roosevelt. Like Theodore, Franklin had served as assistant director of the navy. Like Theodore, he had run for vice-president – part of the Democrat ticket that lost to Warren G. Harding in 1920. Like Theodore, he was a controversial politician within his own party. Many traditional conservative Democrats were suspicious of Franklin D. Roosevelt in the same way as many traditional conservative Republicans had opposed Theodore Roosevelt's progressive views.

> Balance the budget. Stop spending money we haven't got. Cut government spending – like you cut rations when there is a siege. Tax everybody for everything.

 **7**

*Advice to Roosevelt early in 1933 from the conservative Democrat financier, Bernard Baruch*

Roosevelt was a talented politician with drive, self-confidence and speechmaking ability. He had to be. In 1928, he overcome serious disability because of the effects of polio (he could not stand or walk without metal leg braces) to become governor of New York. In 1932, he won the Democratic nomination against a powerful opponent, Al Smith, and then went on to defeat Hoover. On 15 February 1933, Roosevelt showed a steady nerve after an assassination attempt; the mayor of Chicago died after being hit by bullets intended for the president. However, he was not a systematic political thinker and he definitely had no coherent master plan at the start of 1933.

When Roosevelt finally took office on 4 March 1933, the New Deal was not much more than a loose collection of general principles. Some of these had been put to the public during the 1932 election campaign, but others had to be secret in case they caused alarm in the business world:

- Government intervention was urgently needed. The new administration would have to start with a bang.
- Attitudes had to be changed. The people, and businesses, had to be given hope and enthusiasm, and persuaded to believe that the situation was not as desperate as it seemed – even if it was.
- Extreme socialist ideas should be rejected – business should be reformed and regulated, not torn apart.
- The USA would have to come off the gold standard.

### The transition from Herbert Hoover to Franklin D. Roosevelt

One of the important features of the American political system is the long delay between the presidential election and the inauguration of the new president several months later. In November 1932, Roosevelt and the Democrats won a decisive victory, not only capturing the White House but also winning strong majorities in the House of Representatives and the Senate. However, he did not become president until the inauguration in March 1933. In the meantime, there was an awkward interregnum – a vacuum of power – at a time when urgent action was needed to deal with the economic crisis. The outgoing president could not take any strong action; the incoming president did not want to do anything too soon.

Herbert Hoover was keen to meet Roosevelt to discuss what needed to be done. A meeting took place but relations between the two men were stiff, with no real cooperation forthcoming. Hoover bombarded Roosevelt with advice and policy suggestions, but Roosevelt was unwilling. His reasons were partly cynical politics: he did not wish to be tarnished by Hoover's image as a failure and preferred to save himself for a dramatic impact when his presidency began. Another reason was that Roosevelt was not yet sure what his policies would be. Opinions within the Democratic Party were divided and Roosevelt was a politician who always avoided committing himself.

> He is amiable, pleasant, anxious to be of service – and very badly informed. Most of my time in conversation with him was like educating a very ignorant, well-meaning young man.

**8**
*By Herbert Hoover about his meeting with Roosevelt in November 1932*

> Listening to Herbert Hoover at this meeting, it was clear that we were in the presence of the best-informed person in the country on the subject of international debts. He showed a mastery of detail and a clarity of organisation that compelled admiration.

**9**
*By Roosevelt's political adviser, Raymond Moley, about the same meeting*

Key developments took place in the four-month gap between November 1932 and March 1933. Hitler came to power in Germany. Britain announced that it would be suspending payment of war debts. There were plans for a World Economic Conference in London. Decisions needed to be taken about American policy at the Geneva Disarmament Conference. Hoover was pressing Roosevelt to agree what to do about the foreign situation, which Hoover believed to be the chief problem behind the depression.

Roosevelt was more inclined to believe that the root causes of the depression were internal American problems. He also wanted to keep his options open. If he agreed with Hoover's suggestions, he would be saying that Republican policies were on the right lines and he would have to back away from some of his election promises about the New Deal. During the first months of 1933, Roosevelt just waited and watched. In the meantime, the banking crisis got worse, unemployment rose even higher and the farm crisis deepened. The depression was at its lowest point in the winter of 1932–3. In January, a liberal journalist, Walter Lippmann, suggested to Roosevelt that he might have to assume dictatorial powers to get the country on its feet again.

## Summary questions

**1** How important were the problems of agriculture in causing the Great Depression?

**2** Why did Franklin D. Roosevelt win the 1932 presidential election by such a margin?

# 6  Roosevelt and the New Deal

**Fig. 1** *Roosevelt at a New Deal rally*

*In this chapter you will learn about:*

- the aims and policies of Franklin D. Roosevelt's New Deal

- the impact of the New Deal – its successes and the opposition it aroused

- the fight against organised crime in the 1930s

- the USA's situation by 1941.

This is the time to speak the truth, the whole truth, frankly and boldly. This great Nation will endure; it will revive and prosper. So, first of all, let me assert my firm belief that the only thing we have to fear is fear itself – nameless, unreasoning, unjustified terror that paralyses our efforts to turn retreat into advance. In the past, in every dark hour of our national life, leadership of frankness and vigour has been met with the support of the people. I am convinced that you will give that support to my leadership in these critical days. With such a spirit on my part and on yours we can face our difficulties.

Thank God, they concern only material things. Values have shrunk to fantastically low levels; taxes have risen; the withered leaves of industrial enterprise lie on every side; farmers find no markets for their produce; the savings made over many years by thousands of families are gone. More important, a host of unemployed citizens face the grim problem of existence. Only a foolish optimist can deny the dark realities of the moment.

Yet we are not stricken by any plague of locusts. Compared with the perils our forefathers faced and conquered, we have much to be thankful for. The rulers of the exchange of mankind's goods have failed, through their own stubbornness and incompetence. The answer is that we must apply social values more noble than mere monetary profit. Happiness lies not in the mere possession of money, it lies in the joy of achievement and creative effort. Our greatest task is to put people to work. It can be accomplished by direct recruiting by the government itself treating the task as we would treat the emergency of a war.

Hand in hand we need definite efforts to provide better use of the land. We must act to prevent the tragedy of people losing their small homes and farms. It can be helped by unifying relief activities and national planning for all forms of transportation and of communications and other utilities. Finally, we need two safeguards against a return to the evils of the old order: there must be a strict supervision of all banking, and there must be an end to speculation with other people's money.

**1**

*Franklin D. Roosevelt's first inaugural speech,
4 March 1933*

This first speech of Roosevelt's presidency is very different from his election speeches; being in power and responsible for what happens is not the same as attacking your opponent and making promises. This is the speech that launched the New Deal.

The 1930s in the USA was defined by the New Deal. Roosevelt won re-election in 1936 and again in 1940 as the New Deal president – the leader who had rescued the country from the Great Depression and got the American people back to work. However, the New Deal was a complicated affair that leaves many issues for historians to argue over. Some claim that it was not a coherent economic programme, just a hotch-potch of ideas and compromises that Roosevelt made up as he went along; some claim that the economic recovery of the 1930s was directly due to Roosevelt and the New Deal; others that it was just luck that Roosevelt's arrival in the White House coincided with the beginnings of a recovery that would have happened anyway.

Many historians have suggested that the New Deal did not really bring recovery from the depression, it only tinkered at the margins, with real recovery coming with the economic stimulus of the war after 1941. Yet for many liberals in the 1930s and since, Roosevelt was one of the great presidents and the New Deal saved the nation.

There was opposition to the New Deal at the time – from within Roosevelt's own party, from Congress, from conservative business leaders who thought he went too far, from farmers and workers who thought he did not go nearly far enough. The New Deal also ran into trouble with the Supreme Court because aspects of Roosevelt's policies were regarded as unconstitutional. He was a brilliant political salesman. He carried most of the American people with him, most of the time. However, eight years is a long time in politics. Circumstances and policies often change. There were times during the 1930s that he faced major difficulties and times he disappointed his own supporters.

Reaching firm and balanced conclusions about the New Deal, therefore, is not easy. Many of the judgements made about Roosevelt come from very partisan viewpoints – committed liberal New Dealers or hostile conservative commentators who think the USA was 'saved' in the 1980s by the tough conservative economic policies pursued during the presidency of Ronald Reagan. The fact remains that understanding the history of the USA requires careful assessment of exactly how and how far the nation was transformed by the impact of the New Deal between Roosevelt's inauguration in 1933 and the start of American involvement in the Second World War in December 1941.

## Activity

### Source analysis

Study Source 1. Analyse what Roosevelt's aims were in making the speech in the way that he did and assess the extent to which you think it would have been effective.

## Key chronology

### The New Deal

| | |
|---|---|
| **1933 March–June** | The 'Hundred Days' from Roosevelt's inauguration. |
| **1933–4** | First New Deal. |
| **1935 May** | Start of the Second New Deal. |
| **1936 November** | Roosevelt's re-election as president. |
| **1937 March** | Deadlock between the president and the Supreme Court. |
| **1938** | End of New Deal legislation. |
| **1939–41** | Growing opposition to Roosevelt over foreign policy. |
| **1940 November** | Roosevelt's controversial re-election for a third term. |
| **1941 December** | America enters the Second World War. |

## Exploring the detail

### 'Fireside chats'

Roosevelt's 'fireside chats' were a series of 30 evening radio talks given between 1933 and 1944. Sometimes beginning his talks with 'Good evening, friends', he urged listeners to have faith in the banks and support his New Deal measures. The chats were considered enormously successful. He was the first president to reach a mass audience directly over the radio and his conversational style was very effective.

**Fig. 2** *Roosevelt's agenda, 1933*

## Key term

**Alphabet Agencies:** Roosevelt's administration and Congress created dozens of federal recovery programmes. Many of the programmes had long names and therefore became known by their initials. In all, the New Deal spawned 59 Alphabet Agencies between 1933 and 1938.

## The successes of and opposition to the New Deal

### The 'Hundred Days'

From the day of Franklin D. Roosevelt's inauguration, he was a man in a hurry. One of the reasons for this is that he had been planning for weeks to make a psychological impact as soon as possible to convince the American people that things were going to be different. However, the most important reason was the urgency of the banking crisis. Thousands of banks had failed in the weeks before. Symbolically, the New York Stock Exchange suspended trading on the very day of the inauguration.

Roosevelt rushed into action, calling a special session of Congress. The Emergency Banking Act was hurriedly passed on 9 March. It enforced a banking holiday lasting four days. The government and the Federal Reserve were given the power to issue currency and organise the reopening of banks under strict supervision. The night before the banking holiday ended, Roosevelt gave the first of his 'fireside chats' to the American people over the radio, telling them their money would be safe in the banks. The tactics worked. People started depositing money in the banks again. The long banking crisis was over and Roosevelt was an instant hero.

This was the start of the 'Hundred Days' – a rush of action designed to make the maximum impact in the shortest possible time. In reality, Roosevelt's policies were not as new or as radical as they seemed. Many of them were policies Hoover had planned anyway, like the banking holiday. Nevertheless, Roosevelt managed to convey the impression that everything was new. By 15 June, he had rushed through a total of 15 new laws.

### The First New Deal

The New Deal had two broad aims. The first was relief and recovery – helping victims of the depression and trying to get the economy going again. The second was reform and regulation. Government departments known as Alphabet Agencies were set up to implement Roosevelt's policies. One of the problems of studying the New Deal is the sheer number of initiatives that were started in 1933 and 1934. Not all were successful and some were more important than others.

#### Alphabet Agencies: relief and recovery

These agencies were designed to channel subsidies to people in need, create work for the unemployed and stimulate economic recovery. The main relief schemes were as follows.

- The **Agricultural Adjustment Administration** (AAA) 1933 provided farmers with federal subsidies to compensate them for cutting back the production of basic commodities such as pork, wheat, cotton and dairy products. The AAA aimed to bring farm prices back up to profitable levels by eliminating the problem of overproduction.

- The **Civilian Conservation Corps** (CCC) 1933 provided work camps for young men working on conservation projects such as planting trees for windbreaks and improving national parks.
- The **Farm Credit Administration** (FCA) 1933 helped farmers to manage their debts by making loans available from federal funds to pay for seed, machinery and marketing.
- The **Federal Emergency Relief Administration** (FERA) 1933 provided $500 million to State and local agencies that had run out of money so that they could keep making relief payments to the unemployed.
- The **Federal Housing Administration** (FHA) 1934 provided government funding to enable people to keep up their mortgage payments.
- The **National Industrial Recovery Act** (NIRA) 1933 promoted both recovery and reform by setting up the PWA and the NRA.
- The **Public Works Administration** (PWA) 1933 provided more than $3 billion for work-creation projects such as roads and electrification.
- The **Tennessee Valley Authority** (TVA) 1934 was a huge federal government agency providing major conservation and regeneration schemes across the entire Tennessee River valley, covering seven states: Tennessee, Alabama, Mississippi, Kentucky and small parts of Georgia, North Carolina and Virginia. The TVA built dams to provide hydroelectric power, flood control and irrigation and allocated federal money to other social projects including education.

## Alphabet Agencies: reform and regulation

The second aim of the New Deal aim was reform and regulation. Roosevelt's administration wanted to protect the rights of unions and workers, and to use government intervention to impose reforms on private companies. Some people saw this as an attack on the capitalist system. The main agencies were as follows.

- The **Banking Act** 1933 regulated banking and credit. It insured all bank deposits up to $5,000.
- The **Beer-Wine Revenue Act** 1933 legalised some mild alcoholic beverages and paved the way for the end of Prohibition.
- The **Economy Act** 1933 made a commitment to cut the federal budget.
- The **Emergency Railroad Transportation Act** 1934 regulated the railroad companies.
- The **Federal Communications Commission** (FCC) 1934 set up federal government regulation of radio and telegraph services.
- The **National Recovery Administration** (NRA) 1933 encouraged voluntary support from businesses and the public and aimed to improve cooperation between businesses and the government to stop price cutting, wage cuts and job losses. It regulated 'fair competition' between businesses through a code of practice to avoid cut-throat competition with each other and by slackening the anti-trust laws. The NRA code banned child labour and supported the rights of workers to organise trades unions. The NRA used an extensive advertising campaign to promote its slogan 'We do our part' and to persuade people to buy only from companies who had signed up to the code.
- The **Securities and Exchange Commission** (SEC) 1934 extended the powers under the Banking Act. It set up federal government regulation of trading in stocks and shares and strengthened the powers of the Federal Reserve in Washington. It was now illegal to buy stocks on credit.

### Successes and failures of the First New Deal

There were many clear-cut successes in the First New Deal, especially in stabilising banking and the system of credit. One of the most significant decisions was to take the USA off the gold standard, which was done on 10 April 1933. This went against the orthodox economic thinking of the time; Roosevelt himself had previously been against it. However, he became convinced there was no alternative. The results of the decision were mostly beneficial. The financial markets became much more stable – the same thing had happened when Britain had abandoned the gold standard in 1931.

Other successes included the protection of home owners and farmers by giving help to refinance their loans to make them easier to repay. Many public works schemes provided much-needed employment rather than just giving relief payments. These schemes also had beneficial effects for conservation and infrastructure. The Civil Works Administration (CWA), for example, was extremely well managed by Harry Hopkins. It provided temporary employment for 4 million workers in 1933 and built sewers, roads and airports. However, perhaps the greatest achievement of the New Deal was psychological – changing the national mood from hopelessness to optimism.

Nevertheless, in many areas there were failures and adverse side effects. The AAA never achieved what was hoped for it. Wheat production did fall (from 864 million bushels in 1928–32 to about 564 million in 1933–5) but this was not really due to federal policies to cut overproduction. The main reason was the drought. The AAA had a terrible impact on rural poverty, especially in the South. Sharecroppers there suffered as terribly as anyone in the depression and the AAA made their problems worse by reducing the amount of land used to grow cotton. There was little direct action to help the African-American poor. Roosevelt was afraid of antagonising southern politicians and business leaders, who might have obstructed New Deal policies overall.

Fig. 3 *A dust bowl family*

We don't need any Gawd-damned Yankee to tell us how to handle our niggers!

**2**  *Abuse hurled at socialist Norman Thomas on a speaking tour of the South, 1934*

For many people, the First New Deal lessened the impact of the depression, but it did not bring real recovery in either industry or agriculture. By the end of 1934, there were still nearly 22 million unemployed, almost as many as in 1932. As the drought continued and the Great Plains turned into a dust bowl, the long-term decline of agriculture continued. Having raised people's hopes so much, the New Deal was leading to frustration and disillusionment, even among groups who had supported Roosevelt from the beginning.

■ **Activity**

**Thinking point**

Carry out further research to find out more about the impact of the Great Depression and the New Deal on the South.

I wouldn't plough nobody's mule from sunrise to sunset for 50 cents a day, when I could get $1.30 for pretending to work on a DITCH.

**3**  *Angry southern farmer, protesting that New Deal schemes were unfair*

### Opposition to the First New Deal

As Roosevelt had such a strong majority in Congress, he did not need to worry about the Republicans in Congress. He also had quite a lot of success in changing the national mood and gaining popular support for the New Deal. However, this did not mean that there was no opposition. This opposition came from many different people, both on the right and the left.

At first, there was little open opposition from the right. Roosevelt wanted to keep in with business leaders, bankers and the conservative elements in the Democratic Party. So, the First New Deal was full of compromises. In 1934 and 1935, these compromises, and disappointment at the limited results of some early New Deal initiatives, led to opposition and protest from the left – often from people who had originally supported the New Deal. One problem was that Roosevelt was so good at raising hopes and expectations. When reality fell short, the New Deal was blamed for not doing enough. There was pressure on the President to go further and faster.

This opposition included farmers, the labour unions and old-style Progressives like Senator La Follette of Wisconsin, who had last been prominent in running for the presidency in 1924 but now made a political comeback. The 1934 mid-term elections put more liberal reformers into Congress, and there was a sharp increase in the protest votes for socialist and communist candidates.

Strong opposition also came from new movements led by political outsiders. One was the novelist, Upton Sinclair, who founded the End Poverty in California (EPIC) organisation and ran for the state governorship in 1934. Another was Dr Francis Townsend and his popular but unrealistic Old Age Revolving Pensions scheme. An even more effective focus for discontent was the 'Radio Priest', Father Charles Edward Coughlin of Detroit, who reached an audience of more than 30 million listeners via his regular Sunday night radio show (Source 4).

Coughlin was especially popular with Irish-American Catholics and strongly anti-communist. At first, he was on Roosevelt's side. He told his listeners that 'the New Deal is Christ's Deal'. However, by the second half of 1934, he had turned against Roosevelt and was attacking him as 'communistic' and dominated by 'Jewish bankers'. Father Coughlin continued to be a virulent opponent of Roosevelt throughout the 1930s. He was an especially fervent isolationist when the prospect of war in Europe arose after 1936. In 1934–5, Roosevelt faced an even more threatening challenge from the rise of a populist protest movement led by Huey Long of Louisiana.

### A closer look

#### Huey Long

The USA often produces local heroes. The political system makes having a local power base essential for anyone wishing to be a national figure. In the 1930s, Huey Long, governor of Louisiana,

I remember that on March 7, 1930, more than one year and a half ago, the former Secretary of Commerce, Mr Hoover, announced: 'All evidences indicate that the worst effect of the crash of unemployment will have passed within the next sixty days.' That was in the spring of 1930. I recollect that he and hundreds of others to whom 10,000 facts were well-known were busy preaching to us that prosperity was just around the corner. It appears to have been a circular corner to which they referred; a corner which if we could turn, we would not be willing to negotiate if it foreshadows a repetition of these recent occurrences for the children of generations to come.

**4**  *Charles Coughlin in a radio broadcast, 1933*

### Activity

#### Thinking point

Robert Penn Warren's novel *All the King's Men* (1946) is a brilliant fictional account of Huey Long. Read parts of the novel or watch one of the film versions, made in 1949 and 2006.

became for a short while one of the most charismatic and controversial politicians in modern American history. Nobody can know for certain how strongly Huey Long might have challenged Roosevelt if the governor had not been assassinated in 1935. Huey Long was a Populist. Like the Populists of the 1890s, he was hostile to business and the East Coast elites; he played on the grievances and class resentments of ordinary people. One way he gathered political support in the 1930s was by attacking the power of Standard Oil. He became governor of Louisiana in 1928 and was elected to the Senate in 1930, holding both jobs simultaneously until 1933. By this time, he had built up a really powerful political power base in Louisiana using a mixture of popular social policies, corruption and intimidation. His supporters called him 'The Kingfish'.

God smiled on our land and we grew crops of plenty to eat and wear. He called us to come to feast. But then Rockefeller, Morgan and their crowd stepped in and took everything. So now many millions must go hungry and without those good things God gave us.

**5**                             *From a radio talk by Huey Long, 1934*

Long plans to be a candidate of the Hitler type in 1936 … Thus he hopes to defeat the Democratic Party and put in a reactionary Republican. That would bring the country to such a state by 1940 that Long thinks he would be made dictator.

**6**            *Roosevelt's private remarks to the
US ambassador to Germany, 1935*

A NEW CAPTAIN AT THE WHEEL

**Fig. 4** *'A new captain at the wheel.' A contemporary cartoon showing Roosevelt in command of the 'ship of State'*

At first, Huey Long backed the New Deal but then turned against Roosevelt on the grounds that he was too ready to go along with big business. In 1934, Long set up the Share Our Wealth society, promising to tax the rich and redistribute wealth to every household. His claims were totally unrealistic but very popular. He ran his own radio show, which attracted huge audiences. By 1935, Long claimed that Share Our Wealth had 5 million members. Roosevelt disliked him intensely but knew that he was a dangerous opponent. It was clear that Long would be running for president in 1936. Even if he was unlikely to win, he might well take enough votes away from the Democrats to let the Republicans in.

Some people even argue that Roosevelt's fear of Long was his main motive for the radical policies of the Second New Deal. In September 1935, however, Long's career came to a sudden end when he was shot dead in the Louisiana capital, Baton Rouge. No one ever knew for sure what the assassin's motive was. Without the personality of Long to lead it, the populist challenge to Roosevelt lost any momentum. Roosevelt won re-election easily in 1936.

In 1934 and 1935, opposition from conservatives was increasing. Al Smith led complaints against Roosevelt from those in the Democratic Party who had always been suspicious of him. They gave support to the American Liberty League, formed mostly from financiers and business leaders who claimed that Roosevelt was 'Sovietising America'. A number of conservative judges passed injunctions to block New Deal measures. This conservative opposition grew much stronger when the Second New Deal began in 1935.

## The Second New Deal

It is too simplistic to say that Franklin D. Roosevelt was pushed into the Second New Deal by pressure from opponents like Huey Long and Father Coughlin. Many other factors were involved, including Roosevelt's determination to override the obstructive decisions being made by the courts, above all when the Supreme Court ruled against the NIRA in May 1935. However, there was a sense in 1935 that America might face serious problems unless something was done to accelerate reform and recovery. New Deal policies became more radical and took state intervention much further.

Roosevelt was looking for a new political coalition in 1935; he was no longer so concerned about building a consensus by making compromises. The result was a Second New Deal and a second 'Hundred Days', starting in June 1935. Roosevelt pushed through Congress a wave of radical new reforms. He took on the banking system and then the public utility companies. He taxed the rich. He vastly expanded relief schemes through the Works Progress Administration (WPA). He brought in federal social security benefits. He reformed labour relations through the Wagner Act. Many of these measures caused storms of protest, but all were passed. After decisively winning the 1936 election, Roosevelt seemed stronger than ever.

The Second New Deal was taken further in 1937–8 by legislation that helped farmers keep more secure possession of their farms, helped poorer people with housing, and gave industrial workers a minimum wage and a 40-hour working week. Between 1935 and 1938, the Second New Deal made a massive impact on the USA. Nevertheless, the ultimate aim of economic recovery was not achieved and Roosevelt faced a dangerous backlash from the conservatives.

### A closer look

#### Alphabet Agencies of the Second New Deal

The following summarises some of the initiatives.

- Banking Act 1935: centralised control of banking and credit by the Federal Reserve.
- Fair Labor Standards Act 1938: set a minimum wage and a 40-hour week for workers.
- Farm Security Administration (FSA) 1937: introduced federal loans to help farmers keep their land.
- National Housing Act 1938: set up housing projects for poorer families.
- National Youth Administration (NYA) 1935: a scheme for education and training.
- Rural Electrification Administration (REA) 1935: brought electricity to rural areas.
- Social Security Administration (SSA) 1935: federal insurance for the elderly, unemployed and disabled.
- Wagner Act 1935: set up the National Labor Relations Board (NLRB).
- Works Progress Administration (WPA) 1935: major public works scheme to provide relief.

### Activity

#### Thinking point

**1** Make two lists:

a One naming the social groups likely to express opposition to the New Deal in 1934–5 because they were opposed to it on principle.

b One naming the social groups likely to express disappointment with the New Deal in 1934–5 because it had not lived up to their expectations.

**2** Imagine you are a journalist working for a British newspaper in 1935. Write a brief newspaper article explaining the political importance of the assassination of Huey Long.

### Successes and failures of the Second New Deal

There were several long-term successes of the Second New Deal. Labour rights and industrial relations were much improved by government intervention and membership of trades unions more than doubled between 1935 and 1940. There were lasting improvements to the infrastructure, such as rural electrification. However, there was no real economic recovery and the economic situation actually went backwards between 1937 and 1939.

Unemployment, already high, jumped back up to 10 million in 1938, 2 million more than in 1936. The situation facing farmers was still desperate. In 1939, John Steinbeck wrote *The Grapes of Wrath* to dramatise the plight of the 'Okies' who had lost their farms and homes and migrated west seeking temporary work. The drought years came to an end in 1938, but there was no stopping the long-term decline of agriculture.

> **Activity**
>
> **Revision exercise**
>
> Watch the film version of Steinbeck's *The Grapes of Wrath*. It was made in 1940, shortly after the events it describes, and gives a convincing impression of the agricultural disaster.

THE NEW TREND IN EASTER FASHIONS!

**Fig. 5** *A contemporary cartoon about President Roosevelt's approach to farm relief under the New Deal*

Some historians claim that the failures of the Second New Deal were caused by the sheer depth and extent of the depression. Many European countries took years to get out the depression. Others claim that it was due to Roosevelt's own mistakes – that he failed to understand or make effective use of deficit spending and that his policies were inconsistent. Most of all, they argue, Roosevelt made the mistake of provoking divisions and opposition, especially from the Supreme Court.

### Opposition to the Second New Deal

In November 1936, Roosevelt won re-election with a convincing victory over the Republican candidate, Alf Landon. Roosevelt got 27 million votes and won every state except two. The Republicans lost seats in Congress. Out of 33 electoral races for state governors, the Democrats won 26. The election was virtually a referendum on the New Deal and Roosevelt won it. However, his dominance over Congress did not prevent him from running into opposition.

Even before 1936, Roosevelt was already in conflict with the courts. Several legal decisions had gone against the New Deal legislation before, on 'Black Monday' in 1935 when the Supreme Court struck down the Farm Mortgage Act and ruled that aspects of the National Recovery Administration (NRA) were unconstitutional. The Supreme Court contained several conservative justices appointed in the Republican-dominated 1920s. The chief justice, Charles Evans Hughes, had been the Republican presidential candidate in 1916 but was generally regarded as fair and impartial. Roosevelt was furious. The action of the courts in 1935–6 threatened to undermine much of his New Deal.

After his election victory, Roosevelt decided to make a direct attack against the powers of the Supreme Court. In February 1937, he announced plans for new laws allowing him to appoint up to six additional judges to the Supreme Court, one for every judge over the age of 70. This 'court-packing' bill caused outrage among Republicans and conservative newspapers. It also upset many on Roosevelt's own side, such as Senator Wheeler of Montana. Roosevelt's plan was criticised for bringing partisan politics into the Supreme Court, which was supposed to be above politics.

Roosevelt stubbornly persisted with his plan, even after he was warned he would lose. According to Michael Parrish in *Anxious Decades* (1994), this was 'the biggest blunder of his political career'. It lost Roosevelt a lot of political support. It was also unnecessary: between 1937 and 1943, death and retirement gave Roosevelt the chance to appoint six new justices anyway.

Roosevelt faced more problems in 1937–8 as the economy ran into trouble. This increased opposition to him from people who blamed him for the 'Roosevelt recession'. There was also mounting pressure from isolationists attacking him over foreign policy issues. Roosevelt was nothing like as dominant as he had seemed to be after the 1936 election.

**Table 1** *Unemployment in the USA, 1933–43*

| Year | Annual average (percentage of total population) |
|------|------------------------------------------------|
| 1933 | 24.9 |
| 1934 | 21.7 |
| 1935 | 20.1 |
| 1936 | 16.9 |
| 1937 | 14.3 |
| 1938 | 19.0 |
| 1939 | 17.2 |
| 1940 | 14.6 |
| 1941 | 9.9 |
| 1942 | 4.7 |
| 1943 | 1.9 |

**Table 2** *Some successes and failures of the New Deal*

| Successes | Failures |
|-----------|----------|
| Roosevelt was brilliantly adaptable in coherent responding to circumstances and in knowing what was politically possible | There was no consistency of purpose planning in the New Deal |
| Unemployment went down every year except 1938 and jobless people benefited from New Deal initiatives | Unemployment remained high throughout the 1930s despite all the relief schemes |
| Rural areas got a lot of help through things like loans, TVA and the provision of electricity. Without the New Deal, they would have been much worse off | Agriculture remained badly depressed throughout the 1930s and beyond. Many lost their farms and became migrant workers |
| Roosevelt was right to extend government powers in such a crisis situation and his critics were often politically motivated | Many of Roosevelt's schemes were deemed unconstitutional |
| Many schemes did succeed and good government is often about trial and error | Many schemes had limited success and had to be dropped or replaced |
| Roosevelt took power in a crisis situation and then got re-elected in 1936 and 1940 | Many of those who supported Roosevelt in the beginning turned against him later |
| What the USA needed above all in 1933 was a brilliant communicator to 'sell' optimism | Roosevelt was merely a smooth operator, good at public relations |

## The impact of the New Deal by 1941

The Great Depression never really ended until the mobilisation of the American economy for war. In 1939–40, industry was boosted by the needs of Britain's war effort and because the USA committed itself to rapid rearmament. From December 1941, direct involvement in the war brought full employment and maximum industrial production. The beneficial effects of this lasted far beyond the end of the war in 1945 and laid the foundations for a generation of post-war prosperity. This obviously raises questions about the effectiveness of the New Deal before the war.

On the specific issue of unemployment, for example, Hitler's Germany did much better than the USA. There were 6 million unemployed in

### Activity

**Thinking point**

Study Table 2.

1. Add one or two further points of your own to each column.

2. On a scale of 1 to 5, where 1 is weak and 5 is strong, assess the importance of each point. Add up the total score for each column.

Germany in 1933, but by 1938 unemployment had been eliminated and there was a labour shortage in some areas.

Many people attacked Roosevelt at the time for greatly increasing State intervention. He undoubtedly did so, even though the USA did not have a welfare state by 1941. However, this is not really a question of success or failure; it is more a question of opinion as to whether State intervention is a good thing or not. Other critics argue the opposite case that the New Deal was not radical or socialist enough. Any judgement here depends on your political perspective and on an assessment of whether or not Roosevelt could have taken the country with him if he had been more radical.

 **Activity**

**Revision exercise**

Study Table 1 and other evidence in this chapter.

1. Write a paragraph in support of the argument that 'Roosevelt's New Deal achieved significant successes in bringing about economic recovery.'

2. Set out the counter-argument that 'The New Deal achieved remarkably little improvement in the lives of the American people.'

3. Which of these views do you feel is the more convincing? Explain why.

There are many more than two viewpoints on Roosevelt and the New Deal, but Table 2 on page 109 may help to focus the debate on whether the New Deal was overall mostly successful or mostly a failure.

## The fight against organised crime and the reasons for the end of Prohibition

There is a wide gap between the myths and the realities of the fight against organised crime in the 1930s. According to the myths, organised crime was confronted and defeated by heroic figures such as Eliot Ness and his 'Untouchables', and J. Edgar Hoover and the **'G-Men'** of the FBI. The downfall of Al Capone in 1931 and the deaths of leading gangsters such as John Dillinger were landmark events. By the end of the 1930s, violent crime was much less visible; there were no longer any spectacular shoot-outs like the assault on Capone's headquarters by the O'Banion gang in 1926.

### A closer look

#### John Dillinger

John Dillinger (1903–34) was one of the most notorious and violent criminals of the 1930s. Born in Indianapolis, he had a troubled childhood and soon became involved in crime while drifting from place to place and job to job. In 1924, Dillinger and another associate, Ed Singleton, attempted to rob a Mooresville grocer but both were caught. Despite confessing to his crime on the advice of his father, Dillinger served eight and a half years in prison.

On his release in May 1933, Dillinger immediately went on a criminal rampage that left 10 men dead and 7 wounded. In September 1933, he was arrested but on 12 October three of his gangster associates helped him to break out of jail, killing a sheriff in the process. A string of robberies followed as Dillinger and his gang shot and murdered their way across several states. He was

**Key term**

**'G-Men':** short for 'government men'; a nickname for FBI agents.

arrested in January 1934 but once again escaped, this time by bluffing his way out using a fake gun whittled out of wood. By this time the FBI were pursuing him across state lines and the law finally caught up with him on 22 July 1934. He was ambushed when leaving a cinema and shot dead by armed federal agents.

Dillinger achieved the status of a celebrity. One legacy of the Prohibition era was that gangsters could be treated as folk heroes, and Dillinger was depicted in numerous films and stories of the gangster age. His celebrity status also rubbed off on J. Edgar Hoover, who milked the favourable publicity that his Bureau received for hunting Dillinger down.

In reality, there was no clear-cut victory for the forces of law and order. Organised crime was still immensely powerful. Corruption in the police and local government remained widespread. What appeared to be victories in the fight against organised crime were often explained by the fact that bootlegging was no longer an issue after the repeal of Prohibition in 1933 and because organised crime took care to keep up a more respectable image. During the Second World War, organised crime was even able to go into partnership with the federal government: 'Lucky Luciano' and his mafia networks cooperated extensively with US navy intelligence in the war against fascist Italy.

**Fig. 6** *Al Capone (second from the left) after his conviction*

Many factors made it difficult to achieve success in the fight against crime. The money and resources behind law enforcement were pathetically small compared with the vast financial power of organised crime. Bribery and corruption – of police, politicians, court prosecutors and newspaper crime reporters – could protect criminals at all levels. Most crimes, including robbery and murder, came under state law. Law enforcement was often ineffective because local officials were corrupt or criminals were safe from arrest once they had crossed into another state. Public opinion was ambivalent. For many Americans, the enforcement of Prohibition was unpopular and they had sneaking admiration for well-known gangster celebrities.

## The end of Al Capone

When Herbert Hoover became president in 1929, he commissioned his treasury secretary, Andrew Mellon, to go after Al Capone, who was at the time at the peak of his power and influence. Capone had made the mistake of attracting too much publicity, often by feeding quotes to 'tame' crime reporters like Jake Lingle of the *Chicago Tribune*. His high public profile made him a target for the authorities. Normal police methods were no use because Capone had so completely infiltrated local law enforcement. Mellon's strategy focused on the two areas in which the federal authorities could use their powers: income tax evasion and violations of the Volstead Act.

## Cross-reference

Public attitudes towards **Al Capone** are revealed in Figure 9 on page 85. **Andrew Mellon** is discussed on page 74.

For more on the **Volstead Act**, see page 58.

## Exploring the detail

### The IRS

The IRS is responsible for federal taxation. Eliot Ness is more famous than Elmer Irey, but it was the IRS that 'got' Capone in the end.

These methods eventually succeeded in October 1931, when Capone was sentenced to 11 years imprisonment on various charges of income tax evasion and 5,000 offences against the Volstead Act. This was seen as a symbolic victory for the men chiefly responsible – Elmer Irey of the Internal Revenue Service (IRS) and Eliot Ness of the Chicago Bureau of Prohibition – but it should be noted that this victory was only narrowly achieved against the odds. The very name of the hand-picked team working with Ness – 'Untouchables' – shows that corruption was the rule and honesty was the exception. Ness had intended to have a team of 50 agents but in the end there were only 10.

Capone's career was finished but there was more to smashing organised crime than bringing down one individual whose importance had often been overrated. The criminal organisations Capone had operated continued to exist. The new generation of crime bosses carried on much as before, although they learned the lesson of Capone's downfall and avoided attracting too much public attention. In any case, the basis of organised crime was changing because the Prohibition era was coming to an end.

**Fig. 7** *The lesson for Al Capone*

And for the next lesson, we'll look at why I really should have paid my taxes ...

① VIOLATING PROHIBITION

② BRIBING POLICE OFFICERS

③ MURDER

## The reasons for ending Prohibition

Prohibition came to an end in 1933 because there had been a massive shift in public and political opinion. Millions of Americans became convinced that the moral crusade behind Prohibition had been a failure and one of the key reasons why it was seen to have failed was the rise in organised crime.

This shift in public mood was not sudden. There had always been substantial support for the 'Wets'; even though he was defeated, Al Smith gained millions of votes when he ran for president in 1928. Also in 1928, congressional hearings investigated the issue. In 1930, the Wickersham Commission reported its findings on the links between Prohibition and crime. In 1931, the American Federation of Labor (AFL) set up its National Committee for Moderation of the Volstead Act. A host of pressure groups sprang up including the Crusaders, the Molly Pitcher Club and the Women's Moderation Union. Franklin D. Roosevelt's election campaign in 1932 promised repeal.

By 1933, most people were prepared for a change. Some, often known as 'Moists', wanted a halfway house – moderation of the law rather than outright repeal. Congress attempted to pass such a compromise with the Blair Act but the political momentum was too strong. The 'lame-duck' Congress (in the interlude between Roosevelt's election and inauguration) proposed the Twenty-first Amendment in March 1933. Over the following months, the repeal was ratified by individual states; once 75 per cent of them had done this, Prohibition was dead.

## The 'war on crime' and the rise of the FBI

At the start of Roosevelt's presidency in 1933, his attorney general, Homer Cummings, declared a 'war on crime'. Cummings was reacting to the public perception that crime was undermining society. The perceptions of crime were heightened by sensational newspaper reporting and by the popularity and impact of a rush of gangster films that appeared at this time and seemingly glorified the evildoers – *Little Caesar* (1931), *The Public Enemy* (1931) and *Scarface* (1932), which is loosely based on the life of Al Capone. The USA needed someone to lead the fightback; the stage was set for J. Edgar Hoover.

> The country is confronted with a real warfare which is an armed underground is waging on society. It is a real war that must be successfully fought if life and property are to be secure in our country. Organised crime is an open challenge to our civilisation.

 **7**      *Statement by Attorney General Homer Cummings in 1933*

J. Edgar Hoover had started his long career at the Justice Department in 1919 and took a leading role in the Palmer Raids. From 1921, he was deputy director of the Bureau of Investigation, and later acting director. Hoover was a systematic and effective bureaucratic organiser and did a lot to improve discipline and training. He exploited new scientific methods, opening a forensic laboratory in 1932. He was highly effective in winning political support and financial backing. In 1934, the Bureau got jurisdiction over a range of interstate crimes such as kidnapping and car theft. In 1935, the organisation became the Federal Bureau of Investigation (FBI), with Hoover as its director. He kept the job for another 37 years.

Hoover's reputation was enhanced by a series of successes against high-profile criminals such as 'Machine Gun' Kelly in 1933, 'Ma' Barker in 1935, Alvin Karpis in 1936 and, the most publicised of all, John Dillinger in 1934. These successes were backed by a vigorous press campaign by William Randolph Hearst's newspaper empire and by Hollywood. A new censorship code halted the *Little Caesar* style; there was a rush of films glorifying the 'G-Men'. Other films made heroes out of policemen and state prosecutors like Thomas Dewey of New York.

The FBI benefited hugely from Hoover's publicity machine and kept a high reputation in the eyes of Americans through the war years and into the 1950s, when several television series promoted a rosy view of the FBI. In the 1960s, this reputation came under attack. Hoover's critics pointed out that men like Dillinger were essentially individuals and that Hoover had done little to stop real organised crime. One liberal historian claimed: 'Fearing a poor show against the underworld, J. Edgar Hoover chose not to battle against organised crime. He just kept insisting that the mob did not exist in the USA. Meanwhile, organised crime grew and prospered across the country.'

Hoover remains a controversial figure, accused of cutting across civil liberties, bending the truth to exaggerate his success and blackmailing leading politicians by holding secret files. On the other hand, he managed to build the FBI into a large and efficient machine. When he died in 1972, the newspaper columnist Jack Anderson, who had often criticised Hoover fiercely, wrote: 'J. Edgar Hoover transformed the FBI from a collection of misfits and hangers-on into one of the world's most efficient

**Cross-reference**

To recap on the **Palmer Raids**, see pages 62–4.

and formidable law enforcement organisations. Under Hoover's reign, not a single FBI man ever tried to fix a case, defraud the taxpayers, or sell out his country.'

### The USA in 1941

The fight against organised crime was just one feature of American society in the 1930s. In 1941, on the eve of the USA's entry into the Second World War, life for the American people had been shaped by a decade of economic depression and continuing social change. Few people realised then that they were to become involved in another world war – a war that would abolish unemployment and open the way for 30 years of prosperity in the post-war era. In 1941, millions were still unemployed and agricultural communities in the Great Plains remained devastated. However, it is important to remember that the many millions who were not unemployed and had not been ravaged by poverty regarded themselves as lucky to be American citizens.

The 1930s was a decade of mass opportunities for entertainment and leisure, the decade when 'talking pictures' brought the 'American Dream' to every community, however small or remote. This was the decade of Fred Astaire and Ginger Rogers in *Top Hat* and other popular musicals, screwball comedies like *Bringing Up Baby* and Technicolor epics like *Gone with the Wind*. This was the decade of mass radio broadcasts, comedy shows, soap operas and live commentaries on boxing and baseball. Mass unemployment and agricultural problems were terrible things in the 1930s, but life was mostly very good for those who had jobs.

*Learning outcomes*

In this section you have examined the origins of the Great Depression and how American governments struggled to deal with its effects. You have seen how the collapse of the stock market in 1929 led, although not directly or immediately, to deep economic depression, mass unemployment, a banking crisis and desperate conditions for many farming communities. You have looked at the attempts of governments, both Republican and Democrat, to cope with the depression; at the attitudes of those who supported government actions and those who opposed them; and at the impact of government interventions, especially the New Deal, on the people they were intended to help.

**Activity**

### Group activity

Working in groups, use a large sheet of A3 paper to design a poster showing the overall situation of the USA in 1941, on the eve of the war.

# AQA Examination-style questions

(a)   Explain why Roosevelt launched the Second New Deal in 1935.                    *(12 marks)*

  Questions like this are testing understanding of chronology and narrative – what happened before 1935? What aims did Roosevelt have that were different from before? The answer needs to be much more than a list of events with a few reasons attached. A long answer full of detailed information in the right order will be adequate, but not as good as a shorter answer that is more structured and shows differentiation in picking out the key factors.

(b) How important was Roosevelt's personality in shaping the successes and failures of the New Deal between 1933 and 1941?

*(24 marks)*

**AQA**
**Examiner's tip**

Questions like this need to be answered on at least two levels. First, there is the issue of balance and relative importance: was Roosevelt's personality the main factor or were other factors more important? This is the key question – you will need to think about what other factors were involved in making the New Deal and then assess which ones mattered the most and why. Second, there is the issue of success or failure. Did the New Deal succeed overall or not? Remember that the primary task is the first one – depending on your view of its relative importance, you might need rather less on Roosevelt's personal role and more about the other, more important, factors; or almost the whole answer might focus on Roosevelt because you feel he was all-important.

*In this chapter you will learn about:*

- the extent of isolationist feeling in the USA in the 1930s among politicians and the people

- how international developments in the 1930s created pressures for greater American involvement in foreign affairs

- the policies of Franklin D. Roosevelt and the reasons for the end of isolationism

- why the USA entered the Second World War in 1941.

We are not isolationists except in so far as we seek to isolate ourselves completely from war. I have seen war. I have seen war on land and sea. I have seen blood running from the wounded. I have seen men coughing out their gassed lungs. I have seen the dead in the mud. I have seen cities destroyed. I have seen children starving. I have seen the agony of mothers and wives. I hate war. I have passed unnumbered hours, I shall pass unnumbered hours, thinking and planning how war may be kept from this Nation.

**1**
*Extract from Franklin D. Roosevelt's speech in New York City, 14 August 1936*

Roosevelt spoke the words in Source 1 in 1936, three years before the German forces of Adolf Hitler invaded Poland and Europe was plunged into world war. As an assistant secretary to the navy in 1918, Roosevelt had visited the fighting on the Western Front during the First World War, and he had been horrified by the death and conditions that he had witnessed. Nevertheless, by the end of 1941 the USA was plunged into the horror of war once more, fighting against both Germany and Japan in a war that would cost 400,000 American lives.

## The debate concerning the end of isolationism

The USA became a superpower between 1941 and 1945 as a direct result of the Second World War. The demands of the war pushed the American economy to its maximum and unleashed all of its massive productive capacity. The scale of the American war effort between 1941 and 1945 was astonishing. The USA provided massive armies to fight in the Far East against Japan and to take the lead role in the liberation of occupied Europe. At the same time, the American economy produced the resources and the finances to pay for its own war effort, and to pay for a huge part of the war effort of its major allies, Britain and the Soviet Union. On top of all this, the American economy was able to enjoy a consumer boom in the domestic economy.

At the end of the war, all other major powers, whether victorious or defeated, faced the need to rebuild their ruined economies. By contrast, the USA had never experienced bombing, rationing or mass refugees. The war had made the USA the strongest military power in the world, but this was almost entirely accidental. When war began in Europe in 1939, American policymakers, strongly supported by public opinion, were absolutely determined to stay out of it.

It was the surprise Japanese attack on Pearl Harbor in December 1941 that forced the USA unwillingly into the widening world war. Without declaring war, a Japanese task force sailed across the Pacific to launch an assault on the American naval base in Hawaii. In much the same way, Hitler's sudden invasion on 22 June 1941 had dragged the USSR into a war that Stalin had done everything he possibly could to avoid. Yet in the spring of 1945, Soviet and American troops met in the heart of Europe at Torgau on the river Elbe. The age of the European powers was over and the age of the superpowers had begun.

## A closer look

### A brief history of the Second World War

There were three phases in the Second World War. The first phase, from 1938 to 1941, was not a world war at all but a European one: 'the war that Hitler won'. By September 1939, Hitler had already expanded the territories of Nazi Germany by aggressive diplomacy, first by annexing Austria and then by taking over large parts of Czechoslovakia, without being opposed by Western powers. In 1939, he made a non-aggression pact with Stalin's USSR to prepare for a war of conquest. Germany then invaded Poland and began a series of 'Blitzkrieg' victories that led to the fall of France in 1940 and Nazi domination of most of western and central Europe by the middle of 1941. Only Britain remained undefeated, although not capable of mounting any major counter-attack unless and until American help arrived.

The second phase, from the end of 1941 to the middle of 1943, was indeed a world war: 'the war that Hitler lost'. It began with Hitler's decision to break his non-aggression pact with Stalin and launch a surprise invasion of the Soviet Union in June 1941. This invasion did not succeed in knocking Soviet Russia out of the war; by December 1941, Hitler's armies were faced with a long war on two fronts. At the same time as the German invasion of the USSR stalled, Japan's attack in the Pacific forced the USA into joining the war on the side of Britain and the Soviet Union. The balance of military power was completely changed. During 1942 and 1943, the tide of the war turned against the Axis powers (Germany, Italy and Japan). The German invasion of the USSR was blocked at the Battle of Stalingrad; Axis forces were pushed out of North Africa; Japanese advances were halted in the Far East; the Battle of the Atlantic (the fight to protect merchant ships against the U-boats) had been won by May 1943; and Italy changed sides after the overthrow of Mussolini.

During the third and final phase, in 1944 and 1945, the Axis powers were slowly battered to defeat by the greater military and economic power of the USA and the USSR. Mass bombing gradually destroyed the economies of Germany and Japan. Germany was invaded from both east and west. Soviet and US armies met in the heart of defeated Germany, at Torgau on the river Elbe. The war ended with the unconditional surrender of Germany and Japan and the dominance of the two new superpowers.

The Second World War can be seen to have completed a process that had started in 1917. In 1914, just as in 1939, the USA was determined to stay out of the war in Europe. Between 1914 and 1917, just as between 1939 and 1941, the USA provided economic assistance to Britain and its allies in a kind of one-sided neutrality. In 1917, just as in 1941, the USA became militarily involved and had a decisive impact on the ultimate outcome of the war. The difference was that in 1945 the USA accepted its place as a world power, unlike in 1919–20 when the nation rejected Woodrow Wilson and retreated back into isolationism and 'normalcy'.

## American isolationism

From 1920 to 1940, most Americans had supported a policy of isolationism. Some were outright pacifists, opposed to any and all wars. Many were Nationalists, keen to promote American power in the western hemisphere but totally against any involvement in Europe. They felt that the USA should follow a policy of genuine neutrality, putting American interests first. All three Republican presidents – Harding, Coolidge and Hoover – were happy to accept Harding's view that 'We seek no part in directing the destinies of the world.'

Despite the retreat from a world role in 1920, American foreign policy could never be completely isolationist. The USA had hosted the Washington Naval Conference in 1921 to address naval disarmament and to try to secure agreement about the Open Door policy in China. American financiers were involved in restructuring Germany's debts through the Dawes Plan of 1924, a scheme to provide Germany with foreign loans in order to pay its international debts, and the Young Plan of 1929, which extended the time in which Germany must repay those debts. In 1927 and 1928, the American secretary of state, Frank B. Kellogg, together with the French foreign minister, Aristide Briand, had devoted a lot of time and effort to promoting the Kellogg-Briand Pact of 1928 in which 60 nations signed an idealistic agreement to outlaw war. However, in general, the national mood had remained hostile to foreign commitments.

Some Americans regarded isolationism as a terrible mistake. In 1919, Theodore Roosevelt and Henry Cabot Lodge had believed in a formal alliance with Britain and close American involvement in a system of international relations. Woodrow Wilson had believed in collective security and the League of Nations. They felt that the First World War had proved that the world was interdependent; that it was no longer practically possible for the USA to stand aside from world affairs. However, only a small minority of Americans agreed with such views. There was no mood in favour of internationalism in the 1920s.

In the 1930s, Americans were even more preoccupied with domestic issues and the problems of the Great Depression. Public opinion regarded the rise of the dictatorships in Europe as a distant problem, almost as proof that disengagement from Europe was the correct policy. There was a strong pacifist movement, fed by the belief that the American people had been duped into war in 1917 by a conspiracy of politicians, bankers and industrialists. The post-war peace settlement was regarded as unfair and not worth fighting for. This idea was strengthened by the weak response of the League of Nations, failing to take effective action against acts of aggression such as Japan's invasion of Manchuria in China in 1931 and the invasion of Abyssinia by Mussolini's Italy in 1935.

When Franklin D. Roosevelt became president, he did not make any immediate policy changes towards Europe, but he moved quickly to try to change policy in Latin America. Dollar Diplomacy was out; the Good Neighbour policy was begun. The imperialistic Platt Amendment of 1901 was repealed in 1934. For the most part, foreign policy remained in the background as politicians were preoccupied with the problems of the depression and the New Deal. Isolationism grew stronger.

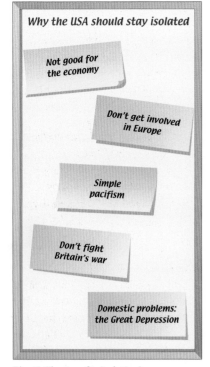

**Why the USA should stay isolated**

Not good for the economy

Don't get involved in Europe

Simple pacifism

Don't fight Britain's war

Domestic problems: the Great Depression

**Fig. 1** *The case for isolationism*

In the late 1930s, isolationist feeling grew even stronger. Congress passed the Neutrality Act in 1935, with further acts in 1936 and 1937. An opinion poll in 1937 produced a 94 per cent vote in favour of keeping out of foreign wars. At the same time, there was strong support in Congress for the Ludlow Amendment, a proposal to change the Constitution to forbid the government from declaring war without first gaining the consent of the people.

In October 1937, President Roosevelt made his Quarantine Speech in Chicago, calling on peace-loving nations to make a concerted effort to oppose conflict by breaking off relations with aggressors and placing them 'in quarantine', like someone with an infectious disease. The speech was clearly aimed at Germany, Italy and Japan, but Roosevelt spoke in general terms and did not even propose economic sanctions, never mind armed intervention. He was conscious of the strength of the isolationists in Congress and in the country.

With the war between Japan and China in 1937 and then the outbreak of war in Europe in September 1939, the Roosevelt administration was in a difficult position. How could Roosevelt do what he thought was necessary to respond to the international situation – to increase American preparedness and keep his options open – without going against the grain of public opinion? In 1938, American isolationism was strengthened by the fact that Britain and France were following a policy of appeasement – making concessions to Nazi Germany and doing everything possible to avoid war. This policy reached a peak in September 1938 when Hitler met leaders of Britain, France and Italy at the Munich Conference. Six months later, Hitler tore up the Munich agreement and German troops entered Prague. From March 1939 onwards, there was increasingly urgent danger of a war in Europe. The scene was set for a confrontation between President Roosevelt and the isolationists.

## The USA and Japan

From the 1890s, American policy in the Far East had always run some risk of conflict with Japan. The main aim of the USA was to maintain the Open Door policy in China and protect American interests in the Pacific. This led to friction at times but relations with Japan were relatively stable. This changed with the rise of the militaristic regime that dominated Japan in the 1930s and heightened American worries, especially after Japan had invaded Manchuria in 1931.

When full-scale war began between Japan and China in 1937, followed by the Japanese proclamation of a New Order in Asia, American attitudes and policies became openly anti-Japanese. In contrast, the leader of the Chinese Nationalists, Chiang Kai-shek, became almost an American folk hero. There was alarm at the growing diplomatic links between Japan and the European dictators. Neither Britain nor the USA wanted confrontation with Japan but both were worried that Japanese expansion would go further.

At first, further Japanese expansion seemed likely to be directed westwards against the Soviet Union. In 1939, a series of major battles took place in Mongolia but the Japanese came up against unexpectedly strong resistance from Soviet armies commanded by General Zhukov. After 1939, Japan left the Soviet Union alone. Japanese expansion looked southwards instead, seeking to control the vital natural resources in the Dutch East Indies and the Asian colonial territories of Britain and France.

### Exploring the detail

**The Neutrality Acts**

There were a series of Neutrality Acts in 1935, 1936, 1937 and 1939. Their main aim was to prevent the USA from being drawn into war (as many people thought had been the case between in 1917) by trading arms to nations fighting a war. The first three acts were drawn very tightly, but the 1939 act relaxed some of the restrictions because of the imminent threat to Britain from Nazi Germany.

### Exploring the detail

**The sinking of the USS** *Panay*

One example of the isolationist trend was the reaction to the Japanese attack on an American gunboat, the *Panay*, off the coast of China in December 1937. This could easily have been seen as an act of war, just like the destruction of the *Maine* in Cuba in 1898, but there was a strong majority in Congress demanding a peaceful outcome. Japan issued an apology, paid a £2 million indemnity and conflict was avoided.

### Key chronology

**Isolationism and US foreign policy**

**1920** Rejection of 'Wilsonism' and election of Warren G. Harding.

**1921** Washington Naval Conference on limitations to battleship construction.

**1922** Nine-Power Treaty in Washington upholds the Open Door policy in China.

**1924** Dawes Plan deals with American loans to Weimar Germany.

**1928** Kellogg-Briand Pact outlaws war.

**1929** Young Plan restructures Germany's reparations payments.

**1934** Termination of the Platt Amendment and withdrawal of US forces from Cuba.

**1935** Neutrality Act passed (further acts were passed in 1936, 1937 and 1939).

**1939** Start of war in Europe.

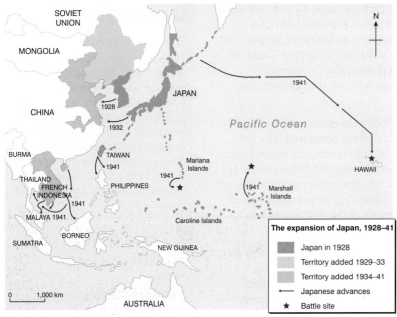

**Fig. 2** *Japanese expansion, 1928–41*

Japan was encouraged to be more aggressive by German military successes in Europe. In June 1940, both France and the Netherlands were overrun, leaving their colonial empires in Asia vulnerable. Japan had ambitions to control the natural resources of French Indo-China and the Dutch East Indies. American policy was to try to prevent this but without risking war to do so.

Japan fortified the Marshall Islands, which strengthened communications between Hawaii and the Philippines. Then, in September 1940, Japan signed the Tripartite Pact with Germany and Italy. This alliance did not mean that Japan was bent on a war with the USA – what the Japanese wanted was to be left alone while they completed the conquest of China – but Roosevelt regarded it as an urgent threat. His response to this threat inevitably caused a clash with American isolationists.

## Key chronology

### Japanese expansion

**1931** Invasion of Manchuria.

**1937** Start of China War.

**1938** Proclamation of the Japanese New Order.

**1939** Inconclusive battles against Soviet armies.

**1940** Establishment of the Greater East Asia Co-Prosperity Sphere.

**1940** The Tripartite Pact with Germany and Italy.

## The USA and the war in Europe

By the summer of 1940, American concerns about the war in Europe were even greater than the problems in the Pacific. From the beginning of the war in 1939, there was no doubt that the USA would aid Britain against Germany. Although public opinion was set on American neutrality, it was hostile to fascist dictators. Neutrality, therefore, was one-sided and Britain was able to acquire war goods easily as long as it was able to pay for them.

In November 1939, Roosevelt persuaded Congress to pass a new Neutrality Act (often known as the Cash and Carry Act) to lift the arms embargo and allow arms shipments to Britain. He also took steps to increase American preparedness. In January, he went to Congress to request a $2 billion increase in defence spending; two further increases pushed the total to above $10 billion by the end of the year.

When France fell to the Nazis in June 1940, the situation became urgent, with Britain apparently on the verge of collapse. From the moment Winston Churchill became prime minister, he pressed Roosevelt hard for emergency aid, particularly stressing Britain's need for more warships for convoy protection. So began the relationship between Roosevelt and Churchill that was to influence American policy for the rest of the war.

As you are no doubt aware, the scene has darkened. The enemy has a marked preponderance in air power. The small countries are simply smashed up one by one, like matchwood. If necessary, we shall continue the war alone and we are not afraid of that. But I trust you realise, Mr President, that the voice and force of the United States may count for nothing if they are held back too long. You may see a Nazified Europe established with astonishing swiftness, and the weight may be more than we can bear. Immediate needs are: first of all, the loan of forty or fifty of your older destroyers. Secondly, we want several hundred of the latest types of aircraft. Thirdly, anti-aircraft equipment and ammunition ... Fourthly, [we need] to purchase steel in the United States. This also applies to other materials. We shall go on paying dollars for as long as we can, but I should like to feel reasonably sure that when we can pay no more, you will give us the stuff all the same. Fifthly, the visit of a United States squadron to Irish ports would be invaluable. Sixthly, I am looking to you to keep that Japanese dog quiet in the Pacific.

*Secret message to President Roosevelt from Winston Churchill, 15 May 1940*

During the war years, wartime propaganda promoted an enduring myth about the 'special relationship' between Britain and the USA, and specifically about the personal link between Churchill and Roosevelt. According to this myth, the two leaders became close almost instantly. However, the reality was different from the myth.

Roosevelt was unsure of Churchill's motives and abilities. Roosevelt was also a tough political realist: he needed to make a judgement of how American interests might be affected by British collapse and by the total domination of Europe by

**Fig. 3** *Winston Churchill and Franklin D. Roosevelt*

Nazi Germany. Before responding to Britain's request for aid, he hesitated for several weeks while considering alternative views of the likelihood of Britain's survival.

The American ambassador in London, Joseph P. Kennedy, was hostile to Britain and reported that it would certainly have to surrender. If this turned out to be the case, any aid sent to Britain would be wasted and doing so would antagonise public opinion, which remained strongly opposed to American involvement in war overseas.

### Key profile

#### Joseph P. Kennedy

Joseph P. Kennedy, Sr. (1888–1969) was the US ambassador to Britain in 1940. He was a strong supporter of the New Deal but opposed Roosevelt's decision to run for a third presidential term. Kennedy was pro-Irish and opposed plans to give aid to Britain in 1940, predicting that it would soon collapse. He remained out of office throughout the war. His son, John F. Kennedy, was elected president in 1960.

## Key chronology

### American response to war in Europe

**1939**
**September** Outbreak of war.

**1939**
**November** Cash and Carry Act.

**1940**
**January** Increased federal budget for defence spending.

**1940**
**May/June** Fall of France.

**1940**
**September** Destroyers for Bases agreement; conscription introduced – the first time ever in peacetime.

## Cross-reference

For more on the **Manhattan Project** and the **atomic bomb**, see pages 133–4.

Eventually, Roosevelt proposed the Destroyers for Bases agreement, lending to Britain 50 surplus warships in return for 99-year leases on eight British bases in Newfoundland, Bermuda and the Caribbean. At first, the deal horrified Churchill and most of the British government, who saw it as a very hard bargain exploiting Britain's weak situation. Roosevelt argued that he needed to gain tangible rewards for giving assistance because isolationists in the USA saw helping Britain as much too dangerous for American interests.

The speed of Hitler's conquests in 1940 pushed Roosevelt into a highly secret executive decision. Having received alarming reports from scientific experts about German plans to build atomic weapons, Roosevelt launched a research programme on nuclear fission. This was the beginning of what later became known as the Manhattan Project, leading to the development of the American–British atomic bomb by 1945.

In September 1940, Roosevelt went ahead with two more public but symbolic decisions. The first was to finalise the Destroyers for Bases deal with Britain. The second was to bring in the draft (military conscription) – the first time this had ever been done in peacetime. Both these steps sharpened political divisions within the USA and brought a powerful backlash from isolationists. In September 1940, the America First Committee was founded in Chicago. The battle lines were drawn for the presidential election campaign.

## A closer look

### Isolationism, Charles Lindbergh and the America First Committee

Isolationism in the USA in the 1930s had many different strands. Many were pacifists, with a long record of opposing any kind of involvement overseas. One of these was Senator William Borah, who had made a notable speech against Woodrow Wilson and the League of Nations in 1919. Several other senators, such as Arthur Vandenberg, had similar views. Some people, like Senator Burton Wheeler of Montana, had originally been strong political allies of President Roosevelt but turned against him on the issue of foreign policy.

There were also groups and individuals who had Irish or German loyalties and were opposed to the USA being linked with Britain again. Several members of the House of Representatives, such as Gerald Nye, were almost obsessed with the idea that the USA had been tricked into war by Britain in 1917 and that this must never happen again. However, the most virulent opposition to Roosevelt came from outside Congress.

One influential voice was Father Charles Coughlin, the Catholic priest-turned-radio star, whose regular broadcasts drew huge audiences. Father Coughlin had once supported the New Deal but then turned against Roosevelt. His broadcasts contained a lot of personal attacks and were strongly isolationist. (Coughlin's influence faded after 1939, when his radio show was stopped.) An even more charismatic and influential figure was Charles Lindbergh, who became a celebrity after his solo flight across the Atlantic in 1927. In the late 1930s, Lindbergh made several visits to Germany and numerous speeches showing admiration for the Third Reich. Roosevelt was convinced Lindbergh was a Nazi.

Lindbergh was given backing by a Chicago newspaper proprietor, Charles McCormick of the *Chicago Tribune*. McCormick was rabidly anti-Roosevelt and anti-New Deal. It was McCormick who took the lead in founding the America First Committee in September 1940. With Lindbergh's national profile and massive financial backing from Henry Ford, America First became a powerful weapon against Roosevelt in his election campaign and for some time afterwards. It gained widespread support, especially in the mid-West. At its peak America First had 850,000 members, with heavy financial backing and editorial support from several newspapers.

Measuring how deep the support for isolationism was is difficult. Some historians claim that its impact seemed greater than it really was, due to the high level of publicity. Certainly, Roosevelt was very worried about the influence of Father Coughlin and especially so about Lindbergh. In his 2004 novel *The Plot Against America*, the novelist Philip Roth depicted the USA ceasing to be a democracy after Lindbergh had defeated Roosevelt in the 1940 election – which, of course, is not what really happened.

## The presidential election of 1940

The issue of isolationism dominated the 1940 presidential election campaign. Almost at the last minute, Roosevelt had decided to run for a third term – something that was unprecedented although it was not then barred by the Constitution. At the beginning of 1940, he told colleagues he would not run again 'unless the situation in Europe becomes very much worse'. Later, he changed his mind, mostly because of the war situation and partly because he thought all other candidates for the Democratic nomination were unsuitable.

The campaign was bitterly fought. He had made many political enemies in the New Deal years. He came under attack from a coalition of influential and well-financed isolationists, including leading Republicans and the America First Committee and its charismatic spokesman, Charles Lindbergh. However, the presidential election did not turn into a straight fight between isolationists and interventionists. First, the Republican candidate, Wendell Willkie, was not an outright isolationist and in fact agreed with many of Roosevelt's policies, including the Destroyers for Bases agreement. Second, Roosevelt was careful not to go against the grain of public opinion.

Fig. 4 *'A slight case of indigestion.' An anti-isolationist cartoon showing how Senator Claude Pepper of Florida exposed support for Nazi Germany from American isolationists*

At the time and afterwards, his opponents accused Roosevelt of fighting a devious and hypocritical campaign. He did everything possible to reassure voters he would put American interests first and that the USA would never go to war unless the country attacked. In the closing days of the campaign, he made a big speech in which he said that 'Your boys are not going to be sent into any foreign wars.' Willkie, who had taken an increasingly isolationist position as the campaign went on, lost ground.

## Activity

### Thinking point

Gather evidence for a newspaper article on the theme that the isolationists were right – that Roosevelt *did* allow Winston Churchill to drag the USA into an avoidable war in Europe.

Roosevelt won the election because he could rely on his image as the 'safe' choice in a time of crisis and on the popularity he had gained from pushing through the New Deal in the 1930s. He gained solid support from the unions, from African-Americans in the North and from the Democrats in the South. The election result was a decisive victory, if not quite a landslide like 1936. Roosevelt won by almost 5 million votes and he now had a much freer hand in foreign policy.

> And while I am talking to you mothers and fathers, I give you one more assurance. I have said this before, but I shall say it again and again and again: Your boys are not going to be sent into any foreign wars.

**3**         *Election promise by Franklin D. Roosevelt, 30 October 1940*

There was (and still is) controversy over Roosevelt's actions and intentions at the time of his re-election. Was he simply following the logic of events at that time, altering his policies later as the situation changed? Or did he deliberately manipulate the situation in 1940, deceiving the American people into believing he would keep them out of a war they did not want while he was already planning for deeper involvement? Whichever view is taken, Roosevelt's policies became much more interventionist in the weeks and months after his re-election.

## Roosevelt and the reasons for US entry into the Second World War

### The end of isolationism

One of the criticisms often made against Roosevelt is that he waited until after he had been re-elected before openly discussing the urgent need for American involvement in the Second World War. It was only in December 1940 that Roosevelt told reporters at a White House press conference how dire Britain's military and financial situation was. Losses of merchant shipping were at frighteningly high levels; Britain was effectively bankrupt, unable to pay for vital war goods.

To be fair to Roosevelt, much of this information had only just been given to him in a secret security briefing, but there is no doubt that he was much more decisive and open about his intentions once his re-election was safely in the bag. Early in 1941, the issue of **Lend-Lease** provided the national debate Roosevelt had sidestepped during the election. The fight against the Lend-Lease Act was the last stand of the isolationists.

### Key term

**Lend-Lease:** the scheme under which the USA supplied Britain, the Soviet Union, France, China and other Allied nations with war material between 1941 and 1945.

> In the present world situation of course there is absolutely no doubt in the mind of a very overwhelming number of Americans that the best immediate defence of the United States is the success of Great Britain in defending itself; and that, therefore, quite aside from our historic and current interest in the survival of democracy in the world as a whole, it is equally important, from a selfish point of view of American defence, that we should do everything to help the British Empire to defend itself.

**4**         *Roosevelt speaking in a radio broadcast, telling Americans about Lend-Lease, 17 December 1940*

Never before have the American people been asked or compelled to give so bounteously and so completely of their tax dollars to any foreign nation. Never before has the Congress of the United States been asked by any president to violate international law. Never before has this nation resorted to duplicity in the conduct of its foreign affairs. Never before has the United States given to one man the power to strip this nation of its defences. Never before has a Congress coldly and flatly been asked to abdicate.

If the American people want a dictatorship – if they want a totalitarian form of government and if they want war – this bill should be steamrollered through Congress, as is the wont of President Roosevelt.

Approval of this legislation means war, open and complete warfare. I, therefore, ask the American people before they supinely accept it – Was the last World War worthwhile?

**5**

*Senator Burton K. Wheeler attacking Lend-Lease in the Senate, 12 January 1941*

In January 1941, Roosevelt proposed lending Britain the resources needed with the terms of repayment to be decided later. The proposed legislation would give massive executive power to the president. It authorised Roosevelt to 'sell, transfer title to, exchange, lease, lend, or otherwise dispose of' any defence material considered vital to the defence of the USA. Congress was also asked for an appropriation of $7 billion dollars to finance Lend-Lease.

The isolationists had a lot of support. America First was well financed and supported by many big names, including the industrialist Henry Ford and the film star Lillian Gish as well as Charles Lindbergh. Influential Republican politicians such as Senator Wheeler and Congressman Hamilton Fish led vociferous opposition from Congress. Other prominent individuals included Senator Borah and Robert La Follette. There was also pressure from Irish-Americans, German-Americans and pacifist groups. However, despite their efforts, Congress passed the Lend-Lease Act on 11 March 1941.

This decision is the end of any attempts at appeasement, the end of compromise with tyranny and the forces of oppression.

**6**

*Roosevelt speaking after the passing of the Lend-lease Act*

Many moderate Republicans supported Roosevelt over Lend-Lease, including Wendell Willkie. Roosevelt was also skilful in accepting amendments in order to compromise and win over doubters. Yet the public mood was changing. In the summer of 1941, far more Americans were in favour of continuing aid to Britain than had been the case a year before. This mood hardened after the German invasion of the Soviet Union in June. The high tide of isolationism had passed its peak.

## Moving towards war

After the German invasion of the USSR in June 1941, Britain had a breathing space. Churchill took the opportunity to host a meeting with

**Key chronology**

### The end of isolationism

**1940 May/June**  Fall of France.

**1940 June**  Start of conscription to the US army.

**1940 September**  Formation of America First Committee; Destroyers for Bases agreement signed.

**1940 November**  Re-election of Roosevelt for a third term.

**1941 February**  Numerous ships sunk off the American coast by German U-boats.

**1941 March**  Lend-Lease Act signed by Congress.

**1941 June**  German invasion of USSR.

**1941 August**  Atlantic Charter announced after the meeting at Placentia Bay.

**1941 December**  Japanese attack on Pearl Harbor and US declaration of war.

**Activity**

### Revision exercise

**1**  Outline the main reasons why many Americans were against the USA becoming involved in the war against Germany in 1940 and 1941.

**2**  Outline the main reasons put forward by those in favour of an interventionist foreign policy.

Roosevelt at Placentia Bay, Newfoundland. The result of this meeting was the Atlantic Charter: a statement of joint war aims. By that stage, the links between Britain and the USA amounted almost to an alliance, with American actions edging closer to direct participation and public opinion increasingly aware of the urgency of the war situation.

There was still considerable opposition to American involvement. Even in late October 1941, despite public outrage against the sinking of US patrol ships by German U-boats, an opinion poll found only 17 per cent in favour of an American declaration of war on Germany. Sensing the drift towards war, Charles Lindbergh made the isolationist case yet again in a speech in September attacking Roosevelt's policies.

> The forces pulling America into war are the British, the Roosevelt administration and the Jews. It is not difficult to understand why Jewish people desire the overthrow of Nazi Germany. But no person of honesty and vision can look upon their pro-war policy without seeing the dangers involved, both for us and for them. Their greatest danger to this country comes from their ownership and influence in our motion pictures, our press, our radio and our government.

**7**            *Lindbergh's speech at an America First rally, September 1941*

**Fig. 5** *The attack on Pearl Harbor*

The reaction to Lindbergh's speech in Source 7 showed how far opinion in the USA had shifted during 1941. The anti-Semitic tone was counter-productive, alienating many who had previously supported him. Many Communists and Socialists who had previously opposed intervention were now in favour of assisting the Soviet Union. It is possible, even probable, that developments in the war in Europe would sooner or later have brought the USA into the conflict. When the declaration of war came, it was not because of Churchill's diplomacy or the German U-boat campaign: it was because of the Japanese attack on Pearl Harbor.

Armed conflict between the USA and Japan was not inevitable in 1941 but it was always likely. Japan was desperate to gain access to vital raw materials such as oil and rubber. After Hitler's victories in Europe, Japan was tempted to seize what it needed from French Indo-China, the Dutch East Indies, or British Malaya and Burma. If and when Japan attempted to do this, the

USA could not stand aside. From an American standpoint, China was all-important. By the summer of 1941, Japan had 2 million troops on the Chinese mainland. Japan would never negotiate to pull them out, whereas the USA would never negotiate to accept Japanese dominance of China.

American policy was to avoid war using economic sanctions against Japan. There were deep divisions within the US government about this. A powerful group led by Henry Stimson pushed for maximum economic pressure to be applied. Roosevelt and his secretary of state, Cordell Hull, wanted to be more cautious, keeping sanctions to a minimum and exempting scrap iron and oil from the list of banned exports to Japan. Despite these American attempts at restraint, Japan's leaders saw any economic sanctions as a provocation, pushing them into a corner.

> I simply have not got enough navy to go around. Every little episode in the Pacific means fewer ships in the Atlantic.

 **8**  *Comment by Roosevelt to a colleague, July 1941*

The tensions between the USA and Japan became more intense in July 1941, when Japanese forces occupied French Indo-China. Roosevelt was convinced that this was the prelude to a Japanese attack on Soviet Russia or the Dutch East Indies. What he did not know was that the Japanese military had already ruled out Russia as a target and were planning to strike south to attack the East Indies. In order to do this, they calculated, it was essential to neutralise British naval forces in Singapore and US naval forces in the Philippines and Hawaii.

At a high-level meeting on 5 November 1941, Japanese Prime Minister Tojo and his government allowed 20 days for last-chance negotiations with the USA. If these failed, Japan would go to war, without any warning, early in December. There was no possibility of the negotiations succeeding. Japan demanded that the USA should begin exporting oil again, but was not willing to make any concessions at all over China. Tojo knew that the talks would almost certainly fail. At the end of November, the Japanese naval task force set out on its way to attack the American battle fleet at its base in Hawaii.

It was the Japanese attack on Pearl Harbor that forced America's entry into the Second World War. Before 7 December 1941, many Americans still regarded the war in Europe as a distant reality. For Japan, however, there were urgent reasons for going to war in the Pacific. In response to Japanese military actions in China and French Indo-China, the USA had imposed an embargo, cutting off vital supplies of raw materials including oil. The Japanese government took the decision to conquer territories in South-east Asia to gain control of desperately needed natural resources. In order to achieve success, Japan needed to neutralise American power by crippling the American Pacific fleet, especially its aircraft carriers. Doing this, the Japanese calculated, would force the USA to the negotiating table.

### A closer look

#### The Japanese attack on Pearl Harbor

A Japanese task force of ships and aircraft carriers set sail from Japan on 26 November 1941 and managed to sail completely undetected to within 400 km (250 miles) of Pearl Harbor. On 7 December, the

Japanese aircraft carriers launched wave after wave of aircraft-carrying torpedoes and bombs, all heading for Pearl Harbor – which was packed with 70 US warships including eight battleships. The US forces at Pearl Harbor, despite extensive warnings that war might break out and that they might be a target, were completely unprepared. It was a Sunday, and the normal laid-back Sunday routine was in operation.

**Fig. 6** *7 December 1941*

### Key chronology

**The road to war, 1941**

| | |
|---|---|
| 22 June | German invasion of the USSR. |
| 24 July | Japanese occupation of French Indo-China. |
| 17 October | Replacement of Konoye by Tojo as prime minister of Japan. |
| 5 November | Meeting of Japanese leadership over war or negotiation. |
| 1 December | Decision to launch assault on Pearl Harbor. |
| 7 December | Japanese attack on Pearl Harbor. |
| 9 December | German declaration of war on the USA. |

The Japanese attack came at about 8 am and was devastating. Over the next hour the Japanese aircraft managed to sink six battleships and damage the other two. Seven other warships were destroyed and nearly 300 US aircraft were lost on nearby airfields. However, the Japanese success was not complete. US aircraft carriers and cruisers had been away at sea at the time of the attack and were not destroyed as Japanese war planners had hoped. Later, these ships, above all the aircraft carriers, would play an important role in the naval war in the Pacific. Furthermore, US industrial might ensured that many damaged vessels were quickly repaired and returned to service and that new ships were manufactured quickly. Most importantly, the surprise Japanese attack united the American people in the need to support the war.

The attack on Pearl Harbor was a tactical victory for Japan. American forces were taken by surprise and suffered heavy losses. On 8 December, the USA declared war on Japan. Almost simultaneously, Hitler declared war on the USA. Without any vote in Congress ever needing to be taken, the USA was fully engaged in a world war, allied to both Britain and the Soviet Union. It was this war, which Americans had tried so hard to stay out of, that would turn the USA into a world power.

### Activity

### Preparing a presentation

Read the following interpretations of Franklin D. Roosevelt and the Second World War. Working either on your own or in small groups, prepare a presentation to the class to explain why the view you have been assigned is the most convincing. For your presentation you should set out three to five key points and produce a poster or cartoon that backs up the main message.

1. **The great statesman**: the wartime myth of Roosevelt presents a picture of a far-sighted statesman, working in close harmony with Winston Churchill, guiding the Western Allies to ultimate victory over the Axis and the forces of evil. This is not a myth but a true reflection of Roosevelt's leadership.

2. **The gullible idealist**: Roosevelt was putty in the hands of Winston Churchill, who bamboozled him into giving vast quantities of money and manpower to fight 'Britain's war'. (Roosevelt was then equally gullible at the end of the war as he allowed Stalin to take over most of eastern and central Europe because he naively trusted Stalin's promises at Yalta.)

3. **The ruthless realist**: Roosevelt was the opposite of gullible. He drove a hard bargain with Britain over Lend-Lease in 1940–1 and waited to see if Britain was defeated in the summer of 1940 before acting to help. Later, he made sure that Britain paid through the nose in terms of bases and long-term debts, opening the way for American economic and strategic domination.

4. **The diplomatic failure**: Roosevelt could have avoided war with Japan but he got it wrong in the diplomatic negotiations of 1940–1. A few sensible concessions about the oil embargo and other Japanese grievances could have prevented war in 1941 and thus avoided the need for the USA to fight two wars at once. He also made a mess of telling the American people about the need to oppose Nazism, not because he was devious but because he was too late to speak out and mishandled his relations with Congress.

5. **The devious conspirator**: Roosevelt knew that the vast majority of Americans were firmly isolationist, so he set out to deceive and trick them into a war they did not want. He connived with Churchill to extend help for Britain that the US Congress would not have voted for and he concealed his true intentions until the 1940 election had been safely won. Some of his enemies even claim he knew in advance about Japan's plan to attack Pearl Harbor but he did nothing about it because it would bring the USA into the war

### Summary questions

1. Why did isolationist feelings in the USA appear to be so strong between 1937 and 1941?

2. Why did Roosevelt develop a close relationship with Winston Churchill in 1940–1?

# The USA and the Second World War

The young Americans who went off to war in 1941 came home to a different country. The war had shaken the American people loose and freed them from a decade of economic and social paralysis. The war had flung them around their country and into new forms of life. It was a war that so richly delivered on the promises of the wartime advertisers and politicians that it nearly banished the memory of the Great Depression. At the end of the depressed Thirties, nearly half of white families and almost 90 per cent of black families still lived in poverty. By the war's end unemployment was negligible. Small wonder that Americans chose to remember it as the Good War.

**1**  *David M. Kennedy, **Freedom From Fear**, 1999*

This rather glowing picture of the USA at the end of the Second World War contains a great deal of truth, but it needs to be evaluated carefully. Wartime myths can be powerful and seductive but there is often a gulf between myths and realities. The war undeniably brought victory and economic prosperity, but the path to victory was not smooth or easy. For many Americans it also brought tragedy, hardships and dashed hopes. It is necessary to look closely at the evidence in this chapter and reach balanced conclusions about the 'good war'.

## The USA and the Second World War

### The rise to world power

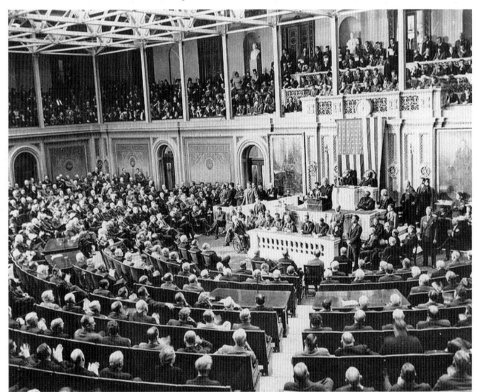

**Fig. 1** *President Roosevelt signs the declaration of war on Japan*

The Japanese assault on Pearl Harbor was recognised at the time as a turning point in American history. The USA declared war on Japan and Germany. Immediately there was a strong sense of national unity and purpose, which lasted throughout the war and into the post-war era. The America First Committee, for example, instantly disbanded and declared full support for the war. Roosevelt faced relatively little political opposition, in either Congress or the country, throughout the war. The power of the federal government greatly increased as the needs of the war economy grew.

Before the war, the USA had rated only 20th in the league table of the world's armies, one place lower than the Netherlands. In 1942, it was necessary to call up, train and equip an army of millions. It was necessary to build thousands of ships, both naval and cargo vessels, to take on Japan and replace the huge losses of merchant shipping in the Battle of the Atlantic. It was necessary to expand American industry to provide the war material required by the USA and its allies. It was necessary to make plans as soon as possible for the invasion of Nazi-occupied western Europe.

Between December 1941 and August 1945, the American contribution to the defeat of the Axis was on a staggering scale. Even though the main American theatre of war was in the Pacific, Roosevelt agreed to give priority to the fight against Nazi Germany, above all supporting Britain in protecting the convoys across the Atlantic but also giving extensive support to the Soviet Union. This decision was not well received by American naval commanders, who wanted greater resources for the war against Japan.

After the war, Stalin pronounced his verdict on the Allied victory over the Axis: 'What the British gave was Time,' he said. 'The Americans gave Money; the Soviet Union gave Blood.' This was a rather barbed comment, stressing how the Soviet people had suffered vast casualties, estimated at 27 million, whereas the USA had lost far fewer lives and had never been invaded. However, it contains a great truth. The USA was indeed the 'Arsenal of Democracy' and without American industrial output the war could not have been won so decisively by 1945. That fact made it certain that the USA would play a dominant role in shaping the post-war world.

## Turning the tide: the Far East

It took time to build up the American war effort. For most of 1942, the Allies were very much on the defensive. The Americans needed to halt Japanese advances in the Pacific. The Soviet Union was fighting desperately to stem the German attacks, in military action and towards Leningrad in the north and the Caucasus oilfields in the south. Britain was mainly concerned with not losing the Battle of the Atlantic. It took until 1943 before the USA could move on to the offensive.

The war in the Pacific commenced with a series of defeats, including the withdrawal from the Philippines and Guam. Britain also lost most of its territories in the Far East, including Hong Kong and the humiliating surrender of its great naval base in Singapore. There were fears that Japan would conquer British India. The American fleet had been badly weakened by Pearl Harbor and took time to recover. Two great aircraft-carrier battles in 1942, the Battle of the Coral Sea and the Battle of Midway, turned the balance of sea power back towards the Americans.

The USA also made a large contribution to aiding the British forces defending Burma and the approaches to India against Japanese attacks. Even more important was American support for the nationalist regime in China. American aircraft kept the supply lines to western China open by flying 'over the hump' of the high Himalayas; American forces under General Stilwell supported the Chinese on the ground. Although outright victory was still a long way off, by November 1943 American forces

### Key chronology

**America's war in the Pacific**

| | |
|---|---|
| **1941** | |
| **December** | Japanese attack on Pearl Harbor. |
| **1942** | |
| **February** | Japanese conquests of British territories and the fall of Singapore. |
| **1942 April** | Withdrawal of US forces from the Philippines and Guam. |
| **1942 May** | Battle of the Coral Sea. |
| **1942 June** | Battle of Midway. |
| **1943 May** | Start of Japanese retreat from Burma. |
| **1944 June** | Battle of the Philippine Sea. |
| **1945** | |
| **February** | American capture of Iwo Jima. |
| **1945 March** | Liberation of Manila. |
| **1945 August** | Japanese surrender after atomic bombs on Hiroshima and Nagasaki. |

were preparing their campaign of island-hopping for the liberation of the Pacific islands and the invasion of Japan.

Victory in the Pacific might possibly have been secured earlier but for the decision to give first priority to the war in Europe in 1942. This decision reflected the urgency of the military situation there and the influence of Roosevelt's Soviet and British allies on American policy. Anglo-American cooperation, the 'special relationship', was at its strongest between late 1941 and early 1943.

## Turning the tide: Europe

The stable Anglo-American relationship was partly because of the increasingly close personal link between Roosevelt and Churchill but also through key personalities such as Harry Hopkins, W. Averell Harriman and General George Marshall. Another important aspect was Churchill's decision to share with the Americans all the secret intelligence obtained at Station X at Bletchley Park by British codebreakers. As the war progressed, of course, the partnership became less equal and more dominated by American power, and there were many significant policy disagreements even in the early stages of the war.

There were two urgent concerns for Allied war planners in 1942. One was the struggle to defeat the U-boats and keep the sea route across the Atlantic secure. Shipping losses were running at 8 million tonnes each month and this threatened to undermine the entire Allied war effort. The second concern was to give support to the Soviet Union by sending supplies and opening a Second Front to divert German forces away from the Eastern Front.

American commanders thought an attack on Nazi-occupied Europe would be possible in 1942, or at the latest 1943. Britain disagreed, emphasising the huge practical difficulties. In the event, American forces made landings in North Africa in 1942 but without any decisive impact. The main invasion of 1943 was in Italy, something many American generals thought too indirect and cautious. Stalin was also critical of his allies about the delay in opening a Second Front. The invasion of western Europe was postponed until June 1944, by which time the Allies had complete superiority in air power.

The Battle of the Atlantic was not won quickly either. Shipping losses remained frighteningly high until May 1943, when the impact of new technologies made the convoy routes safe. From this point, the codebreakers were able to read U-boat signals on a daily basis, new long-range aircraft covered the 'Atlantic gap' so that U-boats could not escape air surveillance and the development of airborne radar turned U-boat commanders from hunters into the hunted.

The war in Europe had also turned decisively by the summer of 1943. After the massive German defeats at Stalingrad and Kursk, the Soviet Union was ready to counter-attack and push the Germans back towards Berlin. The United States Army Air Forces (USAAF) was able to begin a campaign of mass daylight bombing raids on German factories and cities. Italy was knocked out of the war. Barring miracles, the ultimate defeat of Germany and Japan was already certain. Attention turned towards planning for post-war peace.

## The road to victory

The final defeat of the Axis powers took two years after the tide of war turned in 1943 before Germany and Japan were forced into unconditional surrender. The D-Day landings, originally planned for 1943, took place in

Though for decades during the Cold War, Soviet historians played down the role of American and British Lend-Lease aid, its real significance has recently been acknowledged. From 1942 a flow of food, raw materials and equipment sustained the Soviet war effort. Most of the Soviet rail network was supplied with locomotives, wagons and rails made in the USA. One million miles [1.6 million kilometres] of telephone wire, 14 million pairs of boots and 363,000 trucks helped to keep the Red Army fighting.

| 2 | American aid to the USSR, 1942–5. From Richard Overy, *How the Allies Won*, 1996 |

### Activity

**Source analysis**

Study Source 2.

1 Why do you think this issue was 'played down' by Soviet historians?

2 How might this evidence be used to explain the significance of the American contribution to victory in the war?

June 1944. Even after the success of the Normandy landings, it took almost a year for Allied forces to reach Berlin. Recapturing the Pacific islands was also a long and costly process, requiring one amphibious invasion after another. Even in the spring of 1945, American military planners estimated that the final invasion of Japan would take months and cost 1.4 million American lives.

To achieve these victories, the USA developed a vast war machine. The US army mobilised 5 million soldiers. The munitions industry became the biggest the world had ever seen. American air power was reaching a peak, enabling the mass bombing of Germany and Japan as well as keeping vital supply lines open by air. Shipbuilding, for both the navy and the merchant fleets, produced ships faster than U-boats could sink them.

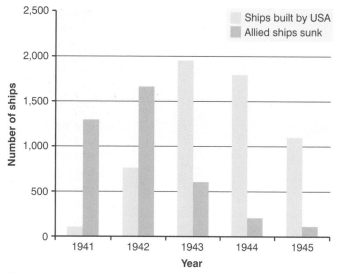

**Fig. 2** *Winning the Battle of the Atlantic*

As the western Allies went on to the offensive, American influence became more and more dominant. The decline in British influence was hidden to some extent by the great personal prestige of Churchill, but there was no question about who called the shots. In late 1943, the appointment of Dwight D. Eisenhower as Supreme Allied Commander Europe (SACEUR) reflected American leadership of the Allied war effort. (It was a close decision as to whether Eisenhower got the job or another American, George Marshall.)

### Key profile

#### Dwight D. Eisenhower

General Dwight D. Eisenhower (1890–1969) was a soldier-politician. He had relatively little battlefield experience and his great skills were in planning, organisation and coordinating the contributions of other people. He was appointed Supreme Allied Commander Europe in December 1943 and led the Allied armies through the invasion and liberation of occupied Europe. He was especially good at handling difficult personalities among his subordinates, such as the American general George Patton and the British commander Bernard Montgomery. He was later president of the USA from 1953 to 1961.

When final victory was achieved in the summer of 1945, American power was dominant. This dominance was enhanced by the possession of atomic weapons.

### A closer look

#### The atomic bomb

The Second World War was a scientific war. Winning the war meant winning the race for the best technologies: the fastest aircraft, the best radar equipment, the cleverest methods of breaking the enemy's secret codes. One of the great fears of the Allies was that Nazi Germany would win the race to develop atomic weapons. Before the war, German physicists had led the world. Ironically, many of the most brilliant scientists in this field were Jewish. A number of them left Germany before the war to escape persecution and ended up working for the Allies.

In 1939, atomic research was on a small scale but it was massively expanded after the USA joined the war in December 1941. Huge financial resources were poured into the Manhattan Project, with a team of scientists headed by Dr Robert Oppenheimer and supervised by General Hodges for the US army. Britain was closely involved in the project but only the Americans could provide the huge amounts of money needed.

The first successful test took place at Los Alamos in New Mexico in 1945. By then it was already clear that the Allied bomb was not needed to win the war in Europe after all. However, the bomb was used against Japan. It is claimed that the use of atomic bombs to destroy Hiroshima and Nagasaki in August 1945 shortened the war, although whether it was absolutely necessary for President Truman to use them remains very controversial. Some historians believe that the decision to use the bomb had more to do with impressing Stalin than with forcing the Japanese to surrender.

The American monopoly of atomic weapons changed the balance of power in the Grand Alliance in the post-war world. American dominance was not only about having a monopoly over the atomic bomb; it was also about sheer economic power. The fact that the Americans had been first to build the bomb was itself proof that the USA could out-spend any power in the world. Table 1 indicates the vast scale of defence spending on America's war effort and how it increased during the course of the war.

Table 1 *American defence spending, 1941–5*

| Year | Spending ($, billions) | Percentage of gross domestic product (GDP) |
|------|------------------------|-------------------------------------------|
| 1941 | 6.1 | 5.1 |
| 1942 | 22.1 | 15.9 |
| 1943 | 46.6 | 32.2 |
| 1944 | 62.9 | 36.0 |
| 1945 | 64.5 | 37.2 |

## The impact of the war on US society

For the American people, the experience of war between 1941 and 1945 was different from all the other nations involved. Outside the USA, the war brought mass destruction, massive casualties and serious economic hardship. Millions of people in Europe and the Far East suffered bombings, food shortages and rationing, and occupation by foreign armies. Millions died and millions became refugees. None of this happened to the American people. For many Americans, military or civilian, the Second World War was a 'good war'.

Table 2 *Comparative living standards, 1939–45 (index of consumer spending)*

| Country | 1939 | 1940 | 1941 | 1942 | 1943 | 1944 | 1945 |
|---------|------|------|------|------|------|------|------|
| Japan | 107 | 109 | 111 | 108 | 99 | 93 | 78 |
| Germany | 108 | 117 | 108 | 105 | 95 | 94 | 85 |
| USA | 96 | 103 | 108 | 116 | 115 | 118 | 122 |

### Key chronology

**America's war in Europe**

| 1942 July | Operation Torch – landings in North Africa. |
| 1943 June | Allied invasion of Italy. |
| 1944 June | Allied landings in Normandy. |
| 1945 April | Meeting of American and Soviet forces at Torgau on the river Elbe. |
| 1945 May | Surrender of German forces in Europe. |

### Activity

**Revision exercise**

Using the evidence in this chapter, create a year-by-year chronological table on American involvement in the Second World War from 1941 to 1945. For each year, think up a key sentence that might be used to summarise the overall importance of that year.

**Table 3** *Comparative wartime casualties*

| Country | Total population (millions) | Military deaths | Civilian deaths | Total deaths | Deaths as a percentage of population |
|---|---|---|---|---|---|
| Germany | 69 | 5,500,000 | 1,800,000 | 7,500,000 | 10.8 |
| Japan | 71 | 2,100,000 | 580,000 | 2,600,000 | 3.7 |
| Britain | 47 | 383,000 | 68,000 | 451,000 | 0.9 |
| Soviet Union | 176 | 11,700,000 | 14,900,000 | 26,600,000 | 15.1 |
| USA | 131 | 408,000 | 12,000 | 421,000 | 0.3 |

In the USA, there was relatively little rationing and the lights were never switched off. There was full employment and living standards went up, not down. Compared with other countries, and compared with their own experiences of the depression years of the 1930s, most Americans found life comfortable in wartime. Cultural life and popular entertainment were thriving. There was a strong sense of national unity and little criticism of the government.

However, casualty levels among American troops were not insignificant. Almost half a million people died far from home and many more were wounded. However, total American military casualties were immeasurably lower than those of Japan, Germany or the Soviet Union. No American cities experienced anything like the firestorms that destroyed Hamburg in 1943 or Tokyo in 1945.

The first and perhaps most important impact of the war was to bring about the full mobilisation of the American economy. It is often claimed that it was not the New Deal that pulled the USA out of the Great Depression; it was the war that kick-started real economic recovery. In 1940, unemployment still stood at nearly 8 million. In the war years there was full employment – and even some severe labour shortages in certain areas of the economy, especially agriculture.

The needs of the armed forces took over the US economy. Millions of new jobs were created, both because of increased production and to fill jobs left by workers called up to the armed forces. The motor industry switched from cars to the production of trucks and tanks. Mass production methods were maximised, with new techniques requiring huge factories and a larger, less-skilled workforce. By the middle of the war, aircraft were being produced at the rate of 1,000 a day. There were government controls on prices and wages. In 1942, the War Production Board (WPB) was set up by Roosevelt to supervise the allocation of key resources such as petrol, rubber and steel.

One effect of this was to strengthen the influence of the trades union organisations. The American Federation of Labor (AFL) and, even more so, the Congress of Industrial Organizations (CIO), grew much stronger. The federal government put pressure on employers to recognise unions – an issue that had caused considerable industrial unrest in the 1930s. The CIO committed itself to a no-strike policy and accepted government arbitration of wage disputes. This produced moderate pay rises and increased fringe benefits. The leadership of the CIO became more centralised and had more influence on government.

There was much more social mobility. Being drafted into the armed forces meant many young men left their home districts for the first time. Large numbers of agricultural workers, including African-Americans, moved to the cities to take up factory jobs. Many women were employed

**Fig. 3** *A woman at war work in a factory*

in the munitions industry and parts of the economy that were previously 'men only'. By 1944, 36 per cent of the workforce was female.

This social mobility raised awareness of race and gender discrimination. The biggest CIO union, the United Auto Workers (UAW), had to deal with several 'hate strikes' by white workers in Detroit. There were similar problems in other industries, such as transport and steel. The federal government made some rather tame efforts to deal with the problem by setting up the Fair Employment Practices Commission (FEPC). Some CIO unions attempted to limit discrimination against African-American and female workers.

The idea of the 'good war' and the image of the whole nation pulling together reflected the success of a sustained official propaganda effort. Government agencies promoted effective poster campaigns – about **Rosie the Riveter**, for example – to encourage women workers in munitions factories; or about the need to buy war bonds; or the need to conserve vital resources. The propaganda images reflected real life to a large extent. Civilian consumption went up by more than 20 per cent. Although there was rationing, people had plenty of food and the gap between rich and poor narrowed. For many Americans, wartime life was a big improvement on life in the 1930s.

There was a surge in mass entertainment. Radio was common in almost every home, providing immediate and extensive news coverage of the war and light relief through music and comedy programmes. Cinemas were packed. After Pearl Harbor, Hollywood films did a huge amount to raise morale and enlist public support for the war effort. The Office of War Information (OWI) was set up by the federal government in 1942 as a propaganda agency to coordinate film coverage of the war. There were many war documentaries, such as *Why We Fight* (a series of films directed by Frank Capra) and John Huston's *The Battle of Midway* (1942). Hollywood stars like Clark Gable, Henry Fonda and James Stewart became high-profile recruits to the armed forces.

Feature films reinforced patriotic messages. Several action films dealt with the battles in the Pacific. *Mrs Miniver* (1942), with Greer Garson starring as a heroic English housewife coping with the tragedies of bombed-out Britain, gave American audiences a favourable picture of Britain at war. *Casablanca* (1942), with Humphrey Bogart outwitting a Vichy police chief and his Nazi allies, was a big hit when it was released. Even films not directly about the war, such as *Meet Me in St Louis* (1944), a happy family film starring the young Judy Garland, helped to influence the national mood of togetherness. Radio and popular music also had a big influence.

Am I an American?

I'm just an Irish, Negro, Jewish, French and English, Spanish, Russian, Chinese, Polish, Scotch, Hungarian, Swedish, Finnish, Canadian, Greek and Turk, and Czech and double Czech American.

And that ain't all.

I was baptised Baptist, Methodist, Congregationalist, Lutheran, Atheist, Roman Catholic, Orthodox Jewish, Presbyterian, Seventh Day Adventist, Quaker, Christian Scientist, and a whole lot more.

 **3**     *Ballad for Americans*, *a song sung on CBS Radio by the famous African-American singer Paul Robeson in 1939*

When Americans looked back at the war after it was over, their memories were shaped as much by these celluloid images as by memories of real-life events.

The rosy national myths about the war obviously covered up some unpleasant realities. Few people heard anything about hate strikes in factories or the serious racial tensions in some units of the armed forces. Beneath the surface, there was a black market, profiteering and pockets of criminal activity.

The treatment of Japanese-Americans was often extremely unpleasant. They were well established by 1941 – about half the population of Hawaii and 1 per cent of the population of California. They had often suffered from discrimination before and the Immigration Acts of 1924 and 1927 had been deliberately framed to cut back on Japanese immigrants. After Pearl Harbor, there were scare stories about the attackers having been assisted by Japanese-Americans. Many of them were rounded up and sent to temporary internment camps. A permanent camp was set up at Manzanar in California.

Conditions were bad and this led to riots. One Supreme Court justice expressed his concerns: 'The government's policy bears a melancholy resemblance to the treatment of the Jewish race in Germany.' That view might seem a bit extreme (although at that time, of course, Justice Murphy knew nothing about the death camps and the Holocaust), but many Americans were troubled by the way the treatment of Japanese-Americans conflicted with the national myth about all kinds of people becoming Americans in the 'melting pot' of integration and the togetherness of the common war effort. Congress tried to ease the nation's guilty conscience in 1948 by awarding nearly $40 million in compensation, but this was only 10 per cent of what had been lost. Much later, in 1988, further legislation provided additional compensation and a belated apology.

**Fig. 4** *'Avenge December 7'*

### The war and African-Americans

When the war began there was still a lot of discrimination, official as well as unofficial. 'We have not had a Negro worker in 25 years,' said a spokesman for the Standard Steel Corporation of Kansas City, 'and we are not going to start now.' Trades unions continued to bar African-Americans from membership. In the armed forces, African-Americans served mostly in segregated units and were rarely used as combat soldiers.

### ■ A closer look

### A. Philip Randolph and the march on Washington

The Brotherhood of Sleeping Car Workers was an all-black union of railroad workers, set up in 1925. Its leader, A. Philip Randolph, had a long record of fighting discrimination. He had been a supporter of the activist Marcus Garvey before the First World War. He had worked for a radical newspaper set up in 1917 to campaign against racial discrimination and American participation in the war. In June 1941, on the eve of another war, Randolph organised a great protest march on Washington by 100,000 African-Americans, demanding that the president issue an executive order to ban racial discrimination in the armed forces and defence industries.

This was an idea ahead of its time. Protest marches were to become regular occurrences in the civil rights movement of the 1960s, but they were seen as radical in 1941, even by other African-American leaders. President Roosevelt was strongly opposed to making any concessions to that kind of pressure, but Randolph stood firm. Democratic Party politicians, especially Fiorello LaGuardia, the mayor of New York, persuaded Roosevelt that he had to give way. He issued Executive Order 8802 stating that 'There shall be no discrimination in the employment of workers in defence industries or government because of race, creed or colour, or national origin. Employers and labour unions have a duty to provide for the full and equitable participation of all workers in defence industries.' The march was called off, but Roosevelt's order was seen as an important victory for Randolph and for the rights of African-Americans.

During the war, there was a huge increase in the membership of the National Association for the Advancement of Colored People (NAACP) and the Committee of Racial Equality (CORE), formed in 1942. Randolph's success in pressuring Roosevelt started a process that ensured the impact of the Second World War on the lives of African-Americans would be very different from that of the First World War in 1917–18.

When I got my first pay cheque, I'd never seen that much money before, not even in a bank, because I'd never been in a bank too much. At Lockheed Aircraft, I worked with a big strong white girl from a cotton farm in Arkansas. We learned that we could open up to each other and get along. She learned that Negroes were people, too, and I saw her as a person also. We both gained from it. Had it not been for the war, I don't think blacks would be in the position they are in now. Some people would never have left the South. They would have had nothing to move for. The war changed my life.

*Sybil Lewis, an African-American woman, compares life in a wartime factory with her pre-war life as a housemaid in Oklahoma*

### Activity

#### Source analysis

Study Source 4. Using other evidence in this chapter, assess the extent to which Sybil's experiences show that the experiences of the war caused a fundamental change in the lives of ordinary people.

The impact of the Second World War undoubtedly led to advances for African-Americans, but there were also severe racial tensions. There were disturbances in 1942 in Texas, Detroit, Baltimore, Los Angeles and many other places. In 1943, a terrible race riot in Detroit saw more than a 100,000 people involved in street violence and 34 were killed. There were racial clashes at army training camps and among US soldiers serving overseas, including a serious riot at Bamber Bridge in Lancashire. Army leaders became so concerned that the army commissioned the famous Hollywood director, Frank Capra, to make *The Negro Soldier* (1944), a film intended to reduce prejudices.

It is difficult to assess the extent of social change during and because of the Second World War. Although extensive shifts took place, they often proved temporary and did not fundamentally change attitudes. Most women workers, for example, left their wartime jobs voluntarily in 1945 and were happy to resume traditional roles. The efforts of the unions to keep women's pay rates high during the war did not reflect a commitment to gender equality; they were mostly aimed at protecting the pay rates of the men who would return to those jobs after the war.

## The USA and international politics

The Grand Alliance between the USA, Britain and the USSR was never a real partnership. There were big ideological differences between the West and the Soviet Union – it can be argued that a 'Cold War' had already existed since the Nazi-Soviet Pact of 1939 or even since the Bolshevik Revolution of 1917. The western Allies and the USSR only came together because of their joint enemy, Hitler. Once fear of Hitler was taken away as Germany came closer to defeat, so the tensions between the Allies came to the forefront. The Cold War did not fully take shape until 1949 but its beginnings can be traced back to well before the end of the war.

Although the main divide was between Stalin and the West, there were deep-rooted differences between the USA and Britain. These tensions became more obvious as the war progressed. Some differences were traditional: in 1919, for example, many Americans were worried that Britain would try to use American power to keep the British Empire intact. Some tensions were due to a clash of personalities – many American generals found the British commander Montgomery very difficult to work with – but the key issue was that America no longer saw Britain as an equal.

There was also a difference between Roosevelt and Churchill in their approach to Stalin. Roosevelt was convinced that he would be able to establish an effective relationship with Stalin and make lasting bargains with him. Roosevelt was often irritated by Churchill's more confrontational approach. It is possible that Stalin had some influence on this by encouraging Roosevelt's view of Churchill as an old-fashioned imperialist. All these tensions played an important part in the series of wartime conferences that took place between January 1943, at Casablanca, and July 1945, at Potsdam.

Before the peace conference at Potsdam, the wartime summit meetings were focused on winning the war as well as planning for its aftermath. At Tehran, for example, an important decision was taken to demand unconditional surrender from Germany, partly to reassure Stalin that there would be no separate peace. Although the Yalta Conference in February 1945 was mostly concerned with agreeing the post-war division of Europe, one key issue was to ensure Soviet involvement in the final defeat of Japan – something that, at the time, was expected to be a long and costly process.

### Activity

**Thinking point**

It is often claimed that 'The Second World War brought about a social revolution in the USA.' Do you agree with this statement? If not, explain why.

### Key chronology

**Wartime conferences**

| | |
|---|---|
| **1943 January** | Casablanca: Roosevelt and Churchill. |
| **1943 May** | Washington: Roosevelt and Churchill. |
| **1943 November** | Cairo: Roosevelt, Churchill and Chiang Kai-shek; Tehran: Roosevelt, Churchill and Stalin. |
| **1944 September** | Quebec: Roosevelt and Churchill. |
| **1945 January/February** | Malta: Roosevelt and Churchill. |
| **1945 February** | Yalta: Roosevelt, Churchill and Stalin. |
| **1945 July/August** | Potsdam: Truman, Stalin, Churchill (replaced by Attlee after the general election). |

**Belligerents:** an individual, group or country that acts in an aggressive manner, such as engaging in warfare.

In 1945, American influence was as important as 'Wilsonism' had been in 1919. The difference was that, this time, American involvement in world affairs was going to be permanent. Ironically, there was no peace settlement, signed by all the **belligerents**, as after the First World War. The Potsdam Conference was inconclusive and no 'final' peace treaty to end the Second World War took place until the reunification of Germany in 1990. In reality, the settlement in 1945 was the Cold War, with the balance of power between the USA and western Europe on one side and the Soviet bloc on the other.

Because there was no final post-war settlement, the provisional agreements made at the wartime summit meeting at Yalta in the Crimea in February 1945 took on great significance. What happened at Yalta, and President Roosevelt's part in it, has been a cause of intense dispute ever since. Many historians consider that Yalta was the best deal Roosevelt could possibly have achieved in the circumstances, but some conservative historians disagree. They claim that Yalta was a great diplomatic failure, a 'betrayal' that sacrificed the freedoms of Poland and the states of east central Europe because a gullible Roosevelt failed to stand up to Stalin's power politics.

■ A closer look

### Roosevelt and the Yalta Conference

Roosevelt was already a dying man when he got to Yalta. Before flying to the Crimea, he had met Churchill at Malta. The British delegation was alarmed to see Roosevelt's visible physical deterioration. The Malta Conference also revealed a lot of the disagreements between the American and British negotiating positions. Roosevelt was sure he could 'make a trade' with Stalin; Churchill wanted to adopt a tough approach.

Historians disagree about the Yalta Conference. Throughout the Cold War, right-wing commentators have criticised Roosevelt as the 'man who lost the peace' – accusing him of failing to stand up to Stalin and therefore sacrificing eastern Europe to future Soviet domination. According to the British historian Norman Davies, 'Poland was handed to Stalin on a plate.' Defenders of Roosevelt saw his policy as a realistic one in the circumstances of February 1945. By then, Soviet troops already controlled most of Poland and eastern Europe anyway. Roosevelt wanted to keep the alliance with Stalin intact because he believed Soviet help was needed to finish off Japan.

One reason why Yalta remains so controversial is that Roosevelt died so soon afterwards, in April 1945. Nobody knows whether he would have been able to make a success of the post-war peace if he had lived long enough. Some historians argue that his successor Harry S. Truman, 'tried to implement Yalta by changing it', and that the Cold War was caused as much by American policy failures as by any deliberate master plan of Stalin.

**Fig. 5** The 'Big Three' at Yalta: Churchill, Roosevelt and Stalin, February 1945

The Russians had the power in eastern Europe; the only practicable course was to use what influence we had to ameliorate the situation.

| 5 | *President Roosevelt on the Yalta Conference* |

The Russians had proved they could be reasonable. There wasn't any doubt in the minds of the president or any of us that we could get along with them peacefully for as far into the future as any of us could imagine.

| 6 | *Roosevelt's adviser, Harry Hopkins, speaking after the war* |

## President Truman and the New World Order

Roosevelt's successor, Vice-President Harry S. Truman, was regarded as having little knowledge of or experience in foreign affairs, but he was plunged into major diplomatic problems. It would be up to Truman to negotiate with the Soviet Union over the fate of liberated Europe. At the same time, he had to bring an end to the war against Japan, something that still seemed a long way off in April 1945.

In July and August 1945, Truman met Stalin and Churchill at Potsdam near Berlin for the last of the great wartime summits. Negotiations were slow and difficult, with deep mutual suspicions between Stalin and the West. No final overall peace settlement could be agreed. Truman's efforts to reopen discussion about borders – which Stalin thought had been agreed previously at Yalta – got nowhere. Admirers of Truman have praised him for his firmness in 'standing up to Stalin' at Potsdam and after. Critics have argued that he was unnecessarily provocative and pushed Stalin too hard to make concessions.

On 24 July, during the Potsdam Conference, Truman received news of the successful test of the atomic bomb. This was kept secret from Stalin, even though he was still an ally and the war against Japan was not yet over. (However, Stalin already knew about the bomb through his spy network.) Shortly after the Potsdam Conference broke up, the war with Japan was brought to a sudden end by the use of atomic bombs in Hiroshima and Nagasaki.

American possession of the bomb altered the balance of power. It alarmed Stalin and made the Soviet Union feel vulnerable. In the years that followed, the combination of American economic might and its monopoly over atomic weapons made the USA a dominant world power. In 1945, unlike in 1919–20, the nation was ready for its role as a superpower.

The USA was the occupying power in Japan, supervising the transition to democracy. The United Nations (UN) was formed, with strong American backing, at the San Francisco Conference. From 1944 onwards, American financiers took the lead in establishing new international economic and trade organisations. The World Bank and the International Monetary Fund (IMF) were set up. The General Agreement on Tariffs and Trade (GATT) was strongly influenced by American policy from 1944. By the end of 1945, the involvement of the USA in shaping the post-war world was an accepted fact.

### Activity

**Talking point**

Marshal the arguments for and against the proposition that 'The USA ended the Second World War as an aggressive imperial power.'

*Learning outcomes*

In this section you have looked at the ways in which the USA and its position in the world changed between 1941 and 1945. Before 1941, the USA mostly looked inward to concerns about the economy and isolationist feeling was strong. You have examined the reasons why isolationism ended and Franklin D. Roosevelt took the nation into war. You have seen how, by 1945, the American people were experiencing abundant prosperity. Unlike in 1919, a national consensus had emerged in favour of the USA taking the lead role in world affairs.

#  Examination-style questions

(a) Explain why the USA was so unprepared for war in December 1941. *(12 marks)*

 Answers to 12-mark questions need to be concise and selective. A differentiated assessment of a few key reasons is better than a long list. You might start by considering exactly how 'unprepared' the USA was at the time of Pearl Harbor: how it was taken by surprise and how it had tried so hard to avoid a war. Then you might look at some key long-term factors, such as isolationism, traditional American hostility to having a standing army in peacetime or the distractions caused by the Great Depression. Finally, decide which factors mattered most and which factors were also important but less than decisive.

(b) 'How important was the influence of government propaganda and the mass media in bringing about a sense of patriotic unity in the American people? *(24 marks)*

 This question makes an assumption – that Americans did indeed have a sense of patriotic unity during the war. You can challenge this idea if you wish (the examiner will reward you appropriately if you do it well) but there is no need to. The main focus of the question is on the relative importance of a range of factors that contributed to national unity, with special reference to the way public opinion was moulded by propaganda and mass entertainment. There is a massive amount of evidence available: radio, films, poster campaigns, etc. You may wish to make maximum use of this because you think it *was* the most important factor and you will need to give only brief attention to other factors. Alternatively, you may feel that other factors were the most significant ones – in which case you will need to assemble less plentiful material on propaganda and the media. As always, avoid writing descriptively and use your knowledge to back up your argument.

When trying to evaluate what happened to the USA between 1890 and 1945, it is a sensible idea to ask the questions all good historians ask about broad periods in history:

- What was the situation in the beginning?
- What was the situation at the end?
- In between, what changed?
- In between, what stayed the same?

It is important to balance change against continuity. Change, and the causes of change, often seems more obvious and easier to explain. However, change is often a slower and more uneven process than it might appear.

## Change

The most obvious change in 1945, of course, was the relationship between the USA and the rest of the world. In a sense, the 'American century' began in 1945. Through the intense news coverage of the war – on radio and in cinema newsreels – and through the experience of the millions of soldiers who had gone abroad to fight, Americans knew far more about the world outside and were more interested in what was happening there. Some isolationist ideas still persisted, but most Americans now accepted the USA's world role.

The Cold War did not freeze solid until the years between 1947 and 1949, with the communist takeover in eastern Europe, the division of Germany, the formation of the North Atlantic Treaty Organization (NATO) and the communist revolution in China. However, the origins of the Cold War were clearly visible in 1945; the tensions of the Cold War and the long-standing American fear of Communism did a lot to keep the USA fully engaged in world affairs. Unlike in 1919, when Wilson's peace settlement was rejected and America retreated into 'normalcy', the Cold War tied the USA tightly into the New World Order.

As a result of the USA becoming the 'world's policeman', politics and government in the USA were changed significantly. There was now a massive standing army in peacetime. The air force became a key element in American military power, with the drive for new weapons and more advanced aircraft requiring massive expenditure. The needs of the armed forces led to huge industrial contracts. The armed forces, big industrial companies and the government were all combined together in what President Eisenhower in the 1950s dubbed the 'military-industrial complex'.

Along with this went the expansion of the so-called national security state. The powers of the presidency and the National Security Council were increased. Agencies like the FBI and the CIA were expanded, as well as diplomatic and cultural links with countries overseas.

## ■ Delayed effects

It is often claimed that fundamental social changes were caused, or at least accelerated, by the Second World War. Many African-Americans served in the armed forces. Many others left the South to take up labour opportunities in the war industries. This also applied to women, who comprised more than one-third of the workforce during the war. However, these changes were mainly temporary.

For most of American society, at least on the surface, life returned to normal after the war. There was a long post-war economic boom, with increased ownership of houses, cars and consumer goods. The impact of the war on social change had delayed effects. The role of women, for example, had changed during the war, with many women taking on jobs formerly considered 'men's work'. After the war, employment patterns and social attitudes towards the role of women returned to conventional pre-war models. The 'gender revolution' did not arrive until the 1960s – some observers claim that it was still far from complete by the end of the 20th century.

Similarly, despite the fact that the war brought greater awareness and more social mobility to African-Americans, there was no immediate radical change in their status. The South continued for a few more years along its separated, segregationist path until the mid-1950s. At that time, the civil rights movement gained momentum from the Supreme Court judgement of 1954 that declared school segregation to be unconstitutional and a decade of protest began that culminated in the Civil Rights Act 1964 and the Voting Rights Act 1965.

Deep social changes did indeed take place in post-war American society, especially in the 1960s. John F. Kennedy, a Catholic, was elected president in 1960; a white southerner, Jimmy Carter, became president in 1976. Both achieved something that would have been thought unlikely in 1945. The 1960s, and especially the symbolic year of 1968, brought about rapid changes in the lives of women and youth. The Second World War no doubt contributed to these changes, but this social change was not sudden and complete after 1945 – and its causes can often be traced back to long before the conflict.

## ■ Continuity

Anyone observing the USA in 1945 would have recognised many things that had been there since 1890 or could easily have been predicted then. The political system, with its two-party structure, the role of the Supreme Court and the prestige of the presidency was still much the same. So was the proud and idealistic self-image of the idea of the USA as a 'melting pot', a land of freedom and opportunity.

The idea of Americans as tough individualists, moulded by the frontier experience, was as strong after 1945 as it had been in the days of Buffalo Bill's Wild West Show. In the 1940s and early 1950s, the epic 'Westerns' directed by John Ford and starring John Wayne, such as *Fort Apache* (1948) and *She Wore A Yellow Ribbon* (1949), were enduring examples of the frontier myth; so were the many patriotic war films of the time, like *Sands of Iwo Jima* (1949).

The USA in 1945 had the same sense of abundance as had been the case in 1890: unlimited economic potential, unlimited natural resources, unlimited space. The nation had the same optimism and the same sense that the future was an American future, more dynamic than tired, war-torn 'Old Europe'. Even the new role of world's superpower can be seen as following on from the ambitions of American imperialists in the 1890s, such as Theodore Roosevelt and Alfred Thayer Mahan.

In post-war USA, as in many other examples in history, continuity was deceptively strong, especially in social attitudes. The revival of the Republican right and the backlash against 1960s liberalism by the so-called 'silent majority' during the presidencies of Ronald Reagan and George W. Bush provided proof of this. Perhaps the USA was not 'transformed' between 1890 and 1945; it was more a case of fulfilling its natural destiny as the great new power of the Western world.

# Glossary

## A

**AFL:** American Federation of Labor, formed in 1886.

**Alphabet Agencies:** organisations established as part of the New Deal in the 1930s.

**America First:** a campaigning organisation founded in Chicago in 1940 promote American isolationism.

**Antitrust Act:** legislation to prevent big business from fixing prices and destroying competition.

**assimilation:** the integration of new immigrants into American society.

**Axis:** the alliance between Germany, Italy and Japan, formed in the late 1930s.

## B

**banking holiday:** a suspension of banking activity to allow financial markets to stabilise and to prevent panic withdrawals.

**bear market:** a time when stock market prices are consistently falling.

**belligerents:** nations legally declared to be at war.

**'Black Monday' (27 May 1935):** the declaration by the Supreme Court that Roosevelt's legislation for the Second New Deal was unconstitutional.

**'Black Thursday' (24 October 1929):** the day the Wall Street stock market collapsed.

**'Black Sunday' (14 April 1935):** a day of exceptionally severe dust storms in the regions affected by drought and wind erosion.

**bootlegging:** importing, transporting and selling illegal booze.

**bull market:** a time when stock market prices are consistently rising.

**Bureau of Investigation:** the forerunner of the FBI.

## C

**call loans:** short-term stock-market loans liable to be instantly repaid ('called in') .

**carpet-baggers:** the name given by resentful southerners to the northern businessmen whom they accused of unfairly exploiting the defeated South during the era of Reconstruction.

**Central Powers:** the alliance between Germany, Austria-Hungary, Bulgaria and the Ottoman Empire during the First World War.

**Confederate flag:** the flag of the 11 southern states which fought and lost the Civil War.

## D

**deficit spending:** the policy of spending federal money to stimulate the economy without raising taxes.

**deflation:** policies to prevent inflation by keeping wages and prices down.

**disfranchisement:** depriving people of the right to vote – many African-Americans in the South were removed from voter registers from the 1880s.

**Dollar Diplomacy:** the policy of using financial power, rather than military intervention, to extend US influence abroad.

**Dow Jones average:** the index of average stock market prices on Wall Street.

**'Drys':** those who supported the temperance movement and Prohibition.

**dust bowl:** the areas of Colorado, Kansas, Oklahoma and Texas hit by drought and wind erosion in the 1930s.

## F

**FBI:** Federal Bureau of Investigation, formed in 1935.

**federal government:** the central government of the United States, based in Washington, DC.

## F

**federal relief:** aid and subsidies from the federal government to relieve economic distress.

**free trade:** the removal of protective tariffs to make international trade freer and more competitive.

## G

**GDP:** gross domestic product – a measurement of the total value of the national economy.

**'G-Men':** 'government men' – agents of the FBI.

**gold standard:** the policy of tying the national currency to the value of gold reserves in order to ensure financial stability.

**Grand Alliance:** the alliance between Britain, the United States and the Soviet Union from 1941 to 1945.

## H

**hyperinflation:** a colossal rise in prices.

## I

**ideology:** a system of ideas and beliefs.

**imperialism:** the idea of overseas expansion to impose Western progress on less-developed peoples.

**inauguration:** the ceremony in Washington, DC when the incoming president is sworn in by the chief justice of the Supreme Court.

**IWW:** Industrial Workers of the World, a radical trades union organisation formed in 1905.

## J

**'Jim Crow':** the nickname for the system of segregation in the South and the suppression of the rights of African-Americans.

## K

**Keynesianism:** the economic theories of John Maynard Keynes.

**L**

**Lend-Lease:** the agreement that Britain would receive American loans to aid its war effort in return for leasing bases to the USA.

**M**

**McCarthyism:** a term used to describe the anti-communist hysteria (sometimes called the 'Second Red Scare') whipped up in the USA after 1949 by Senator Joe McCarthy.

**Monroe Doctrine:** the principle of excluding European influence from the Americas, asserted in 1823.

**moonshine:** illegal homemade alcoholic drink.

**N**

**Nationalists:** people motivated by love of country and the ideals of national independence.

**'normalcy':** the slogan of Warren G. Harding in the 1920 presidential election, promising a less interventionist approach to government both abroad and at home.

**O**

**Open Door policy:** the policy of maintaining equal trade opportunities for all countries, which the USA thought to be especially important in relation to China.

**P**

**Platt Amendment:** passed by Congress in 1903 to justify American intervention in Cuba and other parts of Latin America.

**Prohibition:** the campaign to ban the selling and consumption of alcoholic drinks.

**protective tariff:** higher customs duties on imports in order to protect domestic producers from foreign competition.

**protectorate:** the name used to describe American control over the affairs of overseas territories in order to maintain stability.

**R**

**real wages:** the worth of wages in relation to prices.

**'Red Scare':** anti-communist hysteria whipped up in the USA by A. Mitchell Palmer and others in 1919–20.

**Republican democracy:** the political ideal on which the USA was based, ending monarchy and ensuring government of the people for the people.

**restrictionists:** people who opposed mass immigration into the USA and wanted to introduce a ban or quota system.

**Roosevelt Corollary:** the extension of the Monroe Doctrine to justify American intervention in Latin America, asserted in 1904.

**Rosie the Riveter:** propaganda image of a woman worker used in the poster campaign to glorify the contribution of women in war production during the Second World War.

**S**

**seceding from the Union:** the attempt by the southern states to declare their independence from the United States.

**securitisation:** securing loans against other assets to guarantee repayment will be possible.

**sedition:** actions to undermine lawful government and the security of the State.

**segregationists:** people determined to uphold the system of segregation of the races and suppression of the rights of African-Americans.

**sharecroppers:** poor farmers, often ex-slaves, who rented plots of land and were paid for their crops at prices fixed by the landowners.

**'Solid South':** the electoral dominance of the Democratic Party in the South after 1865.

**SP:** the Socialist Party of America, founded in 1901.

**speakeasies:** clubs and bars selling illegal alcohol during Prohibition.

**standing army:** a permanent, professional army, as opposed to a volunteer army called up only in time of war.

**T**

**Taylorism:** the theories of the 'time and motion' expert, Frederick Winslow Taylor.

**temperance movement:** the campaign to outlaw the production, sale or consumption of alcoholic drinks.

**'trust-busting':** action to break up big industrial monopolies in order to prevent price fixing and ensure fair competition.

**U**

**UMWA:** United Mine Workers of America.

**Uncle Sam:** the nickname for the United States, usually shown by a man wearing Stars and Stripes uniform.

**V**

**veterans' organisations:** organisations to represent the interest of ex-soldiers.

**voluntarism:** the policy of relying on self-help and avoiding the need for government intervention as much as possible.

**W**

**'Wets':** people opposed to Prohibition.

# Bibliography

## ◼ The USA in 1890

### Students

Clements, P. (2008) *Prosperity, Depression and the New Deal 1890–1954*, Hodder.

Farmer, A. and Sanders, V. (2002) *An Introduction to American History 1860–1990*, Hodder.

Murphy, D., Cooper, K and Waldron, M. (1997) *The USA 1776–1992*, HarperCollins.

### Teachers and extension

Boyer, P. *et al.* (2008) *The Enduring Vision: A History of the American People*, Houghton Mifflin.

Brogan, H. (1999) *The Penguin History of the United States*, Penguin.

Dinnerstein, L. (2003) *Natives and Strangers: A Multicultural History of Americans*, OUP.

Evans, H. (1998) *The American Century: An Illustrated History*, Cape.

Graubard, S. (2006) *The Presidents: The American Presidency from Theodore Roosevelt to George W. Bush*, Penguin.

Jones, M. A. (1998) *The Limits of Liberty: The United States 1607–1992*, Macmillan.

Kennedy, D. (1999) *Freedom From Fear: The American People in Depression and War 1929–1945*, OUP.

Rowbotham, S. (1997) *A Century of Women: The History of Women in Britain and the United States*, Penguin.

Walker, M. (2000) *Makers of the American Century*, Chatto & Windus.

Zinn, H. (1995) *A People's History of the United States*, HarperCollins.

Useful source material is provided on the following websites: www.spartacus.schoolnet.co.uk, http://archives.gov

A comprehensive and well-organised specialist bibliography can be found at: www.sussex.ac.uk/americanstudies

## ◼ Section 1 The USA, 1890–1920

### Students

De Pennington, J. (2005) *Modern America: The USA 1865 to the Present*, Hodder Murray.

Gould, L. L. (1991) *America in the Progressive Era 1890–1920*, Longman.

### Teachers and extension

Cooper, J. M. (1992) *The Pivotal Decades: 1900–1920*, Norton.

Daniels, R. (1992) *Not Like Us: Immigrants and Minorities in America 1890–1924*, Ivan Dee.

Ferrell, R. (1983) *Woodrow Wilson and World War One, 1917–1921*, Harper Row.

Holmes, J. (2007) *Theodore Roosevelt and World Order*, Palgrave.

Kraut, A. M. (2001) *The Huddled Masses: The Immigrant in American Society*, Harlan Davidson.

Livesay, H. C. (1999) *Andrew Carnegie and the Rise of Big Business*, Longman.

Morris, E. (1979) *The Rise of Theodore Roosevelt*, Random House.

Painter, N. I. (1988) *Standing at Armageddon: The United States 1877–1919*, Norton.

Porter, G. (2006) *The Rise of Big Business 1860–1920*, Harlan Davidson.

Trask, D. (1996) *The War with Spain in 1898*, Bison.

BBC News website: http://news.bbc.co.uk (search term: 'Trustbusters')

### DVD

Anderson, P. T. (dir.) (2007) *There Will Be Blood*.

Minnelli, V. (dir.) (1944) *Meet Me in St Louis*.

## ◼ Section 2 The USA, 1920–9

### Students

Willoughby, D. (2000) *The USA 1917–1945*, Heinemann.

### Teachers and extension

Allen, F. L. (1931) *Only Yesterday*, Blackwell (reprinted 1997).

Moran, J. P. (2002) *The Scopes Trial: A Brief History With Documents*, Palgrave.

Palmer, N. (2007) *The Twenties in America*, Edinburgh University Press.

Parrish, M. (1992) *The Anxious Decades 1920–1941*, Norton.

## ◼ Section 3 The USA, 1929–41

### Students

Cooper, K. (2001) *FDR*, HarperCollins.

## Teachers and extension

Brinkley, A. (1982) *Voices of Protest: Huey Long, Father Coughlin and the Great Depression*, Knopf.

Fried, A. (2001) *FDR and his Enemies*, Palgrave.

Gallup, G. H. (1972) *The Gallup Poll: Public Opinion 1935–1971*, Random House.

Hixson, W. L. (2006) *Charles A. Lindbergh: Lone Eagle*, Lomgman.

McElvaine, R. (2003) *The Depression and the New Deal: A History in Documents*, OUP.

Renshaw, P. (2004) *Franklin D. Roosevelt*, Longman.

Terkel, S. (1970) *Hard Times: An Oral History of the Great Depression*, New Press.

## Novels

Steinbeck, J. (1939) *The Grapes of Wrath*, Penguin.

Warren, R. P. (1946) *All The King's Men*, Fontana.

## DVD

Ford, J. (dir.) (1940) *The Grapes of Wrath*.

Rossen, R. (dir.) (1949) *All The King's Men*.

Sandrich, M. (dir.) (1935) *Top Hat*.

BBC (1996) *People's Century: Great Escape* (the influence of cinema on people's lives and how governments used film for political purposes).

—*People's Century: Breadline* (the Wall Street Crash and the worldwide economic depression).

## ■ Section 4 The impact of the Second World War on the USA

### Students

Traynor, J. (2001) *Mastering Modern United States History*, Palgrave.

### Teachers and extension

Ambrose, S. (1998) *Rise to Globalism: American Foreign Policy since 1938*, Penguin.

Doenecke, J. D. (2003) *From Isolation to War 1941–1941*, Harlan Davidson.

Kimball, W. F. (1991) *Forged in War: Roosevelt, Churchill and the Second World War*, Morrow.

Overy, R. (1999) *How the Allies Won*, Macmillan.

Terkel, S. (1984) *The Good War: An Oral History of World War Two*, New Press.

Winkler, A.M. (2002) *Home Front USA: America during World War II*, Harlan Davidson.

### Novels

Roth, P. (2004) *The Plot Against America*, Arrow.

### DVD

Dwan, A. (dir.) (1949) *Sands of Iwo Jima*.

Spielberg, S. (dir.) (1998) *Saving Private Ryan*.

Zinnemann, F. (dir.) (1953) *From Here to Eternity*.

# Acknowledgements

**The author and publisher would like to thank the following for permission to reproduce material:**

## Source texts:

p53 Parrish, M., *The Anxious Decades 1920–1941*, Norton, 1992; pp74 and 89 Kennedy D., *Freedom From Fear: The American People in Depression and War 1929–1945*, OUP, 1999; p92 Allen, F. L., *Only Yesterday*, Blackwell, 1931 (reprinted 1997); p130 Kennedy D., *Freedom From Fear: The American People in Depression and War 1929–1945*, OUP, 1999; p132 Overy, R., *How the Allies Won*, Macmillan, 1999

**Photographs courtesy of:**

Edimedia Art Archive pp21, 23, 24, 37, 40, 48, 51, 54 (right), 56, 71, 80, 94, 106, 108, 122, 126, 137, 140; Getty Images piv; Library of Congress, p26 (Public Domain), National Archives p46; National Archives and Records Administration p92; Topfoto pp61, 73, 75, 111; Topfoto/Roger-Viollet p85; World History Archive pp8, 20, 28, 29, 30, 34, 41, 42, 45, 54 (left), 59, 62, 63, 65, 70, 79, 82, 83, 87, 96, 97, 100, 104, 123, 130, 136

Cover photograph: courtesy of Alamy/Michel Friang

For further information concerning any pictures appearing in this book, please email alexander@uniquedimension.com

Photo research by Unique Dimension Limited

Special thanks to Topfoto, Ann Asquith, Dora Swick and Samuel Manning

# Index